Bloom's Modern Critical Interpretations

Bloom's Modern Critical Interpretations

John Steinbeck's

The Grapes of Wrath
Updated Edition

Edited and with an introduction by
Harold Bloom
Sterling Professor of the Humanities
Yale University

CHELSEA HOUSE
P U B L I S H E R S
An imprint of Infobase Publishing

Bloom's Modern Critical Interpretations: The Grapes of Wrath, Updated Edition

©2007 Infobase Publishing

Introduction ©2007 by Harold Bloom

Chelsea House
An imprint of Infobase Publishing
132 West 31st Street
New York NY 10001

Library of Congress Cataloging-in-Publication Data
John Steinbeck's The grapes of wrath / Harold Bloom, editor. — Updated ed.
     p. cm. — (Bloom's modern critical interpretations)
  Includes bibliographical references and index.
  ISBN 0-7910-9305-0 (hardcover)
  1. Steinbeck, John, 1902-1968. Grapes of wrath. 2. Migrant agricultural laborers in literature. 3. Rural families in literature. 4. Labor camps in literature. 5. Depressions in literature. 6. California—In literature. I. Bloom, Harold. II. Title: Grapes of wrath. III. Series.

  PS3537.T3234G8557 2006
  813'.52—dc22   2006020209

Chelsea House books are available at special discounts when purchased in bulk quantities for businesses, associations, institutions, or sales promotions. Please call our Special Sales Department in New York at (212) 967-8800 or (800) 322-8755.

You can find Chelsea House on the World Wide Web at http://www.chelseahouse.com

Contributing Editor: Amy Sickels
Cover design by Ben Peterson
Cover photo © Hulton Archive/Getty Images
Composition by EJB Publishing Services
Cover printed by Yurchak Printing, Landisville, Pa.
Book printed and bound by Yurchak Printing, Landisville, Pa.
Printed in the United States of America

This book is printed on acid-free paper.

All links and web addresses were checked and verified to be correct at the time of publication. Because of the dynamic nature of the web, some addresses and links may have changed since publication and may no longer be valid.

Contents

Editor's Note

My Introduction considers Hemingway's strong influence upon Steinbeck, and then attempts to define both the limitations and the lasting value of *The Grapes of Wrath*.

In Howard Levant's reading, the novel is regarded as a mature prose epic successful on its own terms for its first three quarters, but then yielding to flaws as it nears completion.

Peter Lisca generously overpraises *The Grapes of Wrath*, repeating a reviewer's judgment that it matches any other American book in greatness. I myself think of Hawthorne's *The Scarlet Letter*, Melville's *Moby Dick*, Emerson's *The Conduct of Life*, Whitman's *Leaves of Grass*, Mark Twain's *Adventures of Huckleberry Finn*, Henry James's *The Portrait of a Lady*: is *The Grapes of Wrath* at home in that company?

Ma Joad is judged by Warren Motley as being the dominant personage in the novel, since she incarnates the moral prophecy of Jim Casy, and inspires her son Tom as he goes out to carry Cary's spiritual vision into a dangerous career as a labor organizer.

The Joads as a literary creation are defended by Louis Owens against charges of sentimentalism, after which Mimi Reisel Gladstein argues that John Ford's memorable motion picture version devitalizes the Ma Joad of the novel.

Ma Joad clearly is at variance with current feminism, as Nellie McKay demonstrates, while Stephen Railton eloquently emphasizes the all-too-relevant intimation by Steinbeck that both American Christianity and capitalism are agents of destruction.

Dana N. Cassuto examines the symbolism of water in the novel, after which Brian Railsback clarifies Charles Darwin's influence upon *The Grapes of Wrath*.

In this volume's closing essay, Gavin Cologne-Brooks sees Bruce Springsteen as Steinbeck's heir.

My Afterthought reflects on Steinbeck as a "worthy" writer.

HAROLD BLOOM

Introduction

It is nearly forty years since John Steinbeck died, and while his popularity as a novelist still endures, his critical reputation has suffered a considerable decline. His honors were many and varied, and included the Nobel Prize and the United States Medal of Freedom. His best novels came early in his career: In *Dubious Battle* (1936); *Of Mice and Men* (1937); *The Grapes of Wrath* (1939). Nothing after that, including *East of Eden* (1952), bears rereading. It would be good to record that rereading his three major novels is a valuable experience, from an aesthetic as well as an historical perspective.

Of Mice and Men, an economical work, really a novella, retains considerable power, marred by an intense sentimentality. But *In Dubious Battle* is now quite certainly a period piece, and is of more interest to social historians than to literary critics. *The Grapes of Wrath*, still Steinbeck's most famous and popular novel, is a very problematical work, and very difficult to judge. As story, or rather, chronicle, it lacks invention, and its characters are not persuasive representations of human inwardness. The book's wavering strength is located elsewhere, in a curious American transformation of biblical substance and style that worked splendidly in Whitman and Hemingway, but seems to work only fitfully in Steinbeck.

Steinbeck suffers from too close a comparison with Hemingway, his authentic precursor though born only three years before his follower. I think that Steinbeck's aesthetic problem was Hemingway, whose shadow always hovered too near. Consider the opening of *The Grapes of Wrath*:

> To the red country and part of the gray country of Oklahoma, the last rains came gently, and they did not cut the scarred earth. The plows crossed and recrossed the rivulet marks. The last rains lifted the corn quickly and scattered weed colonies and grass along the sides of the roads so that the gray country and the dark red country began to disappear under a green cover. In the last part of May the sky grew pale and the clouds that had hung in high puffs for so long in the spring were dissipated. The sun flared down on the growing corn day after day until a line of brown spread along the edge of each green bayonet. The clouds appeared, and went away, and in a while they did not try any more. The weeds grew darker green to protect themselves, and they did not spread any more. The surface of the earth crusted, a thin hard crust, and as the sky became pale, so the earth became pale, pink in the red country and white in the gray country.
>
> In the water-cut gullies the earth dusted down in dry little streams. Gophers and ant lions started small avalanches. And as the sharp sun struck day after day, the leaves of the young corn became less stiff and erect; they bent in a curve at first, and then, as the central ribs of strength grew weak, each leaf tilted downward. Then it was June, and the sun shone more fiercely. The brown lines on the corn leaves widened and moved in on the central ribs. The weeds frayed and edged back toward their roots. The air was thin and the sky more pale; and every day the earth paled.

This is not so much biblical style as mediated by Ernest Hemingway, as it is Hemingway assimilated to Steinbeck's sense of biblical style. The monosyllabic diction is hardly the mode of the King James Version, but certainly is Hemingway's. I give, very nearly at random, passages from *The Sun Also Rises*:

> We passed through a town and stopped in front of the posada, and the driver took on several packages. Then we started on again, and outside the town the road commenced to mount. We were going through farming country with rocky hills that sloped down into the fields. The grain-fields went up the hillsides. Now as we went higher there was a wind blowing the grain. The road

was white and dusty, and the dust rose under the wheels and hung in the air behind us. The road climbed up into the hills and left the rich grain-fields below. Now there were only patches of grain on the bare hillsides and on each side of the water-courses. We turned sharply out to the side of the road to give room to pass to a long string of six mules, following one after the other, hauling a high-hooded wagon loaded with freight. The wagon and the mules were covered with dust. Close behind was another string of mules and another wagon. This was loaded with lumber, and the arriero driving the mules leaned back and put on the thick wooden brakes as we passed. Up here the country was quite barren and the hills were rocky and hard-baked clay furrowed by the rain.

The bus climbed steadily up the road. The country was barren and rocks stuck up through the clay. There was no grass beside the road. Looking back we could see the country spread out below. Far back the fields were squares of green and brown on the hillsides. Making the horizon were the brown mountains. They were strangely shaped. As we climbed higher the horizon kept changing. As the bus ground slowly up the road we could see other mountains coming up in the south. Then the road came over the crest, flattened out, and went into a forest. It was a forest of cork oaks, and the sun came through the trees in patches, and there were cattle grazing back in the trees. We went through the forest and the road came out and turned along a rise of land, and out ahead of us was a rolling green plain, with dark mountains beyond it. These were not like the brown, heat-baked mountains we had left behind. These were wooded and there were clouds coming down from them. The green plain stretched off. It was cut by fences and the white of the road showed through the trunks of a double line of trees that crossed the plain toward the north. As we came to the edge of the rise we saw the red roofs and white houses of Burguete ahead strung out on the plain, and away off on the shoulder of the first dark mountain was the gray metal-sheathed roof of the monastery of Roncevalles.

Hemingway's Basque landscapes are described with an apparent literalness and in what seems at first a curiously dry tone, almost flat in its evident lack of significant emotion. But a closer reading suggests that the style here is itself a metaphor for a passion and a nostalgia that is both defensive and meticulous. The contrast between rich soil and barren ground, between wooded hills and heat-baked mountains, is a figure for the lost potency of Jake Barnes, but also for a larger sense of the lost possibilities of life. Steinbeck, following after Hemingway, cannot learn the lesson. He gives us a vision of the Oklahoma Dust Bowl, and it is effective enough, but it is merely a landscape where a process of entropy has been enacted. It has a social and economic meaning, but as a vision of loss lacks spiritual and personal intensity. Steinbeck is more overtly biblical than Hemingway, but too obviously so. We feel that the Bible's sense of meaning in landscape has returned from the dead in Hemingway's own colors, but hardly in Steinbeck's.

If Steinbeck is not an original or even an adequate stylist, if he lacks skill in plot, and power in the mimesis of character, what then remains in his work, except its fairly constant popularity with an immense number of liberal middlebrows, both in his own country and abroad? Certainly, he aspired beyond his aesthetic means. If the literary Sublime, or contest for the highest place, involves persuading the reader to yield up easier pleasures for more difficult pleasures, and it does, then Steinbeck modestly should have avoided Emerson's American Sublime, but he did not. Desiring it both ways, he fell into bathos in everything he wrote, even in *Of Mice and Men* and *The Grapes of Wrath*.

Yet Steinbeck had many of the legitimate impulses of the Sublime writer, and of his precursors Whitman and Hemingway in particular. Like them, he studied the nostalgias, the aboriginal sources that were never available for Americans, and like them he retained a profound hope for the American as natural man and natural woman. Unlike Whitman and Hemingway and the origin of this American tradition, Emerson, Steinbeck had no capacity for the nuances of literary irony. He had read Emerson's essay "The Over-Soul" as his precursors had, but Steinbeck literalized it. Emerson, canniest where he is most the Idealist, barbs his doctrine of "that Unity, that Over-soul, within which every man's particular being is contained and made one with all other." In Emerson, that does not involve the sacrifice of particular being, and is hardly a program for social action:

> We live in succession, in division, in parts, in particles. Meantime within man is the soul of the whole....
>
>   The soul knows only the soul; all else is idle weeds for her wearing.

There always have been Emersonians of the Left, like Whitman and Steinbeck, and Emersonians of the Right, like Henry James and Wallace

Stevens. Emerson himself, rather gingerly planted on the moderate Left, evaded all positions. Social action is also an affair of succession, division, parts, particles; if "the soul knows only the soul," then the soul cannot know doctrines, or even human suffering. Steinbeck, socially generous, a writer on the left, structured the doctrine of *The Grapes of Wrath* on Jim Casy's literalization of Emerson's vision: "Maybe all men got one big soul and everybody's a part of it." Casy, invested by Steinbeck with a rough eloquence that would have moved Emerson, speaks his orator's epitaph just before he is martyred: "They figger I'm a leader 'cause I talk so much." He is a leader, an Okie Moses, and he dies a fitting death for the visionary of an Exodus.

I remain uneasy about my own experience of rereading *The Grapes of Wrath*. Steinbeck is not one of the inescapable American novelists of our past century; he cannot be judged in close relation to Cather, Dreiser, and Faulkner, Hemingway and Fitzgerald, Nathanael West, Ralph Ellison, and Thomas Pynchon. Yet there are no canonical standards worthy of human respect that could exclude *The Grapes of Wrath* from a serious reader's esteem. Compassionate narrative that addresses itself so directly to the great social questions of its era is simply too substantial a human achievement to be dismissed. Whether a human strength, however generously worked through, is also an aesthetic value, in a literary narrative, is one of those larger issues that literary criticism scarcely knows how to decide. One might desire *The Grapes of Wrath* to be composed differently, whether as plot or as characterization, but wisdom compels one to he grateful for the novel's continued existence.

HOWARD LEVANT

The Fully Matured Art:
The Grapes of Wrath

The enormous contemporary social impact of *The Grapes of Wrath*[1] can encourage the slippery reasoning that condemns a period novel to die with its period.[2] But continuing sales and critical discussions suggest that *The Grapes of Wrath* has outlived its directly reportorial ties to the historical past; that it can be considered as an aesthetic object, a good or a bad novel *per se*. In that light, the important consideration is the relative harmony of its structure and materials.

The Grapes of Wrath is an attempted prose epic, a summation of national experience at a given time. Evaluation proceeds from that identification of genre. A negative critical trend asserts that *The Grapes of Wrath* is too flawed to command serious attention: the materials are local and temporary, not universal and permanent; the conception of life is overly simple; the characters are superficial types (except, perhaps, Ma Joad); the language is folksy or strained by turns; and, in particular, the incoherent structure is the weakest point—the story breaks in half, the nonorganic, editorializing interchapters force unearned general conclusions, and the ending is inconclusive as well as overwrought and sentimental.[3] The positive trend asserts that *The Grapes of Wrath* is a great novel. Its materials are properly universalized in specific detail; the conception is philosophical, the characters are warmly felt and deeply created; the language is functional,

From *The Novels of John Steinbeck: A Critical Study*. © 1974 by The University of Missouri Press.

varied, and superb on the whole; and the structure is an almost perfect combination of the dramatic and the panoramic in sufficient harmony with the materials. This criticism admits that overwrought idealistic passages as well as propagandistic simplifications turn up on occasion, but these are minor flaws in an achievement on an extraordinary scale.[4] Relatively detached studies of Steinbeck's ideas comprise a third trend. These studies are not directly useful in analytical criticism; they do establish that Steinbeck's social ideas are ordered and legitimate extensions of biological fact, hence scientific and true rather than mistaken or sentimental.[5]

The two evaluative positions are remarkable in their opposition. They are perhaps overly simple in asserting that *The Grapes of Wrath* is either a classic of our literature or a formless pandering to sentimental popular taste. Certainly these extremes are mistaken in implying (when they do) that somehow, *The Grapes of Wrath* is sui generis in relation to Steinbeck's work.

Trends so awkwardly triple need to be brought into a sharper focus. By way of a recapitulation in focus, consider a few words of outright praise:

> For all of its sprawling asides and extravagances, *The Grapes of Wrath* is a big book, a great book, and one of maybe two or three American novels in a class with *Huckleberry Finn*.[6]

Freeman Champney's praise is conventional enough to pass unquestioned if one admires *The Grapes of Wrath*, or, if one does not, it can seem an invidious borrowing of prestige, shrilly emotive at that. Afterthought emphasizes the serious qualification of the very high praise. Just how much damage is wrought by those "sprawling asides and extravagances," and does *The Grapes of Wrath* survive its structural faults as *Huckleberry Finn* does, by virtue of its mythology, its characterization, its language? If the answers remain obscure, illumination may increase (permitting, as well, a clearer definition of the aesthetic efficacy of Steinbeck's ideas) when the context of critical discussion is the relationship of the novel's structure to materials.

Steinbeck's serious intentions and his artistic honesty are not in question. He had studied and experienced the materials intensely over a period of time. After a false start that he rejected (*L'Affaire Lettuceburg*), his conscious intention was to create an important literary work rather than a propagandistic shocker or a journalistic statement of the topical problem of how certain people faced one aspect of the Great Depression.[7] Therefore, it is an insult to Steinbeck's aims to suggest that somehow *The Grapes of Wrath* is imperfect art but a "big" or "great" novel nevertheless. In all critical justice, *The Grapes of Wrath* must stand or fall as a serious and important work of art.

The consciously functional aspect of Steinbeck's intentions—his working of the materials—is clarified by a comparison of *The Grapes of Wrath* with *In Dubious Battle*. Both novels deal with labor problems peculiar to California, but that similarity cannot be pushed too far. The Joads are fruit pickers in California, but not of apples, the fruit mentioned in *In Dubious Battle*. The Joads pick cotton, and in the strike novel the people expect to move on to cotton. The Joads become involved in a strike but as strikebreakers rather than as strikers. Attitudes are less easy to camouflage. The strikers in *In Dubious Battle* and the Okies in *The Grapes of Wrath* are presented with sympathy whereas the owning class and much of the middle class have no saving virtue. The sharpest similarity is that both the strikers and the Okies derive a consciousness of the need for group action from their experiences; but even here there is a difference in emphasis. The conflict of interest is more pointed and the lessons of experience are less ambiguous in *The Grapes of Wrath* than in *In Dubious Battle*. The fact is that the two novels are not similar beyond a common basis in California labor problems, and Steinbeck differentiates that basis carefully in most specific details. The really significant factor is that different structures are appropriate to each novel. The restricted scope of *In Dubious Battle* demands a dramatic structure with some panoramic elements as they are needed. The broad scope of *The Grapes of Wrath* demands a panoramic structure; the dramatic elements appear as they are needed. Therefore, in each case, the primary critical concern must be the adequacy of the use of the materials, not the materials in themselves.

Steinbeck's profound respect for the materials of *The Grapes of Wrath* is recorded in a remarkable letter in which he explained to his literary agents and to his publisher the main reason for his withdrawing *L'Affaire Lettuceburg*, the hurried, propagandistic, thirty-thousand-word manuscript novel that preceded *The Grapes of Wrath*:

> I know I promised this book to you, and that I am breaking a promise in withholding it. But I had got smart and cagey you see. I had forgotten that I hadn't learned to write books, that I will never learn to write them. A book must be a life that lives all of itself and this one doesn't do that. You can't write a book. It isn't that simple. The process is more painful than that. And this book is fairly clever, has skillful passages, but tricks and jokes. Sometimes I, the writer, seem a hell of a smart guy—just twisting this people out of shape. But the hell with it. I beat poverty for a good many years and I'll be damned if I'll go down at the first little whiff of success. I hope you, Pat, don't think I've double-

crossed you. In the long run to let this book out would be to double-cross you. But to let the bars down is like a first theft. It's hard to do, but the second time it isn't so hard and pretty soon it is easy. If I should write three books like this and let them out, I would forget there were any other kinds.[8]

This is Steinbeck's declaration of artistic purpose—and his effort to exorcise a dangerous (and permanent) aspect of his craft. Much of the motivation for Steinbeck's career is stated in this letter. After all, he did write *L'Affaire Lettuceburg*; and "tricks and jokes," detached episodes, and detached ironic hits, as well as a twisting of characters, are evident enough in much of Steinbeck's earlier work. But the depression materials were too serious to treat lightly or abstractly, or to subject to an imposed structure (mistaken idealism, nature worship, a metaphysical curse, a literary parallel). Such materials need to be in harmony with an appropriate structure.

From that intentional perspective, the central artistic problem is to present the universal and epical in terms of the individual and particular. Steinbeck chooses to deal with this by creating an individual, particular image of the epical experience of the dispossessed Okies by focusing a sustained attention on the experience of the Joads. The result is an organic combination of structures. Dramatic structure suits the family's particular history; panoramic structure proves out the representative nature of their history. To avoid a forced and artificial "typing," to assure that extensions of particular detail are genuinely organic, Steinbeck postulates a conceptual theme that orders structure and materials: the transformation of the Joad family from a self-contained, self-sustaining unit to a conscious part of a group, a whole larger than its parts. This thematic ordering is not merely implicit or ironic, as it is in *The Pastures of Heaven*, or withheld to create mystery as in *Cup of Gold* or *To a God Unknown*. Steinbeck chances the strength of the materials and the organic quality of their structure. And he defines differences: the group is not group-man. The earlier concept is a "beast," created by raw emotion ("blood"), short-lived, unwieldy, unpredictable, mindless; a monster that produces indiscriminate good or evil. The group is quite different—rational, stable, relatively calm—because it is an assemblage of like-minded people who retain their individual and traditional sense of right and wrong as a natural fact. Group-man lacks a moral dimension; the group is a morally pure instrument of power. The difference is acute at the level of leadership. The leaders have ambiguous aims in *In Dubious Battle*, but they are Christ-like (Jim Casy) or attain moral insight (Tom Joad) in *The Grapes of Wrath*.

The Grapes of Wrath is optimistic; *In Dubious Battle* is not. That the living part of the Joad family survives, though on the edge of survival, is less than glowingly optimistic, but that survival produces a mood that differs considerably from the unrelenting misery of *In Dubious Battle*. Optimism stems from the theme, most openly in the alternation of narrative chapter and editorial interchapter. While the Joads move slowly and painfully toward acceptance of the group, many of the interchapters define the broad necessity of that acceptance. Arbitrary plotting does not produce this change. Its development is localized in Ma Joad's intense focus on the family's desire to remain a unit; her recognition of the group is the dramatic resolution.[9] Optimism is demonstrated also in experience that toughens, educates, and enlarges the stronger Joads in a natural process. On the simplest, crudest level, the family's journey and ordeal is a circumstantial narrative of an effort to reach for the good material life. Yet that is not the sole motive, and those members who have only that motive leave the family. On a deeper level, the family is attempting to rediscover the identity it lost when it was dispossessed; so the Joads travel from order (their old, traditional life) through disorder (the road, California) to some hope of a better, rediscovered order, which they reach in Ma's recognition and Tom's dedication. Their journey toward order is the ultimate optimistic, ennobling process, the earned, thematic resolution of the novel.

I do not intend to imply that Steinbeck pretties his materials. He does not stint the details of the family's various privations, its continual losses of dignity, and the death or disappearance of many of its members. On the larger scale, there is considerable objective documentation of the general economic causes of such misery—a circumstantial process that lifts *The Grapes of Wrath* out of the merely historic genre of the proletarian novel. Optimism survives as the ultimate value because of the will of the people to understand and to control the conditions of their lives despite constant discouragement.

This value is essentially abstract, political. Steinbeck deepens and universalizes it by developing the relationship between the family unit and "the people." The family is made up of unique individuals. "The people" embraces a timeless entity, a continuing past, present, and future of collective memory—but free of any social or political function.[10] Time lag confounds the usefulness of "the people" as a guide for the present. The Joads and others like them know they may keep the land or get new land if they can kill or control "the Bank," as the old people killed Indians to take the land and controlled nature to keep it.[11] But "the Bank" is more complicated an enemy than Indians or nature because it is an abstraction.[12] So the Okies submit to dispossession in Oklahoma (forced by mechanized cheaper production of cotton) and to the huge migration into California (encouraged by landowners to get cheap field labor), motivated by the time lag that confuses them, for none of them comprehends the monstrous logic of modern economics. Despite their ignorance, in a process that is unifying in itself and is second only to survival, the families work at some way of preventing against "the Bank." The older, agrarian concept of "the people" is succeeded in time by the new concept of the group, an instrument of technology and political power—an analogue that works. Steinbeck makes this succession appear necessary and legitimate by a representation that excludes alternate solutions.[13] The permitted solution seems a natural evolution, from people to group, because it is a tactic, not a fundamental change in folkways. Its process is long and painful because the emotive entity, "the people," needs to feel its way toward redefinition as the group—the abstract, political entity which emerges as an organic, particularized whole. This is brilliant literary strategy, in its grasp of operative metaphor and its avoidance of an overly obvious, loaded opposition. Steinbeck is scrupulously careful to keep to precise and exact circumstantial detail in this developed metaphor. Concretely, the panicky violence of "the Bank" is the reverse of the fact that (seemingly by habit) the Joads are kind to those who need their help and neighborly to people who are like them. The metaphor is persuasive.

Steinbeck is quite as scrupulous in the use of allegory as a way of universalizing an abstract particular. In his earlier work this method can produce a tangibly artificial, forced result, but allegory is a credible and functional device in *The Grapes of Wrath*. The turtle episode in chapter 3 is justly famous. Objectively, we have a fully realized description of a land turtle's patient, difficult journey over dust fields, across a road and walled embankment, and on through the dust. The facts are the starting point; nature is not distorted or manipulated to yield allegorical meaning. The turtle seems awkward but it is able to survive, like the Joads, and like them it is moving southwest, out of the dry area.[14] It can protect itself against a natural danger like the red ant it kills, as the Joads protect themselves by their unity. The turtle's eyes are "fierce, humorous," suggesting force that takes itself easily; the stronger Joads are a fierce, humorous people.[15] When mismanaged human power attacks, as when a truck swerves to hit the turtle, luck is on the animal's side—it survives by luck. The Joads survive the mismanagement that produced the Dust Bowl and the brutalizing man-made conditions in California as much by luck as by design. The relation to the Joads of the life-bearing function of the turtle is more obscure, or perhaps overly ambitious. The factual starting point is that, unknowingly, the turtle carries an oat seed in its shell and unknowingly drops and plants the seed in the dust, where it will rest until water returns. The most obvious link in the

Joad family is the pregnant Rose of Sharon, but her baby is born dead. Perhaps compassion is "born," as in Uncle John's thoughts as he floats the dead baby down the flooding river in its apple box coffin:

> "Go down an' tell 'em. Go down in the street an' rot an' tell 'em that way. That's the way you can talk.... Maybe they'll know then."[16]

But this appeal is strained, too greatly distanced from the factual starting point. The link works in the restricted sense that Ruthie and Winfield are "planted," and will perhaps take root, in the new environment of California. At this point the careful allegory collapses under its own weight, yet care is taken to join the device to the central narrative. In chapter 4, Tom Joad picks up a turtle, and later Casy remarks on the tenacity of the breed:

> "Nobody can't keep a turtle though. They work at it and work at it, and at last one day they get out and away they go—off somewheres.[17]

This recognition of the turtle's purposeful tenacity interprets and places the preceding interchapter in the central narrative. Tom calls the turtle "an old bulldozer," a figure that works in opposition to the threatening insect life the tractors suggest as self-defeating, destructive tools of "the Bank."[18] Again, a purposeful turtle is opposed to homeless domestic animals, like the "thick-furred yellow shepherd dog" that passes Tom and Casy, to suggest precisely the ruined land and the destruction of the old ways of life on the most basic, animal level, where the wild (or free) animal survives best.[19] These and other supporting details extend the exemplum into the narrative; they continue and deepen Steinbeck's foreshadowing, moralizing insight naturally, within the range of biological imagery. It is true, allowing for the one collapse of the allegory, that none of Steinbeck's earlier work exhibits as profound a comprehension of what can be done to "place" an allegorical narrative device.

The turtle interchapter is masterful enough. Steinbeck does even more with an extended instance of allegorizing—the introduction of the lapsed preacher, Jim Casy, into the Joad family. Casy has a role that is difficult to present within the limits of credibility. Casy may look too much like his function, the Christ-like force that impels the family toward its transformation into the group. If the novel is to have more significance than a reportorial narrative of travel and hardship, Casy's spiritual insights are a necessary means of stating a convincing philosophical optimism. The technical difficulty is that Casy does not have a forthright narrative function. He drops out of the narrative for almost one hundred and fifty pages, although his presence continues through the Joads' wondering at times what had happened to him. When he reenters the novel, he is killed off within fifteen pages—sacrificed for the group in accord with his Christ-like function, with a phrase that recalls Christ's last words.[20] In spite of the obvious technical difficulty in handling such materials, Steinbeck realizes Casy as fully as any of the major Joads. Casy's struggle with himself to define "sin" to include the necessary facts of the natural world lends him a completely human aspect. He earns the right to make moral statements because he bases all judgments on his own experience. This earned right to "witness" serves to keep Casy human, yet it permits him to function as if he were an allegorical figure. This is a brilliant solution, and Casy is Steinbeck's most successful use of a functional allegorical figure in a major role. His narrative sharpness contrasts amazingly with the dim realization of Sir Henry Morgan or Joseph Wayne.

Even Casy's necessary distance is functional rather than arbitrary. He exists outside the narrative in the sense that he travels with the Joads but he is not a member of the family, and there is no danger of confusing his adventures with theirs. Further, by right of his nature and experience, he has the function of being the living moral conscience of "the people." He travels with the Joads to witness the ordeal of the Okies, to understand its causes, and to do what he can to help. Steinbeck's convincing final touch is that, at the end, Tom Joad aspires to Casy's role. In this shift, Steinbeck manipulates allegory, he does not submit to its rigid quality, for Tom is not like Casy. Tom is far more violent, more capable of anger; having been shown the way, however, he may be more successful as a practical missionary than Casy. One might say that if Casy is to be identified with Christ, the almost human god, Tom is to be identified with Saint Paul, the realistic, tough organizer. The allegorical link by which Tom is "converted" and assumes Casy's role is deeply realized and rich with significance, not simply because it is a technical necessity, but because it is a confirmation of Casy's reality as a man and a teacher. The parallels to Christ and Saint Paul would be only and technical facts if they were not realized so profoundly. The trivial fact that Casy has Christ's initials dims beside this more profound and sustained realization.

Function, not mere design, is as evident in the use of characterization to support and develop a conflict of opposed ideas—mainly a struggle between law and anarchy. The one idea postulates justice in a moral world of love and work, identified in the past with "the people" and in the present with the government camp and finally with the union movement, since these are the modern, institutional forms the group may take. The opposed idea postulates injustice in an immoral world of hatred and starvation. It is associated with buccaneering capitalism, which, in violent form, includes strikebreaking and related practices that cheapen human labor.

The Joads present special difficulties in characterization. They must be individualized to be credible and universalized to carry out their representative functions. Steinbeck meets these problems by making each of the Joads a specific individual and by specifying that what happens to the Joads is typical of the times. The means he uses to maintain these identities can be shown in some detail. The least important Joads are given highly specific tags—Grandma's religion, Grandpa's vigor, Uncle John's melancholy, and Al's love of cars and girls. The tags are involved in events; they are not inert labels. Grandma's burial violates her religion; Grandpa's vigor ends when he leaves the land; Uncle John's melancholy balances the family's experience; Al helps to drive the family to California and, by marrying, continues the family. Ma, Pa, Rose of Sharon, and Tom carry the narrative, so their individuality is defined by events rather than through events. Ma is the psychological and moral center of the family; Pa carries its burdens; Rose of Sharon means to ensure its physical continuity; and Tom becomes its moral conscience. On the larger scale, there is much evidence that what happens to the family is typical of the times. The interchapters pile up suggestions that "the whole country is moving" or about to move.[21] The Joads meet many of their counterparts or outsiders who are in sympathy with their ordeal; these meetings reenforce the common bond of "the people."[22] Both in the interchapters and the narrative, the universal, immediate issue is survival—a concrete universal.

On the other hand, the individualized credibility of the Joads is itself the source of two difficulties: the Joads are too different, as sharecroppers, to suggest a universal or even a national woe, and they speak an argot that might limit their universal quality.[23] Steinbeck handles these limitations with artistic license. The narrative background contains the Joads' past; their experience as a landless proletariat is highlighted in the narrative foreground. The argot is made to seem a typical language within the novel in three ways: it is the major language; people who are not Okies speak variations of their argot; and that argot is not specialized in its relevance, but is used to communicate the new experiences "the people" have in common as a landless proletariat. However, because these solutions depend on artistic license, any tonal falseness undermines severely the massive artistic truthfulness the language is intended to present. So the overly editorial tone in several of the interchapters has a profoundly false linguistic ring, although the tonal lapse is limited and fairly trivial in itself.

The Joads are characterized further in comparison with four Okie types who refuse to know or are unable to gain the knowledge the family derives from its collective experience. They are the stubborn, the dead, the weak, and the backtrackers; they appear in the novel in that order.

Muley Graves is the stubborn man, as his punning name suggests. He reveals himself to Tom and Casy near the beginning of the novel. His refusal to leave Oklahoma is mere stubbornness; his isolation drives him somewhat mad. He is aware of a loss of reality, of "jus' wanderin' aroun' like a damn ol' graveyard ghos'," and his blind violence is rejected from the beginning by the strongest, who oppose his pessimism with an essential optimism.[24]

Deaths of the aged and the unborn frame the novel. Grandpa and Grandma are torn up by the roots and die, incapable of absorbing a new, terrible experience. Rose of Sharon's baby, born dead at the end of the novel, is an index of the family's ordeal and a somewhat contrived symbol of the necessity to form the group.

The weak include two extremes within the Joad family. Noah Joad gives up the struggle to survive; he finds a private peace. His character is shadowy, and his choice is directed more clearly by Steinbeck than by any substance within him.[25] Connie has plenty of substance. He is married to Rose of Sharon and deserts her because he had no faith in the family's struggle to reach California. His faith is absorbed in the values of "the Bank," in getting on, in money, in any abstract goal. He wishes to learn about technology in order to rise in the world. He does not admire technique for itself, as Al does. He is a sexual performer, but he loves no one. Finally, he wishes that he had stayed behind in Oklahoma and taken a job driving a tractor. In short, with Connie, Steinbeck chooses brilliantly to place a "Bank" viewpoint within the family. By doing so, he precludes a simplification of character and situation, and he endorses the complexity of real people in the real world. (*In Dubious Battle* is similarly free of schematic characterization.) In addition, the family's tough, humanistic values gain in credibility by their contrast with Connie's shallow, destructive modernity. The confused gas station owner and the pathetic one-eyed junkyard helper are embodied variations on Connie's kind of weakness.[26] Al provides an important counterpoint. He wants to leave the family at last, like Connie, but duty and love force him to stay. His hard choice points the moral survival of the family and measures its human expense.

The Joads meet several backtrackers. The Wilsons go back because Mrs. Wilson is dying; the Joads do not stop, in spite of death. The ragged man's experience foreshadows what the Joads find in California; but they keep on. Some members of the Joad family think of leaving but do not, or they leave for specific reasons—a subtle variation on backtracking. Al and

Uncle John wish deeply at times to leave, but they stay; Tom leaves (as Casy does) but to serve the larger, universal family of the group. Backtracking is a metaphor, then, a denial of life, but always a fact as well. The factual metaphor is deepened into complexity because the Joads sympathize with the backtrackers' failure to endure the hardships of the road and of California, in balance with where they started from—the wasteland—while knowing they cannot accept that life-denying solution. All of these choices are the fruit of the family's experience.

A fifth group of owners and middle-class people are accorded no sympathetic comprehension, as contrasted with the Joads, and, as in *In Dubious Battle*, their simply and purely monstrous characterization is too abstract to be fully credible. The few exceptions occur in highly individualized scenes or episodes (chapter 15 is an example) in which middle-class "shitheels" are caricatures of the bad guys, limited to a broad contrast with the good guys (the truck drivers, the cook), who are in sympathy with a family of Okies.[27] This limitation has the narrative advantage of highlighting the importance and vitality of the Okies to the extent that they seem by right to belong in the context of epic materials, but the disadvantage of shallow characterization is severe. Steinbeck can provide a convincing detailed background of the conditions of the time; he cannot similarly give a rounded, convincing characterization to an owner or a disagreeable middle-class person.

On the whole, then, fictive strength and conviction are inherent in the materials of *The Grapes of Wrath*. The noticeable flaws are probably irreducible aspects of the time context and of narrative shorthand, counterpointed by a complex recognition of human variety in language and behavior.

The ordering of the structure supports this conclusion. *The Grapes of Wrath* has three parts: Tom's return and his witnessing of events; the family's departure and experiences on the road; its arrival and experiences in California. The interchapters "locate" and generalize the narrative chapters, somewhat like stage directions. They supply, in a suitably dramatic or rhetorical style, information the Joads cannot possess, and they are involved more often than not in the narrative.[28] This device provides for both precise detail and epic scope. The imagery fulfills the structural purpose of pitting life against death.

The first part contains ten chapters. The opening is a "location" interchapter. The dead land of the Dust Bowl in Oklahoma provides the imagery of a universal death, but at the close the women watch their men to see if they will break in the stress of that natural disaster. The men do not break; the scene is repeated in California at the close of the novel in a rising rhetoric.[29] The objective imagistic frame sets life against death, and life endures in the will of the people to endure. The following nine chapters center on Tom's return from a kind of death—prison. With Casy, Tom is an external observer, witnessing with fresh eyes the dead land and the universal dispossession. Death seems to prevail. The turtle interchapter is recapitulated ironically in the narrative. Pa carries handbills that promise jobs in California, an analogue to the turtle carrying a head of oats; but the handbills falsely promise renewal; their intention is to cheapen the labor market. Later events prove the group concept is the genuine renewal, the true goal. Immediately, death is associated with "the Bank," an abstraction presented concretely in symbolic form as the tractor—the perfect tool of the abstract "Bank," which dehumanizes its driver and kills the fertility of the land.

When he sees the abandoned Joad home, Tom says, "Maybe they're all dead," but Muley Graves tells Tom the family is alive, with Uncle John, and about to leave without him for California.[30] Tom is reborn or returned to life within the family, but its vital center has shifted (as represented in charged, frankly mystical terms) to a life-giving machine:

> The family met at the most important place, near the truck. The house was dead, and the fields were dead; but this truck was the active thing, the living principle.[31]

The family's certainties develop from an ironically hopeful innocence, a failure to realize that a new basis for life has overtaken them, replacing family with group. The trek is an instinctive flight from death, but the economic system is more deadly than the drouth. The Joads accept the promise of the handbills, they are cheated when they sell their farm equipment, but they do not doubt that they will transplant themselves in California. The real certainty is the death of the past, as in the burning of relics by an unnamed woman in an interchapter, and by Ma herself, just before the trek begins.

All that is not dead is altered. Pa's loss of authority to Ma and Al's new authority (he knows automobiles) represent the shifts in value within the family. They retain a living coherence as farmers. They work as a unit when they kill and salt down the hogs in preparation for the trek. They are innocent of the disgusting techniques of close dealing in business, but Tom explains to Casy how the Joads can deal closely enough in their accustomed agrarian context. Their innocence, therefore, is touching, not comic, and their literal preparations support a symbolic preparation, a blindly hopeful striving to find life. Their journey is an expression, despite all shocks and changes, of the will to survive; hence, it has an epic dignity, echoing their retained, personal dignity.

In all the imagery of life and death, Steinbeck is consistent in that his symbols grow out of objective, literal facts. He thus achieves imagery in a more fully realized texture in this novel than in earlier work. This organically realized symbolism is maintained and developed in the seven chapters of the second section.

With the dead land behind them, the family carries the death of the past on its journey. Grandpa dies on the first night. Probably his stroke is caused, at least in part, by the "medicine" that Ma and Tom dope him with to take him away from the land—for the good of the family as a whole. An incipient group concept emerges in this overriding concern for the whole. Grandpa's death is offset by the meeting of the Joads and the Wilsons. At the beginning, Grandpa's illness and death join the two families in bonds of sympathy. There are other unifying forces; the language bar becomes senseless, and the two families help each other. Casy sees the emergence of the group, the whole absorbing the individual, in his sermon for Grandpa:

> Casy said solemnly, "This here ol' man jus' lived a life an' jus' died out of it. I don't know whether he was good or bad, but that don't matter much. He was alive, an' that's what matters. An' now he's dead, an' that don't matter. Heard a fella tell a poem one time, an' he says, 'All that lives is holy.'"[32]

A modest dignity embodies the vitalistic dogma. As a further push from individual to group, the family decides to break the law by burying Grandpa secretly beside the road; a conventional funeral would eat up the money they need to reach California. Grandma's grisly, circumstantial death is delayed until the end of the section; it outweighs the achievement of reaching their destination and foreshadows the reality of California. True, the family can absorb death, even new kinds of death, into its experience. Ruthie and Winfield react most violently to the dog's death at the first stop on the road; they are less affected by Grandpa's death, still less by Grandma's. Late on the night of Grandpa's death after the Joads and Wilsons have agreed to join forces, Ma remarks: "Grandpa—it's like he's dead a year."[33] Experience breeds a calm in the face of loss that fills in the past. Tom points this harshly realistic network of difference after Grandma's death:

> "They was too old," he said. "They wouldn't of saw nothin' that's here. Grampa would a been a-seein' the Injuns an' the prairie country when he was a young fella. An' Granma would a remembered an' seen the first home she lived in. They was too ol'. Who's really seein' it is Ruthie and Winfiel'."[34]

Life matters. The narrative context supports this fruit of the family's private experience. Between the deaths of Grandpa and Grandma, the Joads meet several symbolically dead people on the road. The gas station owner is incapable of learning the meaning of his own experience even when it is explained to him. The one-eyed junkyard helper lives in a prison of self, inside his ugly face and unclean body. Tom (who was in an actual prison) tries unsuccessfully to force him from his death into life. The several returning sharecroppers have come to accept a living death as the only reality. They have cut themselves off from the inchoate struggle to form a group, admittedly against severe odds, so they have no choice but to return to the dead, empty land.

But to outsiders, seeing only the surface, the Joads are not heroic lifebearers but stupidly ignorant, as in a dialogue between two service station boys when the family leaves on the final lap of the trek, the night trip across the Mojave Desert:

> "Jesus, I'd hate to start out in a jalopy like that." "Well, you and me got sense. Them goddamn Okies got no sense and no feeling. They ain't human. A human being wouldn't live like they do. A human being couldn't stand to be so dirty and miserable. They ain't a hell of a lot better than gorillas." "Just the same. I'm glad I ain't crossing the desert in no Hudson Super-Six...." "You know, they don't have much trouble. They're so goddamn dumb they don't know it's dangerous. And, Christ Almighty, they don't know any better than what they got. Why worry?"[35]

The dialogue is exactly true, but the truth is ironic. The Joads do have the appearance of death, and ignorant, dirty, dispossessed yokels seem to be unlikely carriers of an affirmation of life. The ironic truth defines the heroism of the Joads. The family is aware of the dangers of the desert crossing, and Grandma dies during it, "for the fambly," as Ma says.[36] In general the family is more aware than the boys at the service station are allowed to know. After meeting a second returning sharecropper, the Joads are even aware of the actual conditions in California; Uncle John, the family's weakest moral agent, voices the family's rejection of despair when he says, "We're a-goin' there, ain't we? None of this here talk gonna keep us from goin' there."[37] The service station boys express, so we can dismiss, a superficially sentimental view of the Joads. The ironic truth is that the family goes ahead, knowing the dangers and aware that California may not be Eden. Their genuine heroism and nobility are all the more valid for being tested by irony.

Yet there is no suggestion that the Joads are merely deterministic formulae. They are pawns of circumstance up to a point. They react to events they do not understand fully, and no doubt partial ignorance and pure necessity keep them on the road and get them to California. But Ma and Tom undergo certain developments of character that exclude determinism. Ma's constantly increasing moral authority is her response to the forces that are tearing the family apart, but she acts out of love that is restricted to the family, that is not universalized until very near the end of the novel. Tom's role is more extensive and more complex. He begins by regarding himself as a creature of necessity—"I ruther jus'—lay one foot down in front a the other"—but his quietism relates to a prison experience he does not want to live "over an' over."[38] His natural understanding of why and how people behave forces him into a moral concern that is larger but as intense as Ma's. His knowledge of people is established at the beginning of the novel, in his shrewd, unflattering understanding of the truck driver who gives him a lift, and it widens subsequently with experience on the road. His disdain for the gas station owner precedes his tough moral lecture to the one-eyed junkyard helper and an equally tough lecture to Al. That is to say, Tom is involved. His moral development follows Casy's, with the significant difference that his is the more difficult to achieve. Casy is a relatively simple character; he can express moral concern easily. Tom's emotional numbness following his time in prison does not permit meditation or cancel personality, so the awakening of his moral consciousness on the road is a more rigorous, more painful experience than Casy's time in the desert. Consequently, because of its special quality, Tom's growing awareness of good and evil is a highly credible mirror of the general experience that drives the family toward the group. The logic is paradoxical, but the artistic insight is realized deeply in Tom's circumstantial journey from moral quietism to moral concern for the group.

Enduring all the harsh experiences of their journey, the family gains moral stature and finds that it can function as a unit in the new environment of the road. Its survival in California is a result in part of its redefinition gained on the road.

The interchapters underscore and generalize these particulars. Chapter 14 states the growth of the group concept as a shift in the thinking of the migrants from *I* to *we*. The narrative context is Grandpa's death and the unity of the Joads and Wilsons. Chapter 15 suggests that the Joads' ordeal is a moral experience that affects society at large. Chapter 17 continues the theme that the road furthers the growth of the group concept:

Every night relationships that make a world, established; every morning the world torn down like a circus. At first the families were timid in the building and tumbling worlds, but gradually the technique of building worlds became their technique. Then leaders emerged, then laws were made, then codes came into being. And as the worlds moved westward they were more complete and better furnished, for their builders were more experienced in building them.[39]

The formation of a group is a "technique" with its basis in the older agrarian order. As with the Joads, the experience of building produces a new moral stature and a redefinition of the family.

In the relation of these events and changes, the narrative chapters and interchapters cohere in an organic unity. Their common theme is movement from and through death to a new life inherent in the group concept. The symbolic level extends the narrative level of movement on the road through time and space. The texture is fully realized. No generalization violates narrative particulars or exists apart from them. Steinbeck's work is careful, convincing, flawless.

The third part—the family's arrival and experience in California—marks an artistic decline. The materials alter and at times the structure is defective.

The chief difference in the materials is an absolute focus on man-made misery. In Oklahoma and on the road, survival can seem to be mainly a struggle against natural conditions. Drouth is the cause of the migration. "The Bank" dispossesses the Okies, but it is not the effective cause of the drouth. In California the struggle is almost entirely against men, and there is no possibility of an escape by further migration. The chief difference in structure stems from Steinbeck's need to begin to think of how to conclude the novel, which presents structural choices and manipulations not present in the first two parts of the novel. For a time the narrative thrust remains coherent, an organic unity disguising these changes.

Grandma's undignified burial establishes the pattern of the family's experience in California. Her pauper's funeral by the state contrasts with the full dignity and free will the family expressed in burying Grandpa. Landless poverty is a moral insult to family pride, and it affects their will to survive. For the moment, as their moral spokesman, Ma expresses a will to recover as quickly as possible for the sake of the future:

> "We got to git," she said. "We got to find a place to stay. We got to get to work an' settle down. No use a-lettin' the little fellas go hungry. That wasn't never Granma's way. She always et a good meal at a funeral."[40]

The conserving lesson of the past is negated by the present economic reality. Ma's brave gesture fails as the family learns that California is a false goal. The imagery associated with California indicates these negations. Peter Lisca and Joseph Fontenrose have pointed to the major biblical parallels in *The Grapes of Wrath*, including those associating California and the Promised Land.[41] The parallels are intensive, even more so than Lisca and Fontenrose suggest, and their function is ironic rather than associative. To begin with, California evokes images of plenty to eat and drink. The ironic fact is that California is the literal reverse of Canaan; there is little to eat and drink, at least for Okies; but California is the Promised Land so far as the family's experience there forces the full emergence of the group concept. Appropriately, the family enters California with a foreboding that runs counter to their expectations:

> Pa called, "We're here—we're in California!" They looked dully at the broken rock glaring under the sun, and across the river the terrible ramparts of Arizona.[42]

They have crossed over, but the physical imagery foreshadows their actual human environment. The land is green across the river, but the biblical lists of landscape features are framed by the fact that they have been carrying Grandma's corpse. The human reality of California life is a living death, as the first camp, the Hooverville, suggests: "About the camp there hung a slovenly despair," everything is "grey" and "dirty," there is no work, no food, and no evident means of overcoming "despair."[43] The deadly economic reality is explained by a young man in the Hooverville, when Tom asks why the police "shove along" the migrants:

> "Some say they don' want us to vote; keep us movin' so we can't vote. An' some says so we can't get on relief. An' some says if we set in one place we'd get organized."[44]

That reply announces the political solution, the humanly possible way of countervailing power through organization. But the words are programmatic, not a revelation of character.

The difference in materials and in structure begins to appear at this point. The root of the matter is that Steinbeck is so compelled by the documentary facts that he permits their narration to take precedence over the central theme of the family's transformation into the group. And in moving the novel toward an affirmation of life in response to the facts, Steinbeck allows the Joads' experience in California to become a series of allegorical details within a panoramic structure. The narrowed scope of the materials and the schematic handling of the structure are visible in nearly every event in this part of the novel.

Casy's alternative to "despair," sacrificing himself for "the people," is almost wholly an allegorical solution. It is so abstractly schematic that at first none of the family understands its meaningful allegorical force—that loss of self leads to the group concept and thus to power to enforce the will of the group. Instead, the narrative is largely an account of the family's efforts to avoid starvation. The phrase "We got to eat" echoes through these concluding chapters.[45] Ma's changing attitude toward hungry unknown children is ambiguous: "I dunno what to do. I can't rob the fambly. I got to feed the fambly."[46] Ma grows more positive, later, when she is nagged by a storekeeper in the struck orchard:

> "Any reason you got to make fun? That help you any?" "A fella got to eat," he began; and then, belligerently, "A fella got a right to eat." "What fella?" Ma asked.[47]

Ma asserts finally that only "the poor" constitute a group that practices charity:

> "I'm learnin' one thing good," she said. "Learnin' it all a time, ever' day. If you're in trouble or hurt or need—go to poor people. They're the only ones that'll help—the only ones."[48]

"The poor" are identified with "the people," who, in turn are the emerging group. Their purity is allegorical, and, in its limitation, incredible. Steinbeck's handling of "the poor" in *In Dubious Battle* is much less schematic, and therefore far more credible. In general, romanticizing "the poor" is more successful in an outright fantasy like *Tortilla Flat* but Steinbeck commits himself to a measure of realism in *The Grapes of Wrath* that does not sort well with the allegorical division of "good" from "evil."

Romanticizing "the poor" extends beyond Ma's insight to an idealization of the "folk law" that Tom envisions as the fruit of his own experience in California—at a great distance from the "building" experience on the road:

> "I been thinkin' how it was in that gov'ment camp, how our folks took care a theirselves, an' if they was a fight they fixed it theirself; an' they wasn't no cops wagglin' their guns, but they was better order than them cops ever give. I been a-wonderin' why we

can't do that all over. Throw out the cops that ain't our people. All work together for our own thing—all farm our own lan'."[49]

Presenting the reverse of Tom's beatific vision in an interchapter, Steinbeck draws on the imagery of the novel's title:

This vineyard will belong to the bank. Only the great owners can survive.... Men who can graft the trees and make the seed fertile and big can find no way to let the hungry people eat their produce.... In the souls of the people the grapes of wrath are filling and growing heavy, growing heavy for the vintage.[50]

It is not vitally important that Steinbeck's prediction of some kind of agrarian revolt has turned out to be wrong. The important artistic fact is that "good," divided sharply, abstractly, from "evil," argues that Steinbeck is not interested in rendering the materials in any great depth. Consider the contrast between the people in the government camp and in the struck orchard. Point by point, the camp people are described as clean, friendly, joyful, and organized, while in the struck orchard they are dirty, suspicious, anxious, and disorganized by the police.[51] Credibility gives way to neat opposites, which are less than convincing because Steinbeck's government camp is presented openly as a benevolent tyranny that averages out the will of "the people" to live in dignity and excludes people unable or unwilling to accept that average.

Neat opposites can gather fictive conviction if they are realized through individuals and in specific detail. There is something of that conviction in specific action against specific men, as when the camp leaders exclude troublemakers hired by business interests to break up the camp organization. There is more awkwardness in the exclusion of a small group of religious fanatics obsessed with sin. An important factor is that these people are genuinely Okies, not tools of the interests; another is that the exclusion is necessary, not realistic, if the secular values of the group concept are to prevail. Allowing for his selection and schematic treatment of these materials, Steinbeck does engineer his manipulated point with artistic skill. Fanaticism is considered a bad thing throughout the novel, both as a religious stance and as a social phenomenon. Tom's first meeting with Casy identifies "spirit" with emotional release, not a consciousness of sin, and Casy announces his own discovery, made during his time in the desert, of a social rather than an ethical connection between "spirit" and sexual excitement.[52] Further, fanaticism is identified repeatedly with a coercive denial of life. Rose of Sharon is frightened, in the government camp, by a fanatic woman's argument that dancing is sinful, that it means Rose will lose her baby. The woman's ignorance is placed against the secular knowledge of the camp manager:

> "I think the manager, he took [another girl who danced] away to drop her baby. He don' believe in sin.... Says the sin is bein' hungry. Says the sin is bein' cold."[53]

She compounds ignorance by telling Ma that true religion demands fixed economic classes:

> "[A preacher] says 'They's wicketness in that camp.' He says, 'The poor is tryin' to be rich.' He says, 'They's dancin' an' huggin' when they should be wailin' an' moanin' in sin.'"[54]

These social and economic denials of life are rooted in ignorance, not in spiritual enlightenment, and they are countered by the materialistic humanism of the camp manager. So fanaticism is stripped of value and associated with business in its denial of life. The case is loaded further by the benevolent tyranny of the group. Fanatics are not punished for their opinions, or even for wrongdoing. They are merely excluded, or they exclude themselves.

A similar process is apparent in the group's control of social behavior, as when Ruthie behaves as a rugged individual in the course of a children's game:

> The children laid their mallets on the ground and trooped silently off the court.... Defiantly she hit the ball again.... She pretended to have a good time. And the children stood and watched.... For a moment she stared at them, and then she flung down the mallet and ran crying for home. The children walked back on the court. Pig-tails said to Winfield, "You can git in the nex' game." The watching lady warned them, "When she comes back an' wants to be decent, you let her. You was mean yourself, Amy."[55]

The punishment is directive. The children are being trained to accept the group and to become willing parts of the group. The process is an expression of "folk law" on a primary level. There is no doubt that Ruthie learned her correct place in the social body by invoking a suitably social punishment.

Perhaps the ugliness implicit in the tyranny of the group has become more visible lately. Certainly recent students of the phenomenon of modern conformity could supply Steinbeck with very little essential insight. The real trouble is precisely there. The tyranny of the group is visible in all of Steinbeck's instances (its ambiguity is most evident in Ruthie's case), which argues for Steinbeck's artistic honesty in rendering the materials. But he fails to see deeply enough, to see ugliness and ambiguity, because he has predetermined the absolute "good" of group behavior—an abstraction that precludes subtle technique and profound insight, on the order of Doc Burton's reservations concerning group-man. The result is a felt manipulation of values and a thinning of credibility.

Given this tendency, Steinbeck does not surprise us by dealing abstractly with the problem of leadership in the government camp. Since there is minimal narrative time in which to establish the moral purity of Jim Rawley, the camp manager, or of Ezra Huston, the chairman of the Central Committee, Steinbeck presents both men as allegorical figures. Particularly Jim Rawley. His introduction suggests his allegorical role. He is named only once, and thereafter he is called simply "the camp manager." His name is absorbed in his role as God. He is dressed "all in white," but he is not a remote God. "The frayed seams on his white coat" suggest his human availability, and his "warm" voice matches his social qualities.[56] Nevertheless, there is no doubt that he is God visiting his charges:

> He put the cup on the box with the others, waved his hand, and walked down the line of tents. And Ma heard him speaking to the people as he went.[57]

His identification with God is bulwarked when the fanatic woman calls him the devil:

> "She says you was the devil," [says Rose of Sharon]. "I know she does. That's because I won't let her make people miserable.... Don't you worry. She doesn't know."[58]

What "she doesn't know" is everything the camp manager does know; and if he is not the devil, he must be God. But his very human, secular divinity— he can wish for an easier lot, and he is always tired from overwork—suggests the self-sacrifice that is Casy's function. The two men are outwardly similar. Both are clean and "lean as a picket," and the camp manager has "merry eyes" like Casy's when Tom meets Casy again.[59] These resemblances would be trivial, except for a phrase that pulls them together and lends them considerable weight. Ezra Huston has no character to speak of, beyond his narrative function, except that when he has finished asking the men who try to begin a riot in the camp why they betrayed "their own people," he adds: "They don't know what they're doin'."[60] This phrase foreshadows Casy's words to his murderer just before he is killed in an effort to break the strike: "You don't know what you're a-doin'."[61] Just as these words associate Casy with Christ, so they associate the leaders in the government camp with Casy. Steinbeck's foreshortening indicates that, because Casy is established firmly as a "good" character, the leaders in the government camp must resemble Casy in that "good" identity.

The overall process is allegorical, permitting Steinbeck to assert that the camp manager and Ezra Huston are good men by definition and precluding the notion that leadership may be a corrupting role, as in *In Dubious Battle*. It follows that violence in the name of the group is "good," whereas it is "evil" in the name of business interests. The contrast is too neat, too sharp, to permit much final credibility in narrative or in characterization.

A still more extreme instance of Steinbeck's use of allegory is the process by which Tom Joad assumes the role of a leader. Tom's pastoral concept of the group is fully developed, and as the novel ends, Tom identifies himself through mystic insight with the group. Appropriately, Tom explains his insight to Ma because Tom's function is to act while Ma's function is to endure—in the name of the group. More closely, Ma's earlier phrase, "We're the people—we go on," is echoed directly in Tom's assurance when Ma fears for his life:

> "Well, maybe like Casy says, a fella ain't got a soul of his own, but on'y a piece of a big one—an' then—" "Then what, Tom?" "Then it don't matter. Then I'll be all aroun' in the dark. I'll be ever'where—wherever you look.... See? God, I'm talkin' like Casy. Comes of thinkin' about him so much. Seems like I can see him sometimes."[62]

This anthropomorphic insight, borrowed from *To a God Unknown* and remotely from Emerson, is a serious idea, put seriously within the allegorical framework of the novel's close. Two structural difficulties result. First, Tom has learned more than Casy could have taught him—that identification with the group, rather than self-sacrifice *for* the group, is the truly effective way to kill the dehumanized "Bank." Here, it seems, the Christ/Casy, Saint Paul/Tom identifications were too interesting in themselves, for they limit Steinbeck's development of Tom's insight to a mechanical parallel, such as the suggestion that Tom's visions of Casy equate with Saint Paul's visions of

Christ. Second, the connection between the good material life and Tom's mystical insight is missing. There is Steinbeck's close attention to Tom's political education and to his revival of belief in a moral world. But, in the specific instance, the only bridge is Tom's sudden feeling that mystical insight connects somehow with the good material life. More precisely, the bridge is Steinbeck's own assertion, since Tom's mystical vision of pastoral bliss enters the narrative only as an abstract announcement on Steinbeck's part.

Characterization is, as might be assumed, affected by this abstracting tendency. Earlier, major characters such as Tom and Ma are "given" through actions in which they are involved, not through detached, abstract essays; increasingly, at the close, the method of presentation is the detached essay or the extended, abstract speech. Steinbeck's earlier, more realized presentation of Tom as a natural man measures the difference. Even a late event, Tom's instinctive killing of Casy's murderer, connects organically with Tom's previous "social" crimes—the murder in self-defense, for which Tom has finished serving a prison term when the novel begins, and the parole that Tom jumps to go with the family to California. In all of these crimes, Tom's lack of guilt or shame links with the idea that "the people" have a "natural" right to unused land—not to add life, liberty, and the pursuit of happiness— and that "the Bank" has nothing but an abstract, merely legal right to such land. Tom's mystical vision is something else; it is a narrative shock, not due to Tom's "natural" responses, but to the oversimplified type of the "good" man that Tom is made to represent in order to close the novel on a high and optimistic note. Tom is a rather complex man earlier on, and the thinning out of his character, in its absolute identification with the "good," is an inevitable result of allegorizing.

Style suffers also from these pressures. Tom's speech has been condemned, as Emerson's writing never is, for mawkishness, for maudlin lushness, for the soft, rotten blur of intellectual evasion.[63] Style is a concomitant of structure; its decline is an effect, not a cause. Tom's thinking is embarrassing, not as thought, but as the stylistic measure of a process of manipulation that is necessary to close the novel on Steinbeck's terms.

The final scene, in which Rose of Sharon breastfeeds a sick man, has been regarded universally as the nadir of bad Steinbeck, yet the scene is no more or no less allegorical than earlier scenes in this final part. Purely in a formal sense, it parallels Tom's mystical union or identification with the group: it affirms that "life" has become more important than "family" in a specific action, and, as such, it denotes the emergence of the group concept. In that light, the scene is a technical accomplishment. Yet it is a disaster from the outset, not simply because it is sentimental; its execution, through the leading assumption, is incredible. Rose of Sharon is supposed to become

Ma's alter ego by taking on her burden of moral insight, which, in turn, is similar to the insight that Tom reaches. There is no preparation for Rose of Sharon's transformation and no literary justification except a merely formal symmetry that makes it desirable, in spite of credibility, to devise a repetition. Tom, like Ma, undergoes a long process of education; Rose of Sharon is characterized in detail throughout the novel as a protected, rather thoughtless, whining girl.[64] Possibly her miscarriage produces an unmentioned, certainly mystical change in character. More likely the reader will notice the hand of the author, forcing Rose of Sharon into an unprepared and purely formalistic role.

Once given this degree of manipulation, direct sentimentality is no surprise. Worse, the imagistic shift from anger to sweetness, from the grapes of wrath to the milk of human kindness, allows the metaphor to be uplifted, but at the cost of its structural integrity. The novel is made to close with a forced image of optimism and brotherhood, with an audacious upbeat that cries out in the wilderness. I have no wish to deny the value or the real power of good men, optimism, or brotherhood. The point is that Steinbeck imposes an unsupported conclusion upon materials which themselves are thinned out and manipulated. The increasingly grotesque episodes (and their leading metaphors) prove that even thin and manipulated materials resist the conclusion that is drawn from them, for art visits that revenge on its mistaken practitioners.

To argue that no better conclusion was available at the time, granting the country's social and political immaturity and its economic innocence, simply switches the issue from art to politics. No artist is obliged to provide solutions to the problems of the socio-politico-economic order, however "engaged" his work may be. Flaubert did not present a socioeducational program to help other young women to avoid Emma Bovary's fate. The business of the artist is to present a situation. If he manipulates the materials or forces them to conclusions that violate credibility—especially if he has a visible design upon us—his work will thin, the full range of human possibility will not be available to him, and to that extent he will have failed as an artist.

We must not exclude the likelihood, not that Steinbeck had no other conclusion at hand, but that his predisposition was to see a resolution in the various allegorical and panoramic arrangements that close out *The Grapes of Wrath*; Steinbeck's earlier work argues for that likelihood.

Yet that is not all there is to John Steinbeck. If he becomes the willing victim of abstract, horrendously schematic manipulations as *The Grapes of Wrath* nears its close still he is capable of better things. He demonstrates these potentialities particularly in minor scenes dealing with minor characters, so the negative force of the imposed conclusion is lessened.

Consider the scene in which Ruthie and Winfield make their way (along with the family) from the flooded boxcar to the barn where Rose of Sharon will feed the sick man. The intention of the scene is programmatic: the children's identification with the group concept. The overt content is the essentially undamaged survival of their sense of fun and of beauty. Significantly, the action makes no directly allegorical claim on the reader, unlike the rest of the concluding scenes.

Ruthie finds a flower along the road, "a scraggly geranium gone wild, and there was one rain-beaten blossom on it."[65] The common flower, visualized, does not insist on the identity of the beaten but surviving beauty in pure nature with the uprooted, starved children of all the migrants. The scene is developed implicitly, in dramatic, imagistic terms. Ruthie and Winfield struggle to possess the petals for playthings, and Ma forces Ruthie to be kind:

> Winfield held his nose near to her. She wet a petal with her tongue and jabbed it cruelly on his nose. "You little son-of-a-bitch," she said softly. Winfield felt for the petal with his fingers, and pressed it down on his nose. They walked quickly after the others. Ruthie felt how the fun was gone. "Here," she said. "Here's some more. Stick some on your forehead."[66]

The scene recapitulates the earlier scene on the playground of the government camp. Here, as there, Winfield is the innocent, and Ruthie's cruelty is changed by external pressure (the other children, Ma's threat) to an official kindness that transcends itself to become a genuine kindness when "the fun was gone." The observed basis of the present scene is the strained relationship that usually exists between an older sister and a younger brother. There is no visible effort to make the scene "fit" a predetermined allegorical scheme. Ruthie's kind gesture leads into Rose of Sharon's, as child to adult, and both scenes project the affirmative values—the survival of optimism, brotherhood, kindliness, goodness—that are the substance of the group concept at the conclusion. The children's quarrel and reconciliation is a relatively unloaded action, an event in itself. Tom's affirmation is nondramatic, a long, deeply mystical speech to Ma. Rose of Sharon's affirmation is out of character and frankly incredible. Uncle John's symbolic action derives from his own guilt but expresses a universal anger.

As the scene between the children is exceptional, Steinbeck's development of the flood scene is typical. Allegorical intentions override narrative power: the family's struggle against the flood is intended to equate with its surviving will to struggle against hopelessness; Pa, Uncle John, and

Al are exhausted but not beaten. Tom's insight precedes the flood; Rose of Sharon's agreement to breastfeed the sick man follows it. In the larger frame, neither extreme of drouth or flood can exhaust the will and the vitality of the people. The dense texture of these panoramic materials is impressive. They lie side by side, at different levels of the "willing suspension of disbelief," depending on whether they are convincing narrative actions or palpable links in an arranged allegory. Hence, there is no great sense of a concluding "knot," an organic fusion of parts; there is no more than a formulated ending, a pseudoclose that does not convince because its design is an a priori assertion of structure, not the supportive and necessary skeleton of a realized context. Here structure and materials fail to achieve a harmonious relationship.

These final scenes are not hackwork. We cannot apply to Steinbeck, even here, the slurring remark that F. Scott Fitzgerald aimed at Thomas Wolfe: "The stuff about the GREAT VITAL HEART OF AMERICA is just simply corny."[67] Steinbeck's carefully interwoven strands of character, metaphor, and narrative argue a conscious, skillful intention, not a sudden lapse of material or of novelistic ability. Even in failure, Steinbeck is a formidable technician. His corn, here, if it exists, is not a signal of failed ability.

Steinbeck's feeling that *The Grapes of Wrath* must close on an intense level of sweetness, of optimism and affirmation, is not seriously in doubt. His ability to use the techniques of structure to this end is evident. The earlier novels demonstrate his able willingness to skillfully apply an external structure, to mold, or at least to mystify, somewhat recalcitrant materials. The letter withdrawing *L'Affaire Lettuceburg* suggests that Steinbeck is aware of having that willing skill—"just twisting this people out of shape"—and of having to resist its lures in this most serious work. So for the critic there is a certain horrid fascination in Steinbeck's consistent, enormously talented demonstration of aesthetic failure in the last quarter of *The Grapes of Wrath*.

The failure is not a matter of "sprawling asides and extravagances," or the more extreme motivational simplicities of naturalism, or a lapse in the remarkably sustained folk idiom and the representative epic scope. The failure lies in the means Steinbeck utilizes to achieve the end.

The first three quarters of the novel are masterful. Characters are presented through action; symbolism intensifies character and action; the central theme of transformation from self to group develops persuasively in a solid, realized documentary context. The final quarter of the novel presents a difference in every respect. Characters are fitted or forced into allegorical roles, heightened beyond the limits of credibility, to the point that they thin out or become frankly unbelievable. Scenes are developed almost solely as links in an allegorical pattern. Texture is reduced to documentation, and allegorical signs replace symbolism. The result is a hollowed rhetoric, a manipulated affirmation, a soft twist of insistent sentiment. These qualities deny the conceptual theme by simplifying it, by reducing the facts of human and social complexity to simple opposites.

The reduction is not inherent in the materials, which are rendered magnificently in earlier parts of the novel. The reduction is the consequence of a structural choice—to apply allegory to character, metaphor, and theme. In short, *The Grapes of Wrath* could conceivably have a sweetly positive conclusion without an absolute, unrestrained dependence on allegory. Yet the least subtle variety of that highly visible structural technique, with its objectionably simplified, manipulative ordering of materials, is precisely the element that prevails in the final part of *The Grapes of Wrath*.

Why? Steinbeck is aware of various technical options, and he is able to make use of them earlier in the novel. As we have seen in the previous novels, with the exception of *In Dubious Battle*, Steinbeck draws on allegory to stiffen or to heighten fictions that are too loose—too panoramic—to achieve the semblance of a dramatic structure purely by means of technique. Apparently Steinbeck was not offended aesthetically by the overwhelming artificiality that results from an extreme dependence on allegory. That the contemporary naturalistic or symbolic novel requires a less simple or rigid structure clearly escapes Steinbeck's attention.

On the contrary, Steinbeck is greatly attracted to some extreme kind of external control in much of the immediately preceding work and in much of the succeeding work. During the rest of his career, Steinbeck does not attempt seriously, on the massive scale of *The Grapes of Wrath*, to achieve a harmonious relationship between structure and materials. He prefers some version of the control that flaws the last quarter of *The Grapes of Wrath*.

This judgment offers a certain reasonableness in the otherwise wild shift from *The Grapes of Wrath* to the play-novelettes.

NOTES

1. John Steinbeck, *The Grapes of Wrath* (New York: The Viking Press, Inc., 1939). Hereafter cited as *GW*.

2. Louis Kronenberger, *The Nation*, 148 (April 15, 1939), 440. "It is, I think, one of those books—there are not very many—which really do some good."

3. I list a typical range of such criticism by date of publication.

　　a. James T. Farrell, "The End of a Literary Decade," *The American Mercury*, 48 (December 1939), 408–14.

　　b. Edmund Wilson, "The Californians: Storm and Steinbeck," *The New Republic*, 103 (December 9, 1940), 784–87.

c. Stanley Edgar Hyman, "Some Notes on John Steinbeck," *Antioch Review*, 2 (Summer 1942), 185–200.

d. Maxwell Geismar, *Writers in Crisis* (Boston: Houghton Mifflin Company, 1942), pp. 237–70.

e. Alfred Kazin, *On Native Grounds* (New York: Harcourt, Brace & Co., 1942), pp. 393–94.

f. W. M. Frohock, "John Steinbeck's Men of Wrath," *Southwest Review*, 31 (Spring 1946), 144–52.

g. John S. Kennedy, "John Steinbeck: *Life Affirmed and Dissolved*," in *Fifty Years of the American Novel*, ed. H. C. Gardiner, S.J. (New York: Charles Scribner's Sons, 1951), pp. 217–36.

h. Frederick J. Hoffman, *The Modern Novel in America: 1900–1959* (Chicago: Henry Regnery Company, 1951), pp. 146–53.

i. Edmund Fuller, "The New Compassion in the American Novel," *The American Scholar*, 26 (Spring 1957), 155–63.

j. Walter Fuller Taylor, "*The Grapes of Wrath* Reconsidered," *Mississippi Quarterly*, 12 (Summer 1959), 136–44.

4. I list a typical range of such criticism by date of publication.

a. Harry Thornton Moore, *The Novels of John Steinbeck* (Chicago: Normandie House, 1939), pp. 53–72

b. Frederic I. Carpenter, "The Philosophical Joads," *College English*, 2 (January 1941), 315–25.

c. Joseph Warren Beach, *American Fiction: 1920–1940* (New York: The Macmillan Company, 1941), pp. 327–47.

d. Chester E. Eisinger, "Jeffersonian Agrarianism in *The Grapes of Wrath*," *University of Kansas City Review*, 14 (Winter 1947), 149–54.

e. Peter Lisca, "*The Grapes of Wrath* as Fiction," *PMLA*, 72 (March 1957), 296–309.

f. Eric C. Carlson, "Symbolism in *The Grapes of Wrath*," *College English*, 19 (January 1958), 172–75.

g. Theodore Pollock, "On the Ending of *The Grapes of Wrath*," *Modern Fiction Studies*, 4 (Summer 1958), 177–78.

5. I list a typical range of such criticism by date of publication.

a. Woodburn Ross, "John Steinbeck: Earth and Stars," in *University of Missouri Studies in Honor of A. H. R. Fairchild* (XXI), ed. Charles T. Prouty (Columbia: University of Missouri Press, 1946), pp. 177–91.

b. Frederick Bracher, "Steinbeck and the Biological View of Man," *The Pacific Spectator*, 2 (Winter 1948), 14–29.

c. Woodburn Ross, "John Steinbeck: Naturalism's Priest," *College English*, 10 (May 1949), 432–37.

6. Freeman Champney, "John Steinbeck, Californian," *The Antioch Review*, 7:3 (Fall 1947), 355. Reprinted by permission of *The Antioch Review*.

7. The main sources are:

a. John Steinbeck, "Dubious Battle in California," *The Nation*, 143 (September 12, 1936), 302–4.

b. John Steinbeck, "The Harvest Gypsies," *San Francisco News*, October 5–12, 1936. Reprinted with a 1938 epilogue and retitled *Their Blood Is Strong*, under the auspices of the Simon J. Lubin Society of California, Inc., April 1938. Reprinted in *A Companion to*

"*The Grapes of Wrath*," ed. Warren French (New York: The Viking Press, Inc., 1963), pp. 53–92.

    c. Lewis Gannett, "Introduction: John Steinbeck's Way of Writing," *The Viking Portable Steinbeck* (New York: The Viking Press, Inc., 1946), pp. xx–xxiv.

    d. Moore, pp. 53–54, 85, 88, 90.

    e. Peter Lisca, *The Wide World of John Steinbeck* (New Brunswick: Rutgers University Press, 1958), pp. 144–48.

    8. Gannett, pp. xxii–xxiii.

    9. *GW*, p. 606. "Use' to be the fambly was fust. It ain't so now. It's anybody. Worse off we get, the more we got to do."

    10. *GW*, pp. 37, 45–46, 73, 312, 535–36, 597–98.

    11. *GW*, pp. 45–46, 406–7, 432.

    12. *GW*, pp. 45–46, 50–53, 63–65. That buccaneering capitalism is an abstract or allegorical monster of evil is left to implication in *In Dubious Battle*. Steinbeck is far more directly allegorical in characterizing "the Bank" as an evil, *nonhuman* monster. Consequently there is, I think, a gain in horror but a relative loss of credibility.

    13. It would be too severe to blame Steinbeck for failing to foresee a quite different solution, a war that produced jobs for the Okies. But a cropper does plead to keep his land because with so many wars in sight cotton will go up (p. 44). That logic is rejected, possibly to motivate the emergence of the group—an insight that has turned out to be too shallow or too simple. *The Grapes of Wrath* has lost readers most often in our time because of its serious loss of historic relevance.

    14. I am indebted to Harry Thornton Moore for the directional suggestion. See Moore, p. 55.

    15. *GW*, p. 20.

    16. *GW*, p. 609. The reversal of values is evident in the reversed symbolism; the river bears death—not life, the coffin—not water to seeds in the earth.

    17. *GW*, p. 28.

    18. *GW*, p. 28.

    19. *GW*, p. 29.

    20. *GW*, pp. 364, 520, 527.

    21. *GW*, pp. 6–7, 43–47, 65, 104, 196–97, 206, 236, 259, 264–70, 273, 279, 317–18, 324–25.

    22. *GW*, pp. 165, 171,174–75, 215–20, 245–46.

    23. It is a curious fact that Steinbeck attempts to create a so-called "universal language" in *Burning Bright*, a far more theory-ridden novel than *The Grapes of Wrath*. In any event, the attempt produces a fantastic, wholly incredible language.

    24. *GW*, pp. 67–71, 151.

    25. Noah does not suggest earlier "idiot" characters—the two Burgundians in *Cup of Gold*, Willie in *To a God Unknown*, and Tularecito in *The Pastures of Heaven*. Instead, Noah's shadowy, directed character recalls one aspect of Lennie in *Of Mice and Men*.

    26. *GW*, pp. 170–74, 242, 343–44, 372.

    27. Fifteen years later, Steinbeck detailed this technique in a witty article, "How to Tell Good Guys from Bad Guys," *The Reporter*, 12 (March 10, 1955), 42–44. In that quite different, political context, Steinbeck demonstrates that he knows the technique is too bluntly black and white to permit any but the broadest cartoon characterization. There is every reason to think he knew as much in 1935 or 1939.

28. Because of that involvement, it is incorrect to think of the interchapters as choral. We see the difference in comparing the four detached interchapters in *Cup of Gold* with any interchapters in *The Grapes of Wrath*, and we see as well Steinbeck's artistic growth in the organic integration of chapter and interchapter in the later novel. For an excellent analysis of style in the interchapters, see Lisca, pp. 160–65. The stylistic variety always suited to its content is further evidence of a conscious, intentional artistry.

29. *GW*, pp. 6, 592–94.

30. *GW*, p. 55.

31. *GW*, p. 135.

32. *GW*, p. 196.

33. *GW*, p. 203.

34. *GW*, p. 313.

35. *GW*, pp. 301–2.

36. *GW*, pp. 311–12.

37. *GW*, p. 283.

38. *GW*, p. 241.

39. *GW*, p. 265.

40. *GW*, p. 328.

41. Lisca, pp. 169–70; Joseph Fontenrose, *John Steinbeck: An Introduction and Interpretation* (New York: Barnes & Noble, Inc., 1963), pp. 74–83.

42. *GW*, p. 275.

43. *GW*, pp. 327–29.

44. *GW*, pp. 332–33.

45. *GW*, pp. 479, 483, 487, 497, 512–13.

46. *GW*, p. 351.

47. *GW*, p. 512.

48. *GW*, pp. 513–14.

49. *GW*, p. 571.

50. *GW*, p. 476

51. *GW*, pp. 389–491, 558.

52. *GW*, pp. 27, 29, 30, 31–32.

53. *GW*, p. 423.

54. *GW*, p. 437.

55. *GW*, pp. 433–34.

56. *GW*, pp. 415–16.

57. *GW*, p. 416.

58. *GW*, p. 424.

59. *GW*, pp. 25–26, 415, 512.

60. *GW*, p. 470.

61. *GW*, p. 527.

62. *GW*, p. 572.

63. See references in footnote 3.

64. *GW*, pp. 129–30, 134–35, 175–77, 285–86, 343–44, 366, 371–72, 378–79, 413–14, 420–225, 440, 460–61, 482–85, 504, 508, 537, 539, 548, 580–81, 586–88.

65. *GW*, p. 615.

66. *GW*, pp. 615–16.

67. F. Scott Fitzgerald, *The Letters of F. Scott Fitzgerald*, edited, with an introduction by Andrew Turnbull (New York: Charles Scribner's Sons, 1963), p. 97. Reprinted by permission of Charles Scribner's Sons. Copyright © 1963 Frances Scott Fitzgerald Lanahan.

PETER LISCA

The Grapes of Wrath:
An Achievement of Genius

Steinbeck is frequently identified as a proletarian writer of the nineteen thirties, one whose dominant interest lay in the social and political problems of the Great Depression. But although *In Dubious Battle* and *Of Mice and Men* might generally seem to justify this reputation, neither work is specifically dated either by its materials or by Steinbeck's treatment. Migrant workers and union organizers had long been part of the California scene—and continued so to be. Steinbeck's early short story, "The Raid" (1934), dealing with two labor organizers, similarly avoids identification with its decade. It was not until 1939, at the very end of the period, that he published *The Grapes of Wrath*, a work clearly and specifically grounded in conditions and events that were then making news. In fact, so directly and powerfully did this novel deal with contemporary events that it itself became an important part of those events—debated in public forums, banned, burned, denounced from pulpits, attacked in pamphlets, and even debated on the floor of Congress. Along with such works as Upton Sinclair's *The Jungle* and Harriet Beecher Stowe's *Uncle Tom's Cabin*, *The Grapes of Wrath* has achieved a place among those novels that so stirred the American public for a social cause as to have had measurable political impact. Although thus associated with this class of social-protest fiction, *The Grapes of Wrath* continues to be read, not as a piece of literary or social history, but with a sense of emotional

From *John Steinbeck: Nature and Myth*. © 1978 by Peter Lisca.

involvement and aesthetic discovery. More than any other American novel, it successfully embodies a contemporary social problem of national scope in an artistically viable expression. It is unquestionably John Steinbeck's finest achievement, a work of literary genius.

To appreciate fully this accomplishment, it is important to keep in mind Steinbeck's independence from the extensive literary and political proletarian movements of the period. He took no part in the organized efforts of writers, critics, and scholars to promote leftist or Communist theory as fulfillment of their responsibility to society; nor was he personally committed to any political viewpoint. While this kind of ideological neutrality enabled him to escape the pitfall of being too close to his materials—prejudice and propaganda—Steinbeck's intimate knowledge of his materials contribute greatly to the novel's realism and hence to its authority.

This familiarity had started while he was still a boy working on the farms and ranches surrounding his hometown of Salinas; it had grown through his college years during vacations and drop-out periods. More recently, in the autumn of 1936, he had written an article on migrant labor for *The Nation*, and a series of seven articles on these "Harvest Gypsies" for the *San Francisco News*. Steinbeck's fiction had early shown an absorbing interest in man's relationship to the land. He had explored it in terms of myth and biology in *To a God Unknown*, communally in *The Pastures of Heaven*, and as a factor of maturation in the short stories of *The Red Pony*. But through the field trips he made and the reading he did in preparation for his articles, and through subjecting himself personally to the migrant experience by living and working with the laborers, he was able to extend considerably the range of his terms to include the economic and, in the largest sense, the political. The truth of his observation in these latter dimensions of *The Grapes of Wrath* has long been substantiated by historians, sociologists, and political scientists; the truth of the novel's vision of humanity has been proven again and again in the hearts of its readers.

The novel's main characters are the twelve members of the Joad family: Grampa, Granma, Pa, Ma, their children Winfield, Ruthie, Noah, Al, Tom (just returned from prison), Rosasharn and her husband Connie, and Uncle John, joined by the ex-preacher Jim Casy. Dispossessed of their Oklahoma homestead by the banks having foreclosed the mortgage on their property, after the impoverished soil and dust storms made it impossible for them to support themselves, the group leaves for California, where they expect to find work as field hands. Meanwhile their land is joined to that of other unfortunate neighbors and worked with huge tractors. During the long journey the Joads find that they are part of a large migration of people with whom they share dangers and privations—especially the Wilson family. Grampa and Grandma Joad die, and Noah leaves the group en route. The rest of them arrive in California to find the labor market glutted with families like themselves, resented and disliked by the inhabitants, exploited mercilessly by the large growers and oppressed by the police. Connie deserts the family; Jim Casy is arrested, appears later as a labor organizer but is killed by vigilantes, one of whom is in return killed by Tom, who then becomes a fugitive; Rosasharn's baby is born dead, and the novel ends with the Joads and their new friends, the Wainwrights, being even more hungry, ill, and impoverished than they were at the start.

All the characters are drawn as fully credible human beings, individual yet also representative of their social class and circumstances. This is true even of such clearly unusual and strong personalities as Tom Joad, Jim Casy, Ma Joad, and her daughter Rosasharn. Casy, although a vision-pierced prophet, retains enough elements of his revival-meeting, "Jesus-jumping" sect and cultural folkways to remain specifically human. Ma Joad's heroic maternal qualities reflect the strength and character of those migrant wives who not only survived but nourished as well their children and husbands. Steinbeck may have had these women especially in mind when he chose the title "Their Blood Is Strong" for the republication of his *San Francisco News* articles. Such details as Grampa's senility, Al's abilities as an automobile mechanic, Connie's faith in cheap, correspondence trade schools, Uncle John's guilt complex, and Rosasharn's pregnancy personalize each character in turn and contribute to the reader's involvement. But Steinbeck was not writing a novel of personal adventure and misfortune. His theme is the entire social condition of which his characters are a part, and it is primarily in terms of the total situation that they have existence. Thus their role is collective, representational of the Okies and migrant workers, just as in the novel the Shawnee Land and Cattle Company represents the evicting landlords, and the California Farmers' Association represents the growers.

That Steinbeck succeeds in creating characters capable of bearing such wide responsibility is a brilliant achievement, but the novel's vast subject requires even more. To have put the Joads into the large variety of situations needed to add up to a total picture would have destroyed their necessary credibility as particular and real people. Rather than vastly increasing the number of characters and thus weakening the reader's empathetic response and the novel's narrative line, or digressing from the action with authorial comment, Steinbeck conceived the idea of using alternating chapters as a way of filling in the larger picture. About one hundred pages, or one sixth of the book, is devoted to this purpose. At first glance it might seem that putting these digressions from the Joad family into separate chapters interrupts the narrative line even more, and that such a device breaks the book into two distinct parts, or kinds of chapters; resulting in a monotonous tick tock effect. Of this danger the author was well aware, and he avoided it by using in the interchapters a variety of devices to minimize their interruption of the narrative action, temper their expository nature, and otherwise blend the two kinds of chapters in the reader's mind.

Perhaps the most important of the devices Steinbeck uses is dramatization. Chapter five, for example, deals with the process by which mortgaged lands are taken over by the banks, the small farmers evicted, and these lands combined into vast holdings cultivated with efficient modern machinery by absentee landlords. Whereas such previous writers in the naturalist tradition as Theodore Dreiser and Frank Norris would have addressed the reader directly on these points, giving him a well-researched lecture, Steinbeck presents a series of vignettes in which, through generalized characters, situations, and dialogue, we see these things happening. The device is reminiscent of the medieval mystery plays which dramatized Bible stories and made them real to the common people; or of Greek drama which through familiar figures and a chorus of elders or women gave voice to the people's ethical and religious beliefs. Even the introduction and the transitions between these vignettes share this dramatized quality, as in the opening paragraph of chapter five, in which "owners" are presented walking, talking, touching things, and "tenants" are listening, watching, squatting in the dust which they mark with their little sticks, their wives standing in the doorways, the children wriggling their toes. In similar fashion other chapters present further aspects of the total situation: chapter seven, the buying of used cars for the trip; chapter nine, the selling of household goods; chapters seventeen and twenty-three, the nature of migrant life along the road.

Another device that Steinbeck uses to integrate the two kinds of material is juxtaposition. Of course, everything included in the interchapters is related to the events of the narrative. And each interchapter is so placed that its content is most pertinent to the action in the chapter that precedes or follows it. Highway 66 is the subject of the interchapter that follows the Joads' turning onto that highway; the rain and flood of chapter twenty-nine set the stage for the novel's conclusion. But furthermore, and most effectively, the interchapters are frequently used to develop or complete some specific action initiated in the preceding narrative, or vice versa. Chapter eight ends with the Joads driving off to sell their household goods; the interchapter that follows presents us with generalized characters selling just such goods; in chapter ten the Joads return with the empty truck, having sold their goods, pack the truck, and leave home; chapter eleven describes the gradual deterioration of an abandoned house. A variation of this device is achieved by repetition, in which some specific detail in one kind of chapter reappears in the other, thus further knitting the two together. The anonymous house in an interchapter becomes the Joad house when, in the following chapter, the latter also is seen with one of its corners knocked off the foundation; the anonymous man with a rifle who in the same interchapter threatens the tractor driver becomes Grampa Joad, who in the next chapter is reported to have shot out the headlight of a tractor.

To temper the expository nature of the interchapters and blend them with the rest, Steinbeck works with the prose style itself. The colorful folk idiom and figurative language used by the Joads, Wilsons, Wainwrights, and other migrants reappear in the dramatizations of the interchapters as the language also of the generalized characters. But (except for a brief oversight in chapter five) the conversation in the interchapters is not marked off by quotation marks, thus emphasizing its generalized nature and at the same time further blending it into other elements in these same chapters, weakening the identity and separateness of the more directly expository passages. Finally, through frequent variations in prose rhythm and idiom specifically pertinent to a particular scene, any tendency to group the expository chapters together as different in kind from the narrative ones is discouraged. Consider, for example, the variety of effects presented by chapter three on the turtle, chapter seven on the selling of used cars, chapter twenty-five on the California harvest.

There is, however, another important element of continuity in the prose style, in addition to the spoken idiom of its generalized characters. From the opening chapter, describing the drought, to the penultimate one, describing the flood with which the novel ends, the syntactical structures and rhythms of the narrative voice are those of the King James Bible: "The tractors had lights shining, for there is no day and night for a tractor and the discs turn the earth in the darkness and they glitter in the daylight." Almost disappearing in some of the chapters and totally possessing others, this voice, through its inescapable association with the Bible, becomes the moral center of the novel. It speaks with the force and authority of an Old Testament prophet, some Jeremiah haranguing a sinful people: "There is a crime here that goes beyond denunciation. There is a sorrow here that weeping cannot symbolize. There is a failure here that topples all our success. The fertile earth, the straight tree rows, the sturdy trunks and the ripe fruit. And children dying of pellagra must die because a profit cannot be taken from an orange."

All this is not to say that the sixteen interchapters are equally brilliant or successful. Perhaps three of them (nineteen, twenty-one, twenty-five), concerned with historical information, and a few paragraphs in two or three others, are too direct. But these are exceptions. For the most part, the problem raised by the use of interchapters is fully met by the brilliance of Steinbeck's literary technique.

In themselves, then, the interchapters accomplish several things for the novel. As has been mentioned, they provide an artistically acceptable place for the author's own statements, and they make possible the inclusion of additional materials without overusing the Joads or introducing many other specific characters. Closely related to this latter function is these chapters' capacity for amplification. They present dramatically with a sense of real experience what would otherwise be left to inference—that the situations and actions of the Joad family are typical of a large group of people, that the Joads are caught up in a problem of national dimensions. These are perhaps the chapters' most important uses. In addition, they provide information—the history of land ownership and migrant labor in California, for example. Also, through their depiction of American people, scenes, and folkways, there emerges the portrait of a substantial portion of a people—their political and religious beliefs, their music, manners, stories, jokes; their essentially pioneer character, with its virtues and its limitations. *The Grapes of Wrath* is a "great American novel" in every sense of that phrase.

The brilliance of conception and technique with which Steinbeck manages the larger units of his novel is equally evident in its small details. This is well illustrated by the migrants' frequent use of animals in their figures of speech, as natural to these people as literary references to professors of English. A tractor pushing over a shed "give her a shake like a dog shakes a rat"; Al, in his sexual pride, behaves like "a dung-hill rooster"; when all the Joads are forced to move into one house, Muley describes them as "piled in John's house like gophers in a winter burrow." Casy, the most intellectual of the Joad group, sometimes elaborates these simple figures of speech in his attempt to understand a new idea or express it to others—as when he envisions the socioeconomic forces in terms of a gila monster with its poison and its unbreakable hold, or compares the plight of the migrants to that of a bird trapped in an attic, trying to escape.

The narrative passages also make use of animals, but tend to employ them symbolically rather than figuratively. At the beginning of their journey the Joads' dog is killed on the highway by a "big swift car" which does not even stop. Another dog, the "lean brown mongrel ... nervous and flexed to run" who upon sight of strangers "leaped sideways, and fled, ears back, bony tail clamped protectively" symbolizes the conditions of the "Hooverville," a group of cardboard and tin shanties, in which his owner lives. A jackrabbit that gets smashed on the highway, lean gray cats, birds, snakes, and even bugs—all appear under perfectly natural circumstances and yet serve also as symbols. The most extended example of this is the turtle that is accorded the first interchapter entirely to itself. The indomitable life force that drives the turtle, the toughness that allows it to survive predators and trucks, the efficiency of nature that uses the turtle to unwittingly carry seeds and bury them, are clearly characteristic also of the Joads. They, too, carry their house (the truck) with them, survive the natural catastrophe of drought and flood and the intimidations of police and vigilantes; they, too, pick up life in one place and carry it to another. This correspondence is further strengthened when in the very next chapter Tom picks up a turtle as a present for the younger children, talks about turtles with Casy, and eventually releases it to travel—as the Joads are to do—southwest.

Steinbeck's use of machine imagery, though not so extensive, is similarly brilliant. As the first interchapter was devoted to the turtle, so the second is devoted mostly to the tractor, which through its blind power and lack of feeling comes to symbolize the impersonal industrialization and mechanization which, following the economic collapse of their family homestead, is bringing an end to the Joads' old way of life: "The driver ... could not see the land as it was, he could not smell the land as it smelled; his feet did not stamp the clods or feel the warmth and power of the earth.... No man had touched the seed, or lusted for the growth. Men ate what they had not raised, had no connection with the bread. Behind the tractor rolled the shining disks, cutting the earth with blades—not plowing but surgery.... the long seeders—twelve curved iron penes erected in the foundry, orgasm set by gears, raping methodically, raping without passion." Not that Steinbeck in this chapter, or in the book, is symbolizing the evils of machinery, but rather the evils of its misuse. "Is a tractor bad? ... If this tractor were ours it would be good.... If our tractor turned the long furrows of our land, it would be good.... We could love that tractor then.... But this tractor does two things— it turns the land and turns us off the land."

The tractor as symbol of a new era appears almost exclusively in the first part of the book; the most pervasive machine imagery is that of cars and trucks, from the shiny red transport which brings Tom home from prison to the broken-down jalopies of the migrants and the sleek new touring cars of the wealthy and the landowners. As a man used to be judged by the horse he rode, so now his social position is revealed by his car; as a man used to have to know about galls, chipped hooves, curb chains, saddle sores, he now must know about tires, valves, bearings, and spark plugs. "Funny how you fellas can fix a car. Jus' light right in an' fix her," Casy says to Tom and Al. "I couldn't fix no car, not even now when I seen you do it." "Got to grow into her when you're a little kid," Tom said. "It ain't jus' knowin'. It's more'n that." Survival, whether of man or animals, rests upon the ability to adapt to or master the new factors of environment. The Joads have this ability. Even before the moment comes when they are to leave their home, they instinctively gather around the truck that is to carry them to California: "The house was dead, and the fields were dead; but this truck was the active thing, the living principle.... This was the new hearth, the living center of the family." From this beginning, through various tire punctures, flickering headlights, and boiling radiators, to the ending, in which "the old cars stood, and water fouled the ignition wires and water fouled the carburetors," the condition of the Joads and their fellow migrants is the condition of their machines.

Powerful and unstinting as these machine images are in their reflection of the Joads' physical condition, there is developed at the same time a counterthrust which makes the novel a cry not of despair but of hope and affirmation. This thrust begins with Casy's early self-questioning and ends with Rosasharn breastfeeding—a starving old man. The migrants journey west along Highway 66, but also along the unmapped roads of social change, from an old concept of community lost in the blowing dust of the opening chapter, or forfeited by foreclosed mortgages, to a new and very different sense of community formulated gradually on the new social realities. In an interchapter (seventeen), Steinbeck gives us this process in the abstract, and it is detailed in both kinds of chapters throughout the book.

Not all, however, can participate in this process. Muley Graves (a suggestive name) stays behind in Oklahoma, living in a cave like an animal because he cannot separate his sense of community and identity from the land and its history of personal experiences: "Place where folks live is them folks." As the generalized migrants in one of the interchapters express it to the buyers of their household goods, "You are not buying only junk, you're buying junked lives.... How can we live without our lives? How will we know it's us without our past?" Grampa Joad, like Muley, cannot bear to leave the land. He is given an overdose of painkiller and carried off it, but he does not make it beyond the Oklahoma border. Casy's little funeral speech assures the folks that "Grampa didn't die tonight. He died the minute you took 'im off the place.... Oh, he was breathin', but he was dead. He was that place, an' he knowed it.... He's jus' stayin' with the lan'. He couldn't leave it." As it is expressed in one of the interchapters, "This land, this red land is us; and the flood years and the dust years and the drought years are us."

The old sense of identity and community is invested not only in land and possessions, but in social customs and mores that also must be left behind; for example, traditional male and female roles. Ma Joad may be consulted briefly concerning food and space in the decision to include Casy in the family group, but once that decision is made she goes back to the house and womanly things. It is Casy who takes his place among the planning men grouped around Grampa, whose patriarchal headship must be acknowledged despite his senility. Similarly, when they take their places on the truck, Rosasharn, although pregnant, cannot sit in the cab on a comfortable seat: "This was impossible because she was young and a woman." The traditional distinction in social role is also evident in Ma's embarrassment at Casy's offer to salt down the pork. Ma "stopped her work then and inspected him oddly, as though he suggested a curious thing.... 'It's women's work,' she said finally." The preacher's reply is significant of many changes to come in the sense of community and the individual's changing role: "It's all work," he says. "They's too much of it to split up to men's or women's work." By the end of the book, the male role, deprived of its breadwinner status, loses also its authority. It is Ma Joad who, as woman and Earth Mother, becomes the nucleus of order and survival.

It is fitting that this break with domestic tradition should be announced by Casy, the spiritual leader of his community. He has already abandoned preaching the hell-fire, blood-of-the-Lamb evangelism which is typified in the book through the recollections of Pa Joad, when the spirit took him, "jumpin' an' yellin'" and Granma "talkin' in tongues." This primitive religion is also dramatically presented in Uncle John's sense of guilt and Mrs. Sandry's frightening of Rosasharn with predictions of the horrible penalties God visits on pregnant women who see a play or do "clutch-an'-hug dancin'." Significantly, during the happiest moment in the book, the dance at the federal migrant camp, "The Jesus-lovers sat and watched, their faces hard and contemptuous. They did not speak to one another, they watched for sin, and their faces condemned the whole proceeding."

Casy's new direction rejects such theological notions of sin ("There ain't no sin and there ain't no virtue. There's just stuff people do."); it defines the religious impulse as human love ("What's this call, this sperit? ... It's love."); and it identifies the Holy Spirit as the human spirit in all mankind ("Maybe all men got one big soul ever'body's a part of"). Casy joins the migration not to escape or to preach but to learn from the common human experience: "I'm gonna work in the fiel's, in the green fiel's, an' I'm gonna try to learn.... why the folks walks in the grass, gonna hear 'em talk, gonna hear 'em sing. Gonna listen to kids eatin' mush. Gonna hear husban' an' wife poundin' the mattress in the night. Gonna eat with 'em an' learn." What Casy finally learns, in jail after giving himself up to save Tom and Floyd, is that man's spiritual brotherhood must express itself in a social unity, which is why he becomes a labor organizer. The grace that he reluctantly says before eating his first breakfast with the Joads is already groping in that direction:

"I got to thinkin' how we was holy when we was one thing, an mankin' was holy when it was one thing. An' it on'y got unholy when one mis'able little fella got the bit in his teeth an run off his own way, kickin' an' draggin' an' fightin'. Fella like that bust the holiness. But when they're all workin' together, not one fella for another fella, but one fella kind of harnessed to the whole shebang—that's right, that's holy." It is for this belief in a new sense of community that he gives his life, rediscovering for himself his American heritage of Thomas Paine's *The Rights of Man*, Ralph Waldo Emerson's "The Over–Soul," Walt Whitman's *Democratic Vistas*.

Although varying considerably in their ability to share Casy's spiritual vision, it is the Joads' growing acceptance of the social application of that vision that gives them and the other migrants their strength to endure and their faith in a better future. Even Muley knows why he must share his stringy wild rabbit with Tom and Casy: "What I mean, if a fella's got somepin to eat an' another fella's hungry—why, the first fella ain't got no choice." Mrs. Wilson's answer to Ma Joad's thanks for help puts it differently: "People needs [have the need] to help." A few pages later, Ma Joad's reply to Mrs. Wilson's thanks for help gives the concept a further turn: "You can't let help go unwanted." It is significant that the first example of spontaneous sharing with strangers on the journey is a symbolic merging of two families: Grampa's death in the Wilsons' tent, his burial in one of their quilts with a page torn from their Bible; Ma Joad's promise to care for Mrs. Wilson. As Pa Joad expresses it later, "We almost got a kin bond." Near the end of the novel, Al Joad tears down the tarpaulin that hangs between themselves and the Wainwrights, so that "the two families in the car were one." In one of the most hauntingly beautiful scenes of the book, a family spontaneously shares their breakfast with a stranger (Tom), and their hard-found paying job as well, even though this shortens the time between themselves and starvation.

Consider in contrast the Joads' neighbor who turned tractor driver: "I got a wife an' my wife's mother. Them people got to eat. Fust an on'y thing I got to think about is my own folks." Ma Joad herself starts out on the journey with a ferocious defense of her own family against all things, because "All we got is the fambly"; four hundred pages later she has learned, "Use' to be the fambly was first. It ain't so now. It's anybody. Worse off we get, the more we got to do." Tom Joad has learned in prison to mind his own business and to live one day at a time. As he puts it, "I'm just puttin' one foot in front a the other," and again a few pages later, "I ruther jus' lay one foot down in front a the other"; in another image, "I climb fences when I got fences to climb." By the end of the book he says, "But I know now a fella ain't no good alone"; and he goes out dedicated to work for the improvement of his people, though it may mean his own death: "Then it don' matter. Then I'll be ever'where—wherever you look. Wherever there's a fight so hungry people can eat, I'll be there."

These are only a few of the particulars that key into chapter seventeen's more abstract statement: "They shared their lives, their food, and the things they hoped for in the new country.... twenty families became one family, the children were the children of all." The family of man is established, the change from "I" to "we," the new sense of identity and community through which the people survive. Those who do not share, who continue selfish and distrustful, "worked at their own doom and did not know it."

Of all the abstract statements, generalized examples, and specific acts addressed to this principle of survival, Steinbeck saved the most powerful for the novel's concluding scene. In Rosasharn's feeding of a stranger with the milk from her own breast is reenacted the primal act of human nourishment and the most intimate expression of human kinship. That the stranger is an old man and that, for physical reasons, Rosasharn is glad to give the milk, which continues to gather painfully in her breast although her baby is dead, make its symbolic assertion all the stronger. The significance of this final act is further magnified by the facts that the old man is weak from giving his share of the food to his son, and that the son had "stoled some bread" for him but the father had "puked it all up." The ultimate nourishment is the sharing of oneself, as Rosasharn symbolizes by literally giving of her body. This act takes on religious overtones by the still, mysterious, and lingering quality of the scene as "her lips came together and smiled mysteriously" (the last words of the novel), suggesting a common subject of religious paintings—the Madonna nursing her child whom she knows to be the Son of God.

These overtones do more than enhance a humanistic symbol, however. They bring to conclusion a whole level of the novel that exists in religious terms beginning with the title itself, *The Grapes of Wrath*, a phrase from "The Battle Hymn of the Republic" that alludes to the Book of Revelation in the Bible, containing prophecies of the coming Apocalypse: "And the angel thrust in his sickle into the earth, and gathered the vine of the earth, and cast it into the great winepress of the wrath of God." The reference is reinforced in one of the novel's interchapters: "In the souls of the people the grapes of wrath are filling and growing heavy, heavy for the vintage." From this beginning, the Biblical allusions follow thick and fast, for Steinbeck enlarges the significance of his Okies' experiences by associating them with those of the Israelites (the chosen people) in the Old Testament and thus suggesting their human and historical importance. Although not formally so divided, the novel falls into three parts: the drought and dispossession (chapters 1–11), the journey (chapters 12–18), and the arrival in California (chapters 19–30). This corresponds respectively to the oppression and bondage of the

Israelites in Egypt, their Exodus and wandering in the wilderness, and their entrance into the Land of Canaan. The plagues in Egypt, which released the Israelites, have their parallel in the drought and erosion in Oklahoma; the Egyptian oppressors, in the bank officials; the hostile Canaanites, in the equally hostile Californians. In both accounts the Promised Land is first glimpsed from a mountain top. As there were twelve tribes of Israel, so are there twelve Joads (counting Rosasharn's husband). Even the family name recalls a parallel—the tribe of Judah, or the Jews. Ma Joad's simple faith that "We're the people," is reminiscent of the Jewish faith in God's promise that the Jews are a chosen people, as expressed in Psalm Ninety-five: "For He is the Lord our God; and we are the people of his pasture, and the sheep of his hand." As the Jews formulated new codes of law by which they governed themselves in their Exodus (see the Book of Deuteronomy), so the migrants evolve new codes of conduct (see chapter seventeen). When Uncle John sets Rosasharn's "baby in an apple box among the willow stems of a stream, saying, "Go down an' tell 'em," it is the counterpart of Moses in a basket among the bulrushes. A Negro spiritual completes the allusion for the reader: "Let my people go." These are but a scattered sampling of the many, often quite specific parallels through which Steinbeck—in addition to the recurring Biblical prose style mentioned earlier—sustains in the novel a strong religious presence.

The Biblical parallels of three of the novel's characters, however, is of such significance and complexity that they require further discussion—Casy, Tom, and Rosasharn. Jim Casy is, as his initials suggest, in several ways a Christ figure. He breaks from the old religious beliefs and practices, of which he was an advocate, and after a retreat "in the hills, thinkin', almost you might say like Jesus went into the wilderness," emerges to preach an initially unpopular new testament, rejecting a god of vengeance for an oversoul of love. "You can't hold no church with idears like that," Tom tells him. "People would drive you out of the country...." He dedicates himself to establishing his "church" among the people and is killed uttering as his last words a paraphrase of Christ's "They know not what they do": "You don' know what you're a-doin'"; Tom, who has been a doubter all along, now announces himself as Casy's disciple. It all fits together very neatly, too neatly. Steinbeck, however, like other modern American writers, such as Faulkner, is not content to use elements of Christian myth on the simple level of allegory. Thus Casy's Christ role is deliberately confused in two ways. First, he is given attributes of John the Baptist, such as the description of his speech as "a voice out of the ground," and, of course, his role as a baptizer. One of those he clearly remembers baptizing is Tom Joad, and thus the second area of confusion.

For Tom Joad, too, beginning with his baptism by Casy, is given the attributes of a Christ figure. He is even called "Jesus Meek" by his fellow prisoners because of his grandmother's Christmas card with that phrase on it. Once when he seems to be rebelling against his emerging role and says he wants to "go out like Al.... get mad like Pa.... drunk like Uncle John," his mother shakes her head. "You can't, Tom. I know. I knowed from the time you was a little fella. You can't. They's some folks that's just theirself an' nothin' more.... Ever'thing you do is more'n you.... You're spoke for." In other words, his succession to the role of Christ the Messiah, or Saviour, is complete when, in a scene rife with womb imagery (mother, cave, food, darkness), Tom is figuratively reborn and tells his mother of his vocation to preach and live the words of Casy. His speech paraphrases the words of Christ recorded in Luke 4:18 and Matthew 7:3 and 25:35–45, as well as in Isaiah 65:21–22: "And they shall build houses and inhabit them, they shall not build and another inhabit; they shall not plant and another eat." Tom Joad is a complex figure, and it is possible to see in him also sufficient attributes (a specific act of violence, for example) to identify him as a type of Moses who will lead his people to a better future, or the apostle Paul, particularly in the specific details of his conversion.

Though not so rich a figure, Rosasharn also gathers to herself multiple Christian aspects. To begin with, her real name, Rose of Sharon, from the Song of Solomon ("I am the Rose of Sharon, and the lily of the valleys") is frequently interpreted as referring to Christ. The Song of Solomon also contains the line, "This thy stature is like to a palm tree, and thy breasts to clusters of grapes." Thus the final scene in which she feeds the old man with her milk is symbolic of the Eucharist: "Take, eat, this is my body...." Through this identification, the anonymous old man becomes Grampa Joad, whose image for the plenty of California had been a "big bunch a grapes" which he could squash on his face until the juice ran down his chin. As both Christ and Madonna figures, Rosasharn combines attributes more divergent than does Casy (Christ and John the Baptist) or even Tom (Moses, Christ, Saint Paul).

Probably because of this very diversity of reference, these three characters greatly contribute to the lively tension of Biblical allusions in the novel's prose style, events, and structure. The novel never falls into allegory. Furthermore, and more important, they bring together and make one in their lives the novel's social message and certain precepts of Christianity. Whether *The Grapes of Wrath* as a whole promulgates specifically Christian values is a moot point depending entirely on one's definition of what is essentially Christian. Both sides have been well argued. There is no question, however, that through the abundance, variety, and intensity of its Biblical allusions the novel imbues its social message with a religious fervor and sanction.

When *The Grapes of Wrath* was published in 1939, one reviewer said that it seemed to him "as great a book as has yet come out of America." The passing of time has given no reason for correcting that estimate.

WARREN MOTLEY

From Patriarchy to Matriarchy: Ma Joad's Role in The Grapes of Wrath

As the Joad clan disintegrates under the pressure of dispossession and migration, Ma Joad emerges as a central, cohesive force. However, critics exploring the social thinking behind *The Grapes of Wrath* have tended to give her short shrift. Many of them have looked to the articulate Jim Casy rather than to the reticent Joads to explain the family's gradual realization that their survival depends on communal cooperation.[1] I wish to correct that imbalance now. I shall argue that the Joad family shifts from a patriarchal structure to a predominantly matriarchal one. So doing, they dramatize the influence of the anthropologist Robert Briffault on John Steinbeck as he tried to understand the Depression.

Focusing too closely on the ideas of Jim Casy distorts the critical view of Ma Joad. She is too often, and mistakenly, set in opposition to the preacher, as if she shared the social values of her individualistic husband. In fact, she is receptive to Casy from the beginning and is thus marked as a cohesive rather than a fragmenting force. But the preacher does not have to convert Ma Joad. Her communal feelings emerge independently of his pronouncements. Working from Briffault's theories on the matriarchal origin of society, Steinbeck presents Ma Joad's growing power as a source of communal strength sheltering human dignity from the antisocial effects of individualism.

From *American Literature* 54, 3 (October 1982). © 1982 by Duke University Press.

Steinbeck observed the Okies' migration across the Southwest at first hand and could not accept the human wreckage trailed along Route 66 as an instance of the human species sloughing off unsuccessful lower members. Seeking intellectual support, he turned to those scientists and thinkers who believed that cooperation rather than competition was the basis of both evolutionary and social progress. They strove to heal what they saw as the post-Darwinian split between scientific thinking and ethical experience. Steinbeck read Jan Smuts's *Holism and Evolution* and talked of immersing himself in the works of Jan Elif Boodin, author of *The Social Mind*.[2] In analyzing the shift from patriarchy to matriarchy in the Joad family, Steinbeck's reading in *The Mothers* is particularly important. There, Briffault unfolded a vision of social "solidarity [in the matriarchal clan] almost inconceivable and unintelligible to those who have, like ourselves, developed amid the conditions and ideas created by the strenuously competitive and suspicious individualism of modern societies."[3] As Carol Steinbeck commented to Richard Astro, Ma Joad is "pure Briffault."[4]

Briffault published a three-volume edition of *The Mothers* in 1927. No one ever wished it longer than it is, and in 1931 Macmillan printed a more accessible one-volume edition concentrating on the distinctions between matriarchal and patriarchal societies. Drawing on historical records and contemporary anthropological studies, Briffault argued that society first develops on matriarchal lines and that a matriarchal stage universally precedes the patriarchal structure of more advanced societies. Unfortunately, matriarchy is an awkward term, as Briffault himself understood; to most people it erroneously connotes a topsy-turvy, Amazonian patriarchy in which "women exercise a domination over the men similar or equivalent to that exercised by the men over the women in a patriarchal social order" (p. 179). But to Briffault matriarchy describes a radically different relationship between people based on cooperation rather than power. In defining the stages of social evolution and their economic determinants, Briffault closely parallels Frederick Engels' *The Origin of the Family, Private Property and the State in the Light of the Researches of Lewis H. Morgan*. Briffault and Engels shared a source in Morgan's *Ancient Society* (1877), a study of matriarchal kinship groups among North American Indians. Working from Marx's abstract of *Ancient Society*, Engels declared Morgan's rediscovery of the matriarchal gens to have "the same importance for anthropology as Darwin's theory of evolution for biology and Marx's theory of surplus value for political economy." Hyperbole, no doubt, but Engels, like Briffault and Morgan, was excited to document a society that fostered "'liberty, equality and fraternity'" and that "'in a higher form'" might be revived. Although many anthropologists took up the issue of an earlier matrilineal stage,

Briffault's focus on the actual roles and status of women was original. However haphazardly, he gathered copious evidence of the dominant part often played by women in the political and economic life of primitive societies.[5]

Briffault's insistence on the distinctness and precedence of the matriarchal stage reflects his theory that "all familial feeling, all group-sympathy, the essential foundation, therefore, of a social organization, is the direct product of prolonged maternal care, and does not exist apart from it" (p. 57). Gregariousness, he argues, satisfies a behaviorally conditioned need for companionship. It is not a physiological instinct, like breathing or suckling. During their nurturing period, humans develop a fear of solitude and a habit of dependence. Initially the mother appeases the fear and satisfies the need, but later on siblings are accepted as substitutes. Thus the first social groups, Briffault proposed, evolve from biologically linked maternal clans of brothers and sisters rather than from patriarchal families based on sexual bonds (p. 53).

In early societies, a woman's offspring automatically become "legitimate" members of her clan. Therefore, marriage need not regulate sexual activity. If a man forms any lasting association with a woman at all, he becomes part of her group, but his labor is dispensable: "Those functions which in the patriarchal family are discharged by the husband and father ... are in the maternal group fulfilled by the woman's brothers" (p. 140).

Matriarchal cultures, Briffault observed, are "nothing if not equalitarian" (p. 180). The concepts of authority and domination are "entirely foreign to primitive humanity" because the economic advantages on which power rests do not exist (p. 180). Although labor is divided in matriarchies—men take charge of the hunt and women of the camp—the division is not exploitive. Both men and women work for the community; "the sexes are interdependent, and it is upon that mutual dependence that the association which constitutes society is founded" (p. 175). In fact, if there is a question of advantage, Briffault notes that all the arts and industries of primitive societies—tanning, weaving, potting, home building, and toolmaking—were invented and carried out by women. They then controlled the surplus wealth of the community. Men, on the other hand, had to devote their full energies to providing raw materials for these industries. Consequently, "the disparity in physical power, resourcefulness, enterprise, courage, capacity for endurance, observed in [more advanced, patriarchal] societies and often regarded as organic sexual differences" does not appear between men and women in matriarchies (p. 159).

According to Briffault, most civilized observers, blinded by their assumptions about femininity, misunderstood the status of women in primitive societies. They took a woman's work as a sign of "slavery and oppression" when, on the contrary, the woman in matriarchal societies "is independent because, not in spite of her labour" (p. 189). "Generally speaking," Briffault concluded, "it is in those societies where women toil most that their status is most independent and their influence greatest" (p. 189).

Patriarchy evolved when primitive economies passed from the hunting and gathering stage to the pastoral and agricultural stages and men gained predominate economic power. The domestication of animals, and the later development of advanced agriculture, gave men economic strength and freed them from hunting and the necessity of supplying raw materials for women-controlled production. As men took over home industries and agriculture, then expanding with the growth of trade, the relationship between the sexes underwent a major realignment:

> Woman, instead of being the chief producer, became economically unproductive, destitute, and dependent. The contrast between the toiling primitive woman and the idle lady of civilization, which has been mistaken for an indication of the enslavement of the former and the freedom of the latter, marks the opposite relation. It is the primitive toiler who is independent and the unemployed woman who has lost her freedom and is destitute. (p. 248)

Men's monopoly of economic power allowed them to buy the privilege of taking women into their own camps instead of joining the maternal clan; the patriarchal family, based on sexual coupling, replaced the maternal clan as the controlling unit of society.

A definitive shift in values attends the transition to patriarchy. Individualism emerged, Briffault believed, only at the patriarchal stage, not before. The holding of personal and real property separated individuals both economically and psychologically from the group. Therefore, it is "not the operation of innate individualistic instincts that has given rise to the acquisition of personal property; it is, rather, the acquisition of personal property which has brought about the development of individualistic feelings" (p. 65). Briffault could not imagine that the cooperation necessary to the early evolution of man from the animals could have existed if humanity's earliest representatives had been "hordes of jealous and suspicious individualists, in which every member sought his personal advantage only," or if the incipient human social group had been ruled "by the selfishness of a despotic patriarchal male" (pp. 65, 66).

Finally, Briffault suggests that since patriarchies are based on masculine economic dominance, society could theoretically return to a matriarchal stage if our "forms of industry and wealth-production [were] to revert to the dimensions of household industry" (p. 176). The return might well be incomplete; Briffault cautions that matriarchal elements remain in societies moving into the patriarchal stage, and it follows that patriarchal elements would survive a reversion toward matriarchy. Still, in an economic catastrophe, one might expect to see "the predominance of women ... to a large extent ... automatically restored" (p. 177).

Supplementing his own experience with the migrants, Steinbeck's reading in Briffault offered a theoretical framework on which to measure the changes inflicted on the Joads and their fellow farmers. Steinbeck shows how the shock of dispossession suffered by the toads undermines the frontier patriarchy and throws the family back to a more primitive economic and social stage. Briffault's belief that individualism could not have motivated the members of pre-patriarchal society reinforces Steinbeck's feeling that the Oklahoma farmers could no longer rely on the values of frontier individualism. As long as they continued to think only in terms of the self-sufficient patriarchal family, their efforts to overcome oppression would be doomed.

The patriarchal structure of the Joad family, although shaken, remains intact through the early chapters of *The Grapes of Wrath*. Gathering to plan their trip to California, they arrange themselves in a hierarchical formation. Evidently habitual, it reflects the traditional authority of the pioneer as clearly as would a legislative chamber. The older men cluster around Grampa Joad, "enthroned on the running board" of the family's truck; the next generation of young men extend the semicircle around the patriarch; and the women and children stand as if in a gallery behind them.[6] Although Grampa Joad remains the "titular head" of the family as "a matter of custom," the office of greatest authority has passed to his son. Pa Joad runs the meeting according to a parliamentary procedure as well established as the positions of the participants (p. 137). He defines the meeting's agenda, calls for reports, and asks the members of the family for their opinions beginning with Grampa, who retains "the right of first comment" (p. 137). Women have a voice in the deliberations, but final responsibility for choosing a course of action lies with the older men—the "nucleus" of the family government (p. 136).

Steinbeck describes the squatting posture of the Joad men in unusual detail, as if, like Briffault, he were recording the symbolic ritual of a primitive tribe. He does so because the gesture embodies the intimate relationship between the frontiersman and his property. In times of adversity, the farmer patriarch draws his strength from his connection with the land, not from his association with society. Thus, the position of greatest authority in the Joad's ceremonial hierarchy is the position closest to the soil. The women and children stand; Grampa Joad, deprived of all but token authority by his age, sits on the truck's running board; the men who make the decisions squat. Their authority is rooted in ownership of the land where Grampa "had to kill the Indians and drive them away" and where Pa "killed weeds and snakes" (p. 45).

However, the Joads' actual, much-reduced circumstances now mock the traditional significance of the squatting posture. Banks and corporate landowners have severed the connection between family and land. The Joads gather around a converted Hudson Super-Six instead of the hearth of the patriarchal homestead. The squatting position, once a symbol of strength, has become instead a mark of their downtrodden status. Confrontation with omnipotent owners transforms the Joads and the other farmers from "squatting tenant men" into "squatters" in the traditional sense of men with no property rights and no power (p. 43).

Steinbeck signals the Joads' vulnerability by representing their patriarch as senile. Grampa Joad's incontinence and wandering mind epitomize the ineffectiveness of primitive frontier strengths without discipline and direction. His cantankerousness caricatures the inflexibility of the farmers. In defending their independence, they have clung to their fathers' ways without adjusting to the changing economics of farming. They fall prey to the banks, in part, because they do not fully comprehend that placing a mortgage on their farms deprives them of the full rights of ownership. As Grampa Joad's senility gives him the look of a "frantic child," so, following the pioneer tradition inflexibly makes the farmers childlike in their helplessness before oppression (p. 105).

Above all, the stubborn individualism embodied in the senile patriarch blinds the Joads to the necessity of collective action. When the landowner's tractor cuts across the family homestead, Grampa Joad stands up alone against his enemy with only a gun to guarantee his independence. He levels his rifle steadily at the eyes of the mechanical predator, but the tractor charges forward. The courage and pride Grampa displays mean nothing to the economic forces seizing the farm. The bank puts down the individual family as easily as the tractor caves in the house—as easily as "a dog shakes a rat" (p. 62). United the Oklahoma families might have a chance, but as self-reliant family units, they are defeated one by one.

Steinbeck emphasizes the patriarch's tragically atomistic response by placing another confrontation between tractor and solitary homesteader, similar to Grampa Joad's, in chapter five, the interchapter on the general dispossession of the Oklahoma farmers. According to this classic reading of the relationship between the Joads' saga and the interchapters, the Joad narrative develops on a more intimate level the themes of the interchapters which chronicle the plight of the migrants as a whole. But that relationship can be interpreted more fully. The power of the double narrative depends on the tension between the reader's knowledge that the Joads are representative in their suffering and the failure of the Joad men to recognize their representative status. They act as if their story were unique, when, in fact, it is typical of the tenant farmers' plight.

By establishing parallels between the oppressed and the oppressor throughout *The Grapes of Wrath*, Steinbeck also attributes the external pressures on the Joads, particularly the cruelties of the landowners, to the failure of frontier individualism as a social principle. He argues that both the powerful Californians and the shattered migrants must repudiate those aspects of individualism which deny participation in a larger community. In earlier days, the pioneers of Oklahoma and California had ignored the destructive aspect of their quest because they competed for land with Indians and Mexicans whose humanity they refused to recognize. But now that the frontier has been "closed"—that is, now that the land is owned by other white Americans—American society must confront the antisocial aspects of individualistic competition.

As the older Joad men sink into ineffectiveness and despondency, family authority shifts to Ma Joad. First she aggressively challenges patriarchal decisions that might fragment the family, and by the end of the novel she has taken the initiative. When the men cannot find work at the government camp and have forfeited their patriarchal roles "'either a-thinkin' or a-workin','" Ma Joad makes the decision to move on and rouses "her camp" for their early-morning departure (pp. 481, 491). Later she plans Tom's escape from the peach ranch after he avenges Casy's murder. During the final catastrophic chapters Ma Joad controls the family's money, handles Ruthie's betrayal of Tom's hiding place, finds the family work, leads them away from the flooded railroad car, and finally urges Rose of Sharon to suckle the starving man in the ark-like barn at the top of the hill.

On Briffault's anthropological scale this shift to matriarchal authority represents a regression to a more primitive social organization. But Steinbeck offers the step "back" to matriarchy as a promise of hope. In terms of the Joads' predicament, Ma Joad's emergence signals an essential adaptation: under the economic conditions of the migration, survival depends on the collective security of matriarchal society rather than on patriarchal self-reliance. In broader terms, Steinbeck uses Ma Joad's heightened stature to suggest that the communal values Briffault associates with matriarchy might provide an alternative basis for authority in American society as a whole.

The first extended description of Ma Joad begins in documentary detail and ends in allusions to matriarchal power. Ma Joad is an ordinary tenant farmer's wife and a "goddess" waiting to assume her new role as the representative of a dispossessed people:

> Ma was heavy, but not fat; thick with childbearing and work. She wore a loose Mother Hubbard of gray cloth in which there had once been colored flowers, but the color was washed out now, so that the small flowered pattern was only a little lighter gray than the background. The dress came down to her ankles, and her strong, broad, bare feet moved quickly and deftly over the floor. Her thin, steel-gray hair was gathered in a sparse wispy knot at the back of her head. Strong, freckled arms were bare to the elbow, and her hands were chubby and delicate, like those of a plump little girl. She looked out into the sunshine. Her full face was not soft; it was controlled, kindly. Her hazel eyes seemed to have experienced all possible tragedy and to have mounted pain and suffering like steps into a high calm and a superhuman understanding. She seemed to know, to accept, to welcome her position, the citadel of the family, the strong place that could not be taken.... And from her great and humble position in the family she had taken dignity and a clean calm beauty. From her position as healer, her hands had grown sure and cool and quiet; from her position as arbiter she had become as remote and faultless in judgment as a goddess. She seemed to know that if she swayed the family shook, and if she ever really deeply wavered or despaired the family would fall, the family will to function would be gone. (pp. 99–100)

Steinbeck's portrait of Ma Joad differs in two critical aspects from classic accounts of the pioneer wife by male writers like Cooper, Mark Twain, Howe, Garland, and Rölvaag. He does not take the diurnal chores and unending childbearing as signs of Ma Joad's oppression, nor is he ill at ease with her physical strength and lack of traditional feminine beauty. Although Cooper, for example, admired at a distance the endurance and self-denial of the pioneer wife, he emphasized her sullen submission to her husband. Work and the bearing of fourteen children "amid the difficulties, privations and solitudes of stolen abodes in the wilderness" leave the once beautiful wife of a frontiersman in *The Chainbearer* "sallow, attenuated, with sunken cheeks, hollow, lack-luster eyes, and broken-mouthed." Her preoccupation with feeding and clothing her children makes her anxious and distrustful and, to Cooper's narrator, uncomfortably animalistic, like a "dam overseeing the welfare of its cubs."[7]

Steinbeck, on the other hand, follows Briffault's argument that economically productive labor is a woman's source of power. Ma Joad's work packing away the slaughtered pigs, organizing camp, buying food and cooking it over a succession of improvised stoves represents not submission but the steady shedding of her husband's control. She attains the status of arbiter "as remote and faultless in judgment as a goddess" because, not in spite of, her work. The pioneer woman's roughness threatens earlier writers, but to Steinbeck Ma Joad's thickness, her "strong, broad, bare feet," "her thin, steel-gray hair," her "strong, freckled arms" are not signs of femininity laid waste, but rather of "clean, calm beauty." His portrait places Ma Joad with Willa Cather's frontier heroines and Faulkner's black matriarchs, suggesting there may be an unheralded tradition of powerful women in early twentieth-century American literature who come forward in times of crisis and offer alternatives to the values of an individualistic and patriarchal society.

Thinking of the famous WPA photographs of the Dust Bowl, one might conclude, despite Mark Twain, that Cooper was simply more realistic about the effects of frontier conditions. But throughout *The Grapes of Wrath* Steinbeck acknowledges the reality that "'women's always tar'd'" (p. 147); in the passage on Ma Joad, with its value-loaded vocabulary, Steinbeck works on a mythical level, not to deny reality but to explain the power and endurance that survive Ma Joad's hardships. Briffault opened Steinbeck to a new interpretation of women's experience. Here and later in the novel, Steinbeck suggests that the "pain and suffering" of childbirth and the woman's role as attendant of the sick and dying leave her with an essentially tragic view of life that, in turn, generates a sustaining stoicism. Ma Joad's "high calm" and "superhuman understanding" not only endow her with the mental fortitude to be a "healer," "arbiter," and "citadel," but also spare her the kind of physically debilitating effects of depression suffered by her husband and brother-in-law. Steinbeck's view is thus quite literal. Ma Joad possesses the psychological qualities to govern her family community because she has actually given birth to it and nurtured it.

The family's dispossession deprives Pa Joad of his traditional agrarian labor, but Ma Joad's work continues and she remains strong. The tools of her husband's labor—wagons, horses, plows—are sold before the journey, but Ma Joad's kettles and pans are taken along and become, with the truck, the focus of family life. When the Joads make camp the first night, Ma Joad immediately issues an order to find firewood. Because leaving has not diminished her work, her authority is intact. Tom and Al similarly gain stature because their mechanical knowledge gives them work on the journey. But the older men have "the perplexed manner" Briffault finds common among men in primitive matriarchies (p. 177). Where Ma Joad's eyes convey "superhuman understanding," Steinbeck's initial description of Pa Joad reveals that "his bright dark eyes were failing," and Grampa's eyes move "listlessly" as soon as he leaves the farm (pp. 96, 169).

Because matriarchal strength endures as long as the household industries of camp life can be maintained, it remains available to people cast out of society. Ma Joad is a "citadel," not because she takes action, as Grampa Joad tries to do, but because she can absorb experience and "mount pain and suffering." As the image of an immovable fortress suggests, her strength gives no particular direction to the family. It simply protects the "will to function," to endure, to find some new source of strength for later action. As the family moves west, this citadel replaces the forty-acre farm that sustained the patriarch's individualism. Unlike the farm, Ma Joad's matriarchal citadel is a "strong place that cannot be taken."

Although there are moments of discouragement when Ma Joad reverts to the habits of frontier individualism, from the outset she has a broader understanding of the family's move west than does her husband. She interprets the migration according to the actual experience of the migrants rather than by the inherited and now meaningless patriarchal myth of the frontier. In the West Pa Joad thinks he will find relief from poverty through his individual labor. But his dream depends on land. When he cannot find it, he is crushed. While Ma Joad hopes one day to own a house of her own, a goal of individual fulfillment Steinbeck endorses, she gradually expands her belief that survival until that day depends on keeping the "family unbroke" to include a broader group (p. 231). Independent of Casy's philosophy, she warns her son not to stand up alone against the landowners:

> "Tommy, don't you go fightin' 'em alone. They'll hunt you down like a coyote. Tommy, I got to thinkin' an' dreamin' an' wonderin'. They say there's a hun'erd thousand of us shoved out. If we was all mad the same way, Tommy—they wouldn't hunt nobody down—" She stopped. (p. 104)

When she first asserts her authority over her husband with the jack handle, she places her family first, but even then she is willing to include Casy and the Wilsons, and earlier she speaks up for Tom and Al's idea of traveling with the Wilsons as a "unit" (pp. 202, 222).

Steinbeck suggests that Ma Joad's experience as a woman has made her see the individual as part of a larger whole; when Rose of Sharon grows frightened at her grandmother's illness, Ma Joad soothes her explaining that "dyin' is a piece of all dyin', and bearin' is a piece of all bearin'" (p. 286). As Ma Joad experiences the scorn and savagery of the California deputies, this matriarchal intuition is tempered into political faith. Ma counsels patience: "Why, Tom—us people will go on livin' when all them people is gone. Why, Tom, we're the people that live. They ain't gonna wipe us out. Why, we're the people—we go on" (p. 383).[8]

Ma Joad's matriarchal understanding of unity opens her to the possibility of a new frontier myth founded on the westward migration as a process which brings a dispossessed people together:

> In the evening a strange thing happened: the twenty families became one family, the children were the children of all. The loss of home became one loss, and the golden time in the West was one dream. And it might be that a sick child threw despair into the hearts of twenty families, of a hundred people; that a birth there in a tent kept a hundred people quiet and awestruck through the night and filled a hundred people with the birth-joy in the morning. (p. 264)

To Pa Joad (Job-road), life on the road seems meaningless. Route 66 is a trial by brutality, inhumanity, and contempt. Stretching to an unknown destination from an irretrievable starting point, the road confronts Pa with an image of time slipping by without the reassuring cyclical pattern of farm life to give him a sense of progress or permanence. Without a farm of his own, Pa Joad feels that "life's over an' done," but Ma Joad contradicts him:

> "No, it ain't," Ma smiled. "It ain't, Pa. An' that's one more thing a woman knows. I noticed that. Man, he lives in jerks—baby born an' a man dies, an' that's a jerk—get a farm an' loses his farm, an' that's a jerk. Woman, it's all one flow, like a stream, little eddies, little waterfalls, but the river, it goes right on. Woman looks at it like that. We ain't gonna die out. People is goin' on." (p. 577)

By the time she offers her husband this reassurance late in the novel, she has extended her belief in the importance of collective strength from the family to the migrants as a people: "Use' to be the fambly was fust. It ain't so now. It's anybody" (p. 606). Her statement on the end of the family's primacy has been taken to mark her conversion to Jim Casy's transcendental collectivism, but Ma Joad's sense of belonging to the stream of her race has its deepest origins in her own matriarchal nature.[9]

In his account of the government camp at Weedpatch, where the Joads temporarily find sanctuary from the brutalities of the road, Steinbeck offers an image of a society founded on the communal spirit of the matriarchy. Raising themselves from the more primitive life of roadside bivouacs and Hoovervilles, the migrants return to a life as well ordered as they knew on their farms.

In keeping with Briffault's stages of social development, the more complex government of the camp has shifted back toward patriarchal form. But it has done so without sacrificing the matriarchal impulse to keep the "family unbroke." The migrant men are no longer seen as dull and stupid as they were on the road because organizing the camp and its defenses again gives them a sphere of action. But the division of labor in the camp is consistent with the communal economy of the matriarchy in which the people's needs, instead of being supplied by the accumulation of private property, are provided for by communal division of labor between the sexes. Similarly, while the camp is managed by a male government agent, Steinbeck makes clear that his authority is entirely compatible with the egalitarian character of matriarchal society. He is not a chief, but a representative.

Steinbeck uses the meeting between Ma Joad and the camp manager as his principal metaphor for the matriarchal basis of governmental authority. Unlike the sheriffs and deputies Ma Joad confronts along the way, this man greets Ma Joad without condescension or hostility. With a gesture that Steinbeck has carefully prepared, the government agent squats down beside Ma Joad in the traditional posture of the tenant farmer: "He came to the fire and squatted on his hams, and the last of Ma's resistance went down" (p. 416). The emotional impact of this simple act of kindness and decency after so much insult and brutality drives home the symbolic significance of the gesture: the representative of the government meets the representative of the people's collective strength to "go on" at her own level. As the Oklahoma farmer drew strength from his independent plot of soil, this government will draw strength from the people.

Steinbeck proposes the paradox that a stronger communal government would be necessary to protect individual freedom and dignity and anticipates his readers' suspicions. Taking symbols of the red scare, political committees and barbed-wire fences, he transforms them into symbols of a democracy that protects the propertyless and allows them to participate in government. It is not the imposed patriarchal power of a totalitarian regime that protects the camp from the farmers' associations; it is not "that little guy in the office is a-stoppin' 'em," but the community's own collective strength—" 'cause we're all a-workin' together" (p. 488).

However, Steinbeck doubts that his America will adopt Ma Joad's matriarchal sense of community as a governing principle. He knew where power lay, and his experience forbad optimism. The camp presents only a utopian vision; it cannot provide jobs to the migrants, and the Joads are forced back to the road.[10] As in other accounts of westward migration in our literature, Steinbeck correlates the redemption of American values with the rescue of the distressed patriarchal family. For the Joads the outlook is bleak. Ma Joad retards the family's disintegration but cannot prevent it.

At the end of the novel, Steinbeck preserves some hope, however, by insisting that Ma Joad's legacy passes on to Rose of Sharon, to Tom, and, by extension, to a future generation of Americans that might incorporate her values into democratic society. The significance of Ma Joad's bequest differs according to the sex of the two children; traditional male and female roles persist in Steinbeck's working out of matriarchal values. Rose of Sharon inherits her mother's sense of community through her womb; Tom through his mind. When Rose of Sharon offers her breast to a starving man, her smile announces her initiation into a matriarchal mystery: the capacity to nurture life. The scene confirms Ma Joad's belief that family unity can be extended to the wider community, and its shock, springing from the denial of sexuality in the meeting of man and woman, asserts Briffault's thesis that society originates not in sexual union but in maternal nurturing.[11] As Steinbeck wrote to his editor, Rose of Sharon's offering is "a survival symbol": as a woman, she represents not the alleviation of oppression but the ability to endure it.[12]

Tom Joad carries communal values into a more active mode. From the beginning of the novel, Tom is Ma Joad's chosen child; the core of the Joad family, as of the matriarchal clan, becomes mother and offspring rather than husband and wife. After his years in jail, Tom shares his mother's ability to live day by day on the road. Hunting down Uncle John or calming Al, Tom executes his mother's belief that the family must stay "unbroke." His eventual conversion to the labor cause is convincing in part because his new faith is firmly rooted in his mother's values. When he explains his plans to join the union—"maybe like Casy says, a fella ain't got a soul of his own, but on'y a piece of a big one," his language is not only Casy's. He follows as well his mother's more humble expression of faith—"people is goin' on" (pp. 572, 577). In the last days before Tom begins his mission as a labor organizer, Ma Joad claims the task of carrying food to his hiding place among the rushes. When he leaves, he receives the family's meager savings, not from his father but from Ma Joad—not when he takes over as patriarch of the family, but when he leaves the family to work for the people. Tom will tap strength that has come to the migrants by the shared experience of dispossession rather than by the individualism of his frontier heritage.

Tom's chances of staying alive, much less of relieving his people's oppression, are slim. The uncertainty of his future reflects Steinbeck's pessimism not only about the labor movement's prospects, but also about curbing the antisocial effects of individualism. However, the final image of Tom disappearing into the rushes at night has a power independent of his realistic chances of success. In the symbolic drama of the novel, his decision to follow Jim Casy and to act on the matriarchal sense of community represents the potential of the oppressed to take action—of passive endurance to become active resistance.

NOTES

1. Frederic I. Carpenter, "The Philosophical Joads," *College English*, 2 (1941), 315–25; rpt. in *Steinbeck and His Critics: A Record of Twenty-Five Years*, ed. E. W. Tedlock, Jr. and C. V. Wicker (Albuquerque: Univ. of New Mexico Press, 1957), pp. 241–49; Chester E. Eisinger, "Jeffersonian Agrarianism in *The Grapes of Wrath*," *University of Kansas City Review*, 14 (1947), 149–54; in Viking Critical Library edition of *The Grapes of Wrath*, ed. Peter Lisca (New York: Viking, 1972), pp. 720–28; Woodburn O. Ross, "John Steinbeck: Naturalism's Priest," *College English*, 10 (1949), 432–38; rpt. in Tedlock, pp. 206–15; Peter Lisca, "The Dynamics of Community in *The Grapes of Wrath*," in *From Irving to Steinbeck: Studies of American Literature in Honor of Harry R. Warfel*, ed. Motley Deakin and Peter Lisca (Gainesville: Univ. of Florida Press, 1972), pp. 125–40; Richard Astro, *John Steinbeck and Edward F. Ricketts: The Shaping of a Novelist* (Minneapolis: Univ. of Minnesota Press, 1973); Jackson J. Benson, "John Steinbeck: Novelist as Scientist," *Novel*, 10 (1977), 248–64.

2. Astro, pp. 47–52; I am indebted throughout to Astro's uncovering of Steinbeck's reading.

3. *The Mothers: The Matriarchal Theory of Social Origins* (New York: Macmillan, 1931), p. 59; subsequent quotations will be taken from this edition and noted in the text.

4. Astro, p. 133.

5. *The Origin of the Family, Private Property and the State*, introd. Eleanor Burke Leacock (New York: International Publishers, 1972), pp. 83, 237 (Engels quotes Morgan), 30, 37; to trace Briffault's debt to Engels see particularly three chapters of *The Origin of the Family*, "The Stages of Prehistoric Culture," "The Family," and "Barbarism and Civilization"; for a review of the anthropological research on matriarchy see Leacock's helpful Introduction.

6. *The Grapes of Wrath* (New York: Viking, 1939), p. 140; subsequent quotations will be taken from this edition and noted in the text.

7. *The Chainbearer* (New York: Stringer & Townsend, 1857), p. 228.

8. Lisca refers to this passage as evidence of Ma Joad's sense of participation in a historical community, p. 133.

9. Warren French, *John Steinbeck* (New York: Twayne, 1961), pp. 103–07.

10. French, p. 110.

11. Astro, p. 1;3; Joseph Fontenrose, *John Steinbeck: An Introduction and Interpretation* (New York: Barnes & Noble, 1963), pp. 73–74.

12. "To Pascal Covici," 16 January 1939, *Steinbeck: A Life in Letters*, cd. Elaine Steinbeck and Robert Wallsten (New York: Viking, 1975), p. 178; Steinbeck explains his refusal to change the ending as Covici had requested.

LOUIS OWENS

The American Joads

T hat Steinbeck should keep the Bible firmly in both the background and the foreground of this great American novel is essential, for he is writing not simply about an isolated historical and sociological event—the Dust Bowl and the "Okie" migration—but about a nation founded solidly upon a biblical consciousness, as the novel's title indicates. From the first writings of the colonial founders, America was the New Canaan or New Jerusalem, and the colonists, such as William Bradford's pilgrims at Plymouth, were the chosen people who consciously compared themselves to the Israelites. Their leaders were repeatedly likened to Moses, for they, too, had fled from persecution and religious bondage in England and Europe for the new promise of a place called America. Thus Bradford, in *Of Plymouth Plantation* (1620–50), felt compelled to compare his pilgrims to "Moyses & the Isralits when they went out of Egipte."[43] Out of this acutely biblical consciousness arose what has come to be called the American myth, a kind of national consciousness with which Steinbeck was fascinated throughout his life.

Within this mode of thought, if America was the New Eden, within the wilderness of that Eden lurked the Serpent. Almost at once, in their battle to wrest a continent away from wilderness and from the inhabitants of that wilderness, the colonists imagined themselves embroiled in a desperate struggle with Satan. They saw themselves as the Army of Christ. The Indian in the forest, in resisting the colonists' invasion, appeared to be in league with Satan himself. In his book *The Wonder-Working Providence of Sion's Savior in New England*, describing without compunction the beheading of Pequot Indians, Captain Edward Johnson, in 1653, exhorted the Puritans to "take up your arms and march manfully on till all opposers of Christ's kingly power be abolished."[44]

In *The Grapes of Wrath* Jim Casy has spent his life prior to our meeting with him as just such a Calvinistic fire-and-brimstone fundamentalist embattled with Satan, as he tells Tom Joad: "Here's me that used to give all my fight against the devil 'cause I figured the devil was the enemy. But they's somepin worse'n the devil got hold a the country" (421). It is in the wilderness that Casy has his revelation about man and God, and quickly he moves from Calvinism to a kind of transcendentalism, from that pattern of thought which places the earth under man's dominion and looks at wilderness as the unreclaimed haunt of Satan to that philosophy which makes man inseparable from the natural world and finds in wilderness a direct relationship with truth.

From his past battle with the devil to his declaration that "There was the hills, an' there was me, an' we wasn't separate no more" (88), Casy has taken an enormous stride away from what Steinbeck defines in this novel as the short-sighted and destructive historical pattern of American thought and settlement. Within the Christ-like Casy, commitment to man and to nature becomes a single driving force toward a unity with what Steinbeck and Ricketts in *The Log from the Sea of Cortez* defined mystically as "the whole thing, known and unknowable."

The settlement of America may be seen as a process of ever westward expansion in search of that Eden which seemed to recede always before the eyes of the first colonists. The process became one of despoiling the Garden in the search for the Garden until, finally, Americans stood at the edge of the Pacific, having slaughtered and driven from their lands the original inhabitants, having deforested enormous portions of the continent, and having fought and gouged with all other claimants to the continent in order to reach the western shore. Surely, if there were ever to be a Garden it must be at the western edge. And the beauty and fecundity of California seemed to fulfill that promise. Still, Americans were left with a feeling of loss, emptiness, summed up in Walt Whitman's great poem, "Facing West from California's Shores," in which he concludes with a parenthetic question that resounds throughout American history and American literature: "But where is what I started for so long ago? / And why is it yet unfound?"

Whitman's question is central to *The Grapes of Wrath*. Grampa exclaims, "Gonna get me a whole big bunch of grapes off a bush, or whatever, an' I'm gonna squash 'em on my face an' let 'em run offen my chin" (90). And the faceless, representative owner voices of chapter 5 advise the evicted tenants, "Why don't you go on west to California? There's work there, and it never gets cold. Why, you can reach out anywhere and pick an orange" (35). Both Grampa's dream of grapes and the owners' vague visions of plenty underscore the crucial association between California and the biblical Canaan. And when the Joads arrive at Tehachapi Pass and look down on the fertile San Joaquin Valley, often referred to as the Great Central Valley, California indeed seems to be the New Canaan, the Promised Land sought after for nearly four centuries:

> They drove through Tehachapi in the morning glow, and the sun came up behind them, and then—suddenly they saw the great valley below them. Al jammed on the brake and stopped in the middle of the road, and, "Jesus Christ! Look!" he said. The vineyards, the orchards, the great flat valley, green and beautiful, the trees set in rows, and the farm houses. And Pa said, "God Almighty!" The distant cities, the little towns in the orchard land, and the morning sun, golden on the valley....
>
> Ruthie and Winfield scrambled down from the car, and then they stood, silent and awestruck, embarrassed before the great valley. The distance was thinned with haze, and the land grew softer and softer in the distance. A windmill flashed in the sun, and its turning blades were like a little heliograph, far away. Ruthie and Winfield looked at it, and Ruthie said, "It's California." (250)

It is Winfield who puts the valley into perspective and locates it firmly within the American dream of Eden rediscovered: "'There's fruit,' he said aloud" (251).

When a rattlesnake crawls across the road and Tom drives over it and crushes it as the family starts down into the valley, the way has been cleared for entry into the Garden; the serpent—the symbolic evil of this Promised Land—has at long last been removed. To emphasize the quintessentially American idea of a new beginning, a kind of return to the Garden, Steinbeck has Tom laugh and say, "Jesus, are we gonna start clean! We sure ain't bringin' nothin' with us" (254). With these words, Tom defines the most dangerous flaw within the dream of America as the new beginning: the Joads, like the Dutch sailors who look longingly at the continent at the end of F. Scott Fitzgerald's *The Great Gatsby*, and like all of us, are indeed bringing their pasts with them. This Garden is inhabited by flawed men, men who, like Tom with his scar at the novel's end, are marked. The Eden- and Canaan-like valley that spreads so wonderfully beneath the Joads will prove to be filled with hatred, violence, greed, and corruption—the fruits of man's wisdom and knowledge lying rotting in the fields and orchards. It is a heavily ironic entrance into the Promised Land.

Steinbeck's use of and fascination with what has been termed the American Myth—the myth of this continent as the new Eden and the American as the new Adam—appear again and again throughout his fiction. *Cup of Gold* (1929), Steinbeck's first novel, offers a fictionalized account of the pirate Henry Morgan's conquest of Panama. The primary symbol of this new world in the novel is the chalice or golden cup that suggests the Holy Grail. Purity, promise, and innocence all come together in the symbol of the Grail but, as Steinbeck's conqueror discovers, the New World—America—loses its innocence in the process of being discovered. In *The Pastures of Heaven*, (1932) Steinbeck's early episodic novel, the author makes a small California valley a microcosm for America and the people of that valley, with their fatal insistence upon a kind of illusory innocence, microcosmic Americans. Characters in that novel (Steinbeck's second published though third written) look upon the valley called Pastures of Heaven and they dream of starting over in all innocence, of leaving their flawed selves and the fallen world behind. Steinbeck's message in the novel, of course, is that such illusions of innocence are impossible to realize and dangerous to harbor. Fallen man brings his own flaws into Eden.

Throughout his career, Steinbeck was obsessed with America as a subject. The myths deeply ingrained in our national consciousness and the patterns of thought that have carried us from wilderness to world power appear again and again in Steinbeck's writing, not only in such obvious studies of the nation as *America and Americans* or *Travels with Charley*, but also throughout the novels.

In *The Short Reign of Pippin IV* (1957), Steinbeck, like Henry James before him, but on a lighter note, takes a young "ideal" American to France in order to contrast the public and private moralities of the two nations. Four years later, in his final novel, *The Winter of Our Discontent*, Steinbeck turns his scrutiny squarely upon his own nation in a dark study of the American conscience. Here, Steinbeck evokes American history in the name of his protagonist, Ethan Allen Hawley, who lives in a home with "Adam" decorations. Again Steinbeck creates in Ethan a character who refuses, as long as possible, to recognize humanity's flaws. And in the most allegorical of his major novels, *East of Eden* (1952), Steinbeck creates an explicit American Adam in the character of Adam Trask, who, in a self-destructive search for his own unfallen Eden, flees from his Calvinistic, Jehovah-like father on the eastern seaboard and settles in the Salinas Valley in California.

Steinbeck recognized deep within the American and the universally human psyche a need to believe in the possibility of beginning anew, of returning symbolically from the exile of maturation and experience to a lost Eden and lost innocence. The original English colonists saw America very consciously as this new Eden, and Americans have ever since translated that dream of recovering Eden into the American dream, the dream of shedding the past and starting over. For Walt Whitman this meant an outright denial of original sin, a chance to proclaim himself Adam—the representative American—newly born into innocence. For Benjamin Franklin it meant a chance to create oneself in the pattern of one's imagination, free of any burden of guilt. It is no coincidence that, as a boy, Fitzgerald's Gatsby wrote notes to himself reminiscent of Benjamin Franklin's *Autobiography*. It is this refusal to see the evil we do and the belief in an Eden just west of the next mountain range that Steinbeck saw as the most dangerous flaw in the dream. In *East of Eden*, Adam Trask refuses to see the evil within his wife or within others. He is doomed by that self-willed innocence.

In *The Grapes of Wrath*, Steinbeck evokes this pattern of American thought and American expansion, a pattern that begins with thoughts of a new Eden and moves inexorably westward. This is the illusory hope voiced by a representative migrant in one of the novel's interchapters: "Maybe we can start again, in the new rich land—in California, where the fruit grows. We'll start over" (95). The impossibility of such a dream is made clear in the answering voice: "But you can't start. Only a baby can start.... The bitterness we sold to the junk man—he got it all right, but we have it still. And when the owner men told us to go, that's us; and when the tractor hit the house, that's us until we're dead. To California or any place—every one a drum major leading a parade of hurts marching with our bitterness" (95).

Steinbeck takes pains to place the Joads and the Dust Bowl migrants as a whole securely within this pattern of American history and simultaneously to avoid the sin with which he has often been charged: sentimentalizing his characters. Certainly Steinbeck makes it clear that the sharecroppers are victimized by an inhuman economic monster—personified by the enormous, impersonal tractors raping the land—that tears at the roots of the agrarian life Thomas Jefferson so highly prized for Americans. When Steinbeck causes his representative migrant voice to plead with the owners for a chance to remain on the land, however, he qualifies the celebrated Jeffersonian agrarianism and love-for-the-land in this novel by tainting the sharecroppers' wish: "Get enough wars and cotton'll hit the ceiling" (32), the cropper argues. While the reader is likely to sympathize with the powerless tenant farmer, the tenants' willingness to accept war and death as the price for a chance to remain on their farms and thus further "cotton out" the land is difficult to admire on any level.

Steinbeck goes a step further, to make it clear that the migrants are firmly fixed in a larger, even more damning American pattern. Though the tenants have tried to persuade the owners to let them hang on, hoping for a war to drive up cotton prices, the tenant voice also warns the owners: "But you'll kill the land with cotton." And the owners reply: "We know. We've got to take cotton quick before the land dies. Then we'll sell the land. Lots of families in the East would like to own a piece of land" (33). It is the westering pattern of American history laid bare: people arrive on the Atlantic seaboard seeking Eden only to discover a rocky and dangerous paradise with natives who aggressively resent the "discovery" of their land; Eden must lie ever to the west, over the next hill, across the next plain; then only the Pacific Ocean is there and, along with Jody's grandfather in Steinbeck's *The Red Pony*, we end up shaking our fists at the Pacific because it stopped us, and broke the pattern of displacement. As long as we believe there is a Garden to the west we feel justified in using up and abandoning the place we inhabit today. Tomorrow we will pick up and go, always in the direction of the setting sun, always with the belief that we can put the past behind us, that the ends will be justified by the means. We believe that such acts as passing out smallpox-infested blankets to Indian tribes and the massacre at Wounded Knee and, finally, the theft of the continent from the Indians can be put behind us in the quest for new land and new self.

That the croppers are part of this pattern becomes even more evident when the representative tenant voice informs us that their fathers had to "kill the Indians and drive them away." And when the tenant voice adds, "Grampa killed Indians, Pa killed snakes for the land" (34), Steinbeck is attempting to ensure that we hear a powerful echo of the Puritan forebears who wrested the wilderness from the serpent Satan and his Indian servants, killing and displacing the original inhabitants of the New Canaan.

It is difficult to feel excessive sorrow for these ignorant men who are quite willing to barter death to maintain their place in the destructive pattern of American expansion—a pattern that has ravaged a continent. That Steinbeck thought long about the American phenomenon of destroying the Garden in the search for the Garden is suggested in his declaration (recorded more than a decade later in *Journal of a Novel*, the journal he kept while writing his great investigation of the American myth, *East of Eden*) that "people dominate the land, gradually. They strip it and rob it. Then they are forced to try to replace what they have taken out."[45]

Although Steinbeck makes it clear that man draws sustenance from close contact with the earth, through touching it and feeling a part of it, and in spite of Tom Joad's final wish that the people will one day "all farm our own lan'" (463), Steinbeck is not making a case for Jeffersonian agrarianism in this novel. Jeffersonian agrarianism, as defined succinctly by Chester E. Eisinger in his influential essay "Jeffersonian Agrarianism in *The Grapes of Wrath*," was "essentially democratic: it insisted on the widespread ownership of property, on political and economic independence, on individualism; it created a society in which every individual had status; it made the dignity of man something more than a political slogan."[46] Drawing parallels between Thomas Jefferson's insistence upon the small farmer as the foundation of an ideal society and the philosophy developed in *The Grapes of Wrath*, Eisinger suggests that "Steinbeck was concerned with democracy, and looked upon agrarianism as a way of life that would enable us to realize the full potentialities of the creed."[47]

The "essentially inhuman and unproductive nature of the machine age," according to this reading of the novel, is destroying "a way of life that was based on the retention of the land."[48] Such a reading, while persuasive, leads even Eisinger to question the value of agrarianism itself: "It remains to inquire if agrarianism, its form and substance, is the part of the Jeffersonian tradition that we should preserve."[49] The Jeffersonian ideal is bankrupt, the critic declares, and thus Steinbeck's conclusions in the novel are of dubious value.

If we look more closely at attitudes toward America and, in particular, the small farmer in *The Grapes of Wrath*, it should become clear that Steinbeck, too, saw fully illuminated the "bankruptcy of Jefferson's ideal." By carefully and precisely placing the tenants within the historical pattern that has led to the destruction of the land, Steinbeck is making it obvious that agrarianism alone is insufficient. In fact, the ideal of the independent small farmer, the Jeffersonian image of the heroic individualist wresting an isolated living from the soil, is very firmly scuttled in *The Grapes of Wrath*. Muley Graves points to an aspect of this failure when he tells Tom and Casy, "I know this land ain't much good. Never was much good 'cept for grazin'. Never should a broke her up. An' now she's cottoned damn near to death" (50).

The small farmers of this novel proudly proclaim their grandparents' theft of the land from the Indians, freely acknowledging that murder was their grandparents' tool. They argue that they should be allowed to stay on and raise more cotton because war will boost the price of cotton. Then they tell the owners that they will kill the land with cotton. These small farmers are far from anyone's ideal. They are clearly a part of a system that has failed and in the process has violated the continent. Steinbeck sends them on the road so they may discover a new relationship with their fellow man and with the land itself. The Jeffersonian ideal is one of individuals working the land on isolated farms; Steinbeck's ideal is one of all men working together, committed to man and land, to "the whole thing." It is, in fact, precisely the dangerous idea of man as isolated and independent that Steinbeck is attempting to expose. He is no Jeffersonian.

Once the Joads and their fellow migrants have reached California, they can go no farther. The Joads are the representative migrants, and the migrants are the representative Americans. The migrants' westward journey is America's, a movement that encapsulates the directionality of the American experience. The horrors confronting the migrants to the California Eden have been brought on by all of us, Steinbeck implies; no one is innocent. When, near the novel's conclusion, Uncle John places Rose of Sharon's stillborn baby in an apple box and releases it upon the flood waters with the words, "Go down an' tell 'em" (493), Steinbeck is emphasizing the new consciousness. This Moses—in the Edenically suggestive apple box—is stillborn because the people have no further need for a Moses. There is no Promised Land and nowhere else to go, no place for a Moses to lead his chosen people. The American myth of the Eden ever to the west is shattered, the dangers of the myth exposed. The new leader will be an everyman, a Tom Joad, who crawls into a cave of vines—the womb of the earth—to experience his rebirth, who emerges committed not to leading the people somewhere but to making this place, this America, the garden it might be. This is the Tom who, early in the novel, says to Casy, "What the hell you want to lead 'em someplace for? Jus' lead 'em" (21).

At the novel's end, Tom has become such a leader, one who will not lead the people "someplace" but will lead them toward a new understanding of the place they inhabit here and now. For the same reason, Steinbeck has left Noah behind at the Colorado River, the boundary of this garden, because, in spite of the impending flood, there is no place for a Noah in the new country. Two symbols of mankind's new beginnings from the Bible are rejected in the exclusion of Noah and the stillborn Moses. Through these two rather heavy-handed allusions, Steinbeck is declaring that there is no second chance, no starting over.

The Grapes of Wrath is Steinbeck's jeremiad, his attempt to expose not only the actual, historical suffering of a particular segment of our society, but also the pattern of thought, the mind-set, that has led to far more than this one isolated tragedy. In this novel, with the Bible very much in mind, Steinbeck sets out to expose the fatal dangers of the American myth of a new Eden, and to illuminate a path toward a new consciousness of commitment instead of displacement. And in making his argument, Steinbeck is careful not to sentimentalize his fictional creations, careful to emphasize the shared guilt and responsibility—a new sensibility, not sentimentality, is Steinbeck's answer.

In spite of howls of outrage from the states at the opposite ends of the novel's journey—both Oklahoma and California—however, and in spite of his care to avoid sentimentalizing his characters, America took the Joads to heart, forming out of *The Grapes of Wrath* a new American archetype of oppression and endurance. And in spite of his care to make the Joads and the migrants as a whole far less than perfect, and to place his protagonists squarely within the destructive pattern of American expansion, as soon as the novel was published critics who read less carefully than they should have began to accuse Steinbeck of sentimentality in his portrayal of the downtrodden migrants. Edmund Wilson was one of the first influential critics to take such a position, declaring that in this novel Steinbeck learned much from films, "and not only from the documentary pictures of Pare Lorentz, but also from the sentimental symbolism of Hollywood."[50] Bernard De Voto had anticipated Wilson when he complained that the novel's ending was "symbolism gone sentimental."[51] Still a third major American critic, R. W. B. Lewis, found Steinbeck's fiction "mawkish" and "constitutionally unequipped to deal with the more sombre reality a man must come up against...."[52]

There is much in *The Grapes of Wrath* to ward off such accusations if a reader goes beyond mere surface story. In addition to showing the reader the tenant farmers' willingness to continue to use up the land with cotton and their eagerness for war, Steinbeck consistently shows us the flaws in his characters. As Steinbeck scholar Warren French pointed out long ago, Steinbeck takes care to undercut the nobility and "goodness" of the migrants. Although Casy, in sacrificing himself for the people, and Tom, in dedicating his life to the same cause, move close to heroism, no one in the novel is seen through a sentimental lens.

One of the most obvious examples of Steinbeck's care to avoid sentimentality can be found in the novel's final chapter. Just before the Joads reach the barn and discover the starving man and young boy, Ruthie discovers a "scraggly geranium gone wild." Plucking the flower, she sticks one of the petals onto her forehead, "a little bright-red heart." With this symbol of delicate beauty and love surviving amidst the devastation of ravaged and ravaging nature, Steinbeck could have left his reader with a soft and sentimental portrait-in-miniature of hope. Instead, he deftly undercuts the sentimentalism of the moment through the verisimilitude of his characters. "Come on, Ruthie!" the girl's younger brother, Winfield, begins at once to whine, "Lemme have one." Ruthie, in keeping with the character the reader has come to expect, "banged him in the face with her open hand" (498). A moment later she "wet a petal with her tongue and jabbed it cruelly on his nose. 'You little son-of-a-bitch,' she said softly" (499). In the children's attraction toward the bright-red petals Steinbeck illuminates an image of the enduring life-force and the wellspring of hope in the novel. In Ruthie's convincing cruelty the author refuses to allow his characters to succumb to the potential sentimentalism inherent in the image. The romantic symbol and its ironic deflation prepare for the novel's emotional and critically controversial finale.

NOTES

43. William Bradford, *Of Plymouth Plantation*, ed. Harvey Wish (New York: Capricorn Books, 1962), 36.

44. Edward Johnson, *Johnson's Wonder-Working Providence*, ed. J. Franklin Jameson (New York: Barnes & Noble, 1959), 30.

45. Steinbeck, *Journal of a Novel* (New York: Viking Press, 1969), 39.

46. Chester E. Eisinger, "Jeffersonian Agrarianism in *The Grapes of Wrath*," in *The Grapes of Wrath: Text and Criticism*, 723.

47. Ibid., 722.

48. Ibid., 725.

49. Ibid., 728.

50. Edmund Wilson, *The Boys in the Back Room: Notes on California Novelists* (San Francisco: Colt Press, 1941), 61.

51. Bernard De Voto, "American Novels: 1939," *Atlantic Monthly* 165 (January 1940):68.

52. R. W. B. Lewis, "John Steinbeck: The Fitful Daemon," *Steinbeck: A Collection of Critical Essays*, 171.

MIMI REISEL GLADSTEIN

From Heroine to Supporting Player:
The Diminution of Ma Joad

John Ford's movie version of *The Grapes of Wrath* is generally considered to be one of the few successful film adaptations of an acclaimed novel. The movie is honored as a classic, firmly ensconced on lists of landmark films.[1] Perhaps that is because there had been so much concern among fans of *The Grapes of Wrath* that the book's grim vision would be softened beyond recognition by the Hollywood dream machine and that concern proved to be only partially well-founded. Or perhaps because the film version of Steinbeck's novel has so many virtues as a work of cinematic art: the commanding but underplayed acting of Henry Fonda; the gemlike performances of Charley Grapewin as Grandpa and John Qualen as Muley Graves; the extraordinary cinematography of Gregg Toland with its sensitive use of light and shadow, memorable particularly in such scenes as the opening shot of a long, long road bordered by telephone poles and in Muley Graves's recounting of his family's dispossession, culminating in a shot of tractor treads traversing their hapless shadows.

Robert Morsberger, speaking at the Second International Steinbeck Congress, noted that *The Grapes of Wrath* was the first film translation of a Steinbeck novel to be both an artistic and a commercial success.[2] *Tortilla Flat*, which attempted to make Spencer Tracy, John Garfield, Hedy Lamarr, and Akim Tamiroff believable as California paisanos, had been a commercial

From *Critical Essays on Steinbeck's* The Grapes of Wrath, John Ditsky, ed. © 1989 by John Ditsky success, but an artistic failure. *Of Mice and Men*, on the other hand, bolstered by the strong performances of Burgess Meredith and Lon Chaney, received high critical praise, but did poorly at the box office. *The Grapes of Wrath* opened to near-universal acclaim. Steinbeck, himself, called the film "hard" and "truthful," and "a harsher thing than the book."[3] In the face of all this approbation, particularly that of the original creator, it is no wonder that negative evaluations have been minimal.

Perhaps the voices of dissatisfaction have been few because the field of criticism that encompasses serious fiction and filmmaking is not a crowded one.[4] This is bound to change in the near future. Films, particularly old ones, have been, until the last few years, generally unavailable. Unless one happened on a late night television rerun, the only other access to the movie version of *The Grapes of Wrath* was through either purchase or rental of the four-reel film, an expensive and cumbersome undertaking for any individual. The advent of video cassettes has changed this situation. Every shopping center video store has copies of *The Grapes of Wrath* on its shelves, where for as little as one dollar, one can take the movie home and there, complete with rewinds and fast-forwards, watch to one's heart's content. Soon, *The Grapes of Wrath* may be watched as often as it is read. The power of visual images is strong. It is not unlikely that many people will substitute watching the film for reading the book. Therefore it seems appropriate, in view of this technological bonanza, to voice some misgivings about a troublesome aspect of the film that, though touched upon by a few critics, has not been thoroughly explored: John Ford's reduction and devitalization of the role of woman in his film version of *The Grapes of Wrath*. This enervation would be evident even if one were viewing the film without reference to the novel, but when the film is compared with the novel, the full dimensions of this diminishment are more clearly revealed.

Why Ford did this is not clear. It might have been a result of studio politics, of Ford's strong patriarchal bent, or of the practical constraints of film time. Whatever the reason, Ford reduced and softened the character of Ma Joad, and thereby diluted Steinbeck's depiction of woman's strength, durability, and significance in the human struggle for survival, a depiction that is distinctly embedded in the many layers, both realistic and mythic, of the book.[5] This diminishment of woman's character is also evident in Ford's version of Rose of Sharon, who in the book matures from a self-centered girl into a woman nearly ready to inherit Ma's mantle.

Steinbeck described Ma as the Joad family "citadel, "the strong place that could not be taken."[6] Her significance in the novel cannot be overemphasized. Tetsumaro Hayashi's perceptive analysis, in "Steinbeck's Women in *The Grapes of Wrath*: A New Perspective," clearly articulates the importance not only of Ma, but also of Rose of Sharon, in conveying Steinbeck's message: "The men in the novel articulate the theme, but it remains for women like Ma and Rose to provide the continuity of generations by translating the thought into action."[7] Leonard Lutwack, building on Steinbeck's description of Ma as "remote and faultless in judgment as a goddess; envisions Ma as the mother-goddess who inspires and protects her hero-son, much like the goddesses of ancient myth.[8] Warren Motley calls her the "central, cohesive force" in the novel and argues that the movement from patriarchy to matriarchy in the novel is a result of the influence of Robert Briffault's *The Mothers* on Steinbeck's thinking.[9] Motley convincingly argues that Tom, as Ma's chosen child, functions as a means to bring about a matriarchal sense of community.

The Ma of director John Ford, screenwriter Nunnally Johnson, and actress Jane Darwell is a very different creature. Though she maintains a central role in the Joad saga, she is hardly the "citadel," in no way suggests a goddess, and her cohesiveness is a sticky sweet kind, like honey, instead of the fiercely binding kind practiced by Steinbeck's jack handle–wielding woman. She delivers the movie's message, but it, like the woman who speaks it, is a weaker, more conciliatory, Pollyannaish vision than the one posited by Steinbeck's Ma. Whatever plaudits the screen version of Ma has earned, as an interpretation of the novel's heroine she falls short on many counts.

The diminution of Ma begins with her first scene in the movie. In the novel, Tom hears Ma's voice before the reader is introduced to her by the narrator. Her voice is "cool ... friendly and humble." Her first words reflect her hospitality. Without knowing who the "coupla fellas" are who "wonder if we could spare a bite," she responds with an immediate "Let 'em come." This, although the Joads have just lost their homes and have little to sustain them on their impending journey. Ma's strong sense of sharing with strangers in this scene foreshadows her behavior in inviting Casy along with the family. Neither action is shown in the film. In the novel Casy asks Ma, Grandpa and Tom if he can go along. When none of the men answers, it is Ma who tells Casy she would be proud to have him along. Later, in the family council, when Pa worries about the extra mouth to feed, it is Ma who firmly pronounces the code of hospitality and neighborliness: "I never heerd tell of no Joads or no Hazletts, neither, ever refusin' food an' shelter or a lift on the road to anybody that asked" (139). A sense of community that reaches beyond the boundaries of kinship is an important aspect of Steinbeck's message, a message that is considerably blunted in the movie. Cutting out Ma's articulation of these values early in the film presages their loss in the rest of the script.

There is high drama in Steinbeck's staging of Ma's and Tom's first encounter. Tom sees Ma before she knows who he is. What he sees is a heavy, "but not fat" woman, a woman who is "thick with child-bearing and work." "Strong, broad, bare feet" move "quickly and deftly over the floor." Ma's arms are described as "strong" and "freckled." Her full face is "not soft," but is "controlled, kindly" (99–100). All of these adjectives suggest a hardy and rugged woman, one who knows that her imperturbability and sure-handedness are counted on by her family. She is shocked and relieved to see Tom and her first words to him are "Thank God." When she runs to him she does so "lithely, soundlessly in her bare feet" (101). She touches him, feeling his arm; then her fingers touch his cheek. The emotion between the two is so intense that Tom bites his lip till it bleeds. Only when Ma sees the blood does she pull back from the intensity of the moment in order to normalize the situation. The recurrent word in her description is "strong"; both feet and arms are described with that word. In her scene with Tom, the reader is shown the powerful feelings generated by their relationship.

The first glimpse of the movie Ma is of Jane Darwell standing by the family table. The commanding presence in the room is not Ma, but Grandpa. Charley Grapewin's Grandpa, whether quarreling with Grandma or imagining himself sitting and "scrooging around" in a tub of grapes, steals this scene, even from such traditional scene-stealers as the children.[10] Darwell's Ma is a soft and dumpy-looking woman. Just in terms of outward appearance, she is a great disappointment. Russell Campbell tells us that John Ford would have preferred Beulah Bondi's "gaunt, stringy resilience" in the role, but had to accept Jane Darwell in return for getting Henry Fonda to play Tom instead of Don Ameche or Tyrone Power, whom the studio had on hand as contract players.[11] John Baxter concedes that Jane Darwell is "perhaps too plump, too matriarchal, too *Irish*, for her role," but he counters that "so effective is Ford's use of the actress that one can no longer imagine anyone else playing it."[12] Baxter's point is a good one, but I think it has more to do with the impact of visual images than with the limits of imagination. It is just such concession to the power of the movie that I am arguing against.

The reunion of Tom and Ma is awkwardly handled in the film. Though Johnson's published script version follows the novel closely, preserving Steinbeck's dialogue, word for word, and includes directions for Ma to touch Tom's arm and cheek and for Tom to bite his lip with emotion, in the film it does not happen that way. Instead, there are two close-ups in which both Fonda and Darwell express the joy of seeing each other. But then, as they are impelled toward each other, for some unfathomable reason, rather than reaching to touch her son, to feel the muscle under the flesh, Darwell's Ma sticks her hand out to shake his hand. The action is awkward and establishes

Ma as peculiarly undemonstrative. Later, she does touch Tom's arm and then his lapel, but the initial handshake aborts the intensity of the reunion. If Ford was trying to show that such quaint peasant types maintained certain formal distances between mother and son, then for the sake of consistency he should never have included the dance scene later in the movie. A Ma who will dance with her son, while he sings to her, is not a Ma who shakes hands with him after he has been away in prison for years. Later, when Tom is about to leave, as if to explain the early handshake, the movie Ma asks for a goodbye kiss, although she explains, "We ain't the kissin' kind." This line is in neither the novel nor the published screenplay.

The novel's movement from patriarchy, identified with power relationships and individualism, to matriarchy, associated with cooperation and communal feelings, as the family becomes uprooted and dispossessed, is carefully traced by Warren Motley. Motley explains that Ma has been receptive to Jim Casy's ideas about community from the beginning.[13] Andrew Sarris, seeing a similar plot structure in the film, describes its movement as "nothing less than the transformation of the Joad family from a patriarchy rooted in the earth to a matriarchy uprooted on the road."[14] Ma's appropriation of the role of head of the family as the story progresses is read by both Motley and Sarris as strong evidence of that movement. What is apparent in the novel and what has not been noted by most critics is that Ma has been the de facto head of the family all along. Her power does not grow; only the overt expression of it does. That Ma is the real head of the family is strongly suggested in the panegyrical first description of her, a description that equates her position in the family not only to citadel and goddess, but also to healer and arbiter. She is the locus of the family's will, and she knows that "if she swayed the family shook, and if she ever really deeply wavered or despaired the family would fall" (100).

Ma is not unaware of her power in the family, but her sense of tradition prevents her overt expression of it except when necessary. When the family council meets before setting out for California, she takes her place with the women and children, outside the circle of squatting men. Ritual is observed; Grandpa as titular head of the family is given right of first comment. The men all speak, giving their reports. During this process, Ma works on the periphery of the group, and even leaves to go into the house. However, when the question of whether or not Jim Casy can accompany the family to California comes up, after all the figuring by Pa and comment by Grandpa, it is Ma who makes the decision, one based not on practicalities but on a sense of sharing and community. Pa is shamed by Ma for what she sees as his meanness. After she has had her say in front of the whole group, he turns away, and "his spirit was raw from the whipping." Once that decision is made and Casy is asked to join the group, Ma goes into the house again. This time the council waits for her return, "for Ma was powerful in the group" (140).

The family council scene is deleted from the screenplay, and with it both incident and indication of Ma's eminent position in the family and her sympathy with the kind of communal values that Jim Casy comes to represent. Instead there is a scene where Grandpa is lifted onto the loaded truck, in a semi-conscious state, and when the truck starts to move, Casy is asked by Pa, "Ain't you goin' with us?" (345). When Casy voices his desire to accompany them, it is the men who pull him onto the truck, expressing the sentiment that there is always room for one more.

One of the most touching scenes in both the novel and film is the scene in which Ma must dispose of her mementos, something she does in private where the family members cannot see the toll it takes on her. Steinbeck's Ma, barefoot and haggard from packing and food preparation, is seen by Casy at this moment as looking "real tar'd, like she's sick-tar'd" (147). Ma, hearing these words, tightens her face, straightens her shoulders, and goes into the stripped room for her lonely task. It is this barefoot and tired woman who must waken her family, deal with Grandpa's sudden refusal to go, and then get in the truck whose load prevents her looking back. While the scene is still touching in the movie, certain costuming decisions greatly reduce the magnitude of Ma's task and the audience response to it. For reasons that will probably never be unearthed, the costumer in the film decided to put Jane Darwell in a silly-looking hat for this and many other scenes. Not only is she burdened with a hat that gives her face a decidedly porcine cast as she puts the earrings to her ears and looks at her reflection, but an apron and a sweater are chosen to complete her outfit. Perhaps this costuming decision came from the same impulse that saw Ma as a woman who would shake hands with her favorite son. The hat makes Ma look ridiculous in the context of the family situation. It is also emblematic of the very different kind of woman the film Ma is from the novel Ma. Steinbeck's Ma is taut and muscular, her feet bare and her hands encrusted with salt. The movie Ma not only wears shoes, but bedecks her head with a hat. The result is a quaint country woman, whose strength is softly muted, rather than a tough pioneer who can work all night and leave her home behind with nary a whimper. To be sure, Darwell speaks Steinbeck's words about the change brought about in her by having her house pushed over and her family stuck out in the road. But because she has had time to dress for the occasion in such droll finery, the words do not hit with the same impact.

The filmmakers wisely decided to leave out the Wilsons; there is not time in a two-hour film for too many subplots. This choice also dictated the deletion of one of the most significant scenes in the revelation of Ma's iron will and family domination. When the Wilson touring car breaks down on the road, Pa and Tom decide it would be best if all but Tom and Casy go on to California so that the rest of the group can start earning money and not lose the extra time it will take Tom and Casy to fix the car. The men consider the idea, gathering together: "Uncle John dropped to his hams beside Pa" (228). But when Pa tells the group to "get a-shovin'," Ma revolts. She challenges his authority openly and violently, threatening to hit him with a jack handle or knock him "belly-up with a bucket" (230). Ma does this to prevent the separation of the family. "The eyes of the whole family shifted back to Ma. She was the power. She had taken control" (231). Tom's good-natured suggestion that no more than two or three of them would be killed if they tried to rush her, only serves to underline the completeness of her takeover. With her authority thus established, Ma reverts back to her traditional role as the angel of the hearth, sending bread and meat to Tom and Casy as they work on the Wilson car.

The importance of the jack handle scene was not entirely lost on Nunnally Johnson. His published screenplay retains it in altered form, though he has had to create a new rationale for it because of the deletion of the Wilsons. In the Johnson version, Ma challenges Pa when it appears as if Al is about to run off and thus break up the family. Johnson's scene retains much of Steinbeck's dialogue. Ma challenges Pa to "whup" her; she brandishes the jack handle and insists that the family must stay together. Her concern is for the "fambly unbroke" (360). This scene is interrupted by Tom's return with the information that the Hooverville they are in is going to be burned down by some pool-room boys. Tom takes the jack handle from Ma with the admonition that she and Pa can fight it out later. Ma then tells him that Connie has "lit out," and Tom goes in the tent to comfort Rose of Sharon. Ford's movie omits most of this scene. All that is left is Tom's interruption of a squabble between Ma and Pa. Neither why they are fussing nor why Ma has the jack handle is established. It might be any family quarrel and it certainly does not show Ma in control. Perhaps the scene, as handled by Jane Darwell, was not convincing. Perhaps John Ford, who was to make so many pictures with John Wayne, could not convincingly direct a woman beating a man in a challenge to combat. For whatever reason, since the scene is not in the movie, Ma's overt ascension to the position of head of the family is not accomplished.

As Ma never does take over, there is little motivation for the last scene in the movie when Pa tells Ma: "You're the one who keeps us goin' Ma. I ain't no good anymore, an' I know it." This statement launches Ma into her "Woman can change better'n a man" speech, a recitation often cited as the embodiment of Steinbeck's message about the nature of womanly endurance, of the flexibility and timelessness of matriarchal values. However, since there are few scenes in the movie to illustrate that Pa or any of the men have lost any stature in the family, this speech has little context. It is not well-motivated and certainly is not foreshadowed. The men seem fine. In the beginning of this last part of the movie Pa, Al, and Uncle John are shown loading up the truck. Pa is described as "beaming" when he hollers to everybody, "All aboard for Fresno." He expresses confidence when he says, "Be glad to get my han' on some cotton. That's the kin' a pickin' I understand" (377). Al is chipper enough to be "grinning" when he asks Ma if she is "Gettin' scared?" (377). The only one who is unable to stand on her own two feet and seems thoroughly beaten in this scene is Rose of Sharon.

In the novel the family's experiences with the Wilsons, their working together in times of need, illustrate the already strong sense of hospitality and sharing among these country people. Sairy Wilson responds to Ma's offer to repay the Wilsons for the quilt Grandpa died on: "We're proud to help. People needs—to help" (192). When the Joads can return the favor by repairing the Wilson car and caravanning with them, Ma speaks the formula of the need to work together. "Each'll help each, an' we'll all git to California" (202).

Steinbeck's interchapter following this scene clearly underscores the implications of the Wilson/Joad scenes. In it he explains the power of peoples banding together, the danger to those who own things, of "I" becoming "we," for revolutionary thinkers such as Paine, Marx, and Jefferson, are results, not causes, according to John Steinbeck. So Casy first, and then Tom, are results of the terrible treatment of the dispossessed. They learn that the only way for the migrant workers to be paid a living wage is by transcending the "I" and working together as "we." This whole idea of the larger family of humanity is also greatly diminished in the movie.

Ma's conversations with Sairy Wilson give her the opportunity to articulate her family pride in "holdin' in." Ma quotes her father's dictum that anybody can break down, but it takes a man not to. It is significant that the "men" who do not break down in this scene are women: Sairy, Grandma, and Ma. The deletion of the Wilsons, though practical in terms of cinematic necessities, removes the opportunity to express in word and action the values of hospitality and holding in, values that Ma exemplifies.

Furthermore, it is in the scenes with the Wilsons that Rose of Sharon is shown both helping Ma and learning from her. Rose of Sharon peels the potatoes and does the cooking while Sairy and Ma prepare Grandpa for burial. After dinner, Rose of Sharon goes and lies with her Grandma, comforting her and whispering with her in the night.

Perhaps there was no need for the movie's Rose to be shown doing anything to contribute to the family's sustenance since her role in the screenplay is essentially truncated. Rather than a Rose of Sharon who drags herself out of bed though she is sick, pregnant, and undernourished, in order to pick cotton or try to help her mother with the cooking and cleaning chores, the film gives us a whiney, helpless creature who is last seen being loaded, half-dead, onto the truck by the able-bodied men in the family (377). There is no preparation for this. In the scene that takes place the night before at the dance, Rose of Sharon is pictured sitting prettily beside Ma. Tom even comments on how good she looks and Ma responds that a girl with a baby always gets prettier (374).

Dorris Bowdon plays Rose of Sharon in the movie. She later became the wife of Nunnally Johnson. Acting was obviously not her métier. Whereas most of the other members of the family have good approximations of Oklahoma accents, Bowdon's initial "Hi Tom! How 'ya doin'?" sounds like a sophomore rendition of Scarlett O'Hara. In most of the other scenes that are left to her, she is portrayed as either petulant or passive. Since the pregnancy is never completed in the movie, and the controversial final scene is never played, Rose has no role in the survival of either the Joad or the whole human family. Though we see her at the dance, wearing the earrings Ma salvaged in the memento scene, there is no scene that shows Ma giving them to her. Nunnally Johnson includes such a scene in the screenplay, though it is quite different from the scene in the novel (372). But it was obviously edited out. In the novel, in order to coax Rose of Sharon out of her depression, Ma gives her the earrings and entices her to go to the dance. But before Rose of Sharon can wear the earrings, she must have her ears pierced. Symbolically, Rose must learn to bear pain in order to inherit Ma's role. Ma comments to Rose of Sharon that she "very near let you have a baby without your ears pierced" (484). The statement suggests that having the ears pierced is an initiation rite, indicating readiness to assume the womanly role. Now that she will be a mother also, Rose of Sharon must not only learn to behave like Ma, but she also is ready to wear Ma's jewelry. Rose asks Ma, "Does it mean sompin'?" And Ma responds, "Why, 'course it does. 'Course it does." Rose's contributions to Steinbeck's themes in the novel are significant. Learning from Ma and acting with her, Rose is an agent of survival of the species.[15] In the film, not only does she contribute little, but Bowdon's acting is so poor that one is grateful her scenes are so few.

Ford's Ma is a pacifier, whereas Steinbeck's Ma is a fierce woman who faces people down and speaks her mind. The difference in the two Ma's is patently illustrated in the scene where, after their first day of picking peaches, Ma tries to purchase enough food to feed her family. In the novel,

Steinbeck shows us Ma at the company store. This scene clearly demonstrates how the migrant workers are exploited at every turn. The prices at the company store are outrageously high, and the quality of the food poor. Ma does not react kindly to this situation. She looks at the clerk "fiercely," she moves "menacingly toward him" (511). His treatment of her is cavalier; whenever she complains about the high prices, he reminds her sarcastically that she can always go to town, which is too far away, to get better prices. But Ma will not be whipped. She confronts the clerk about his nasty behavior, which she realizes is a defense against the anger of those he must help exploit. "Doin' a dirty thing like this. Shames ya, don't it? Got to act flip, huh?" (512). Her tone at this point is gentle and she wins the clerk's respect. Ma shows her psychological astuteness and she inspires the clerk to a gesture of charity and defiance. Though Ma does not have enough credit to pay for sugar after buying meat, potatoes, bread, and coffee, the clerk takes ten cents out of his own pocket in order to give her credit until the next day. The scene is germinal for Steinbeck's "we the people" theme, for in this encounter with the clerk, Ma reminds him that he is one of them. When she asks him why he does this nasty job, he replies "a fella got to eat." Ma responds, "What fella?," thus allying all of the hungry and dispossessed. After the clerk has taken money from his own pocket so Ma can have sugar, she articulates the lesson of group interdependentness: "If you're in trouble or hurt or need—go to poor people. They're the only ones that'll help—the only ones" (514).

The store scene is left out of the film. All we see is the eating scene that follows it. The dialogue, though chronologically rearranged, is straight from the novel. Tom expresses his desire for more hamburgers. Ma explains that the prices at the company store are high and that what they have is all a dollar will buy. Her tone is conciliatory. She suggests that tomorrow there will be more food since they can get in a full day's work, thus earning more money. Because the store scene has been deleted, Ma's fierceness and perceptive manipulation of the clerk are also omitted and all that is left is a Pollyannish woman emitting empty optimistic reassurances. There is no indication that Ma understands the exploitative system and its toll on individuals. All the film Ma knows is that if they work more, there will be more money and more to eat.

Steinbeck's Ma is not a soother; she cajoles, prods, pricks, and angers her family into action. In the novel Ma insists that the family must leave the comfort and relative safety of the Weedpatch camp because of the scarcity of work in that area. Their food is running out. She tells Pa, "You ain't got the right to get discouraged. This here fambly's goin' under. You just ain't got the right" (479). When the men in the family don't react swiftly enough for Ma, she decides "We'll go in the mornin'." Pa's pride is hurt by her assertion of authority and he sniffs, "Time was when a man said what we'd do. Seems like women is tellin' now. Seems like it's purty near time to get out a stick" (481). Ma's response is immediate and challenging. She tells him that when he returns to fulfilling his responsibilities as head of the household, then he can use his stick. However, since he is not, she defies him with the information that she has a stick all laid out too. This is the second scene in the novel where Ma challenges Pa to some kind of physical combat and he backs away. As in the jack handle scene, Ma's reason is not a selfish grab for power, but concern for the welfare of the family. She explains to Tom that if you can make a man mad he will react better than if he just worries and "eats out his liver." Ma's perspicacious handling of Pa is not unlike her astute maneuvering of the company store clerk.

In the novel there are many occasions where Steinbeck shows us Ma's assertive strength and sagacity. The aggressive nature of Ma's strength even becomes an occasion for jokes. Tom teases Al that he better have the truck ready or "I'll turn Ma on ya" (481). The stick scene is in neither screenplay nor film. Its loss is not crucial in and of itself, except when added to the loss of other scenes that illustrate Ma's assertiveness, natural wisdom, and family authority. The combined losses significantly affect the nature of Ma's character. Ford's Ma is sweet, good, and reassuring, but there is little evidence that she understands their situation, nor is she assertive about her beliefs. She does not act to effect her values.

Her lack of action helps account for much of the devitalization of the image of woman in the movie. The movie Ma does not determine the judgment of the family council about Casy's accompanying them, she does not face down the company store clerk, she does not wield a jack handle to keep the family together, and she does not threaten Pa with a stick to anger him lest he become too dispirited. All such scenes in which Ma acts assertively are absent from the movie.

Not only is the movie Ma less active than Steinbeck's Ma, but she also understands less. In the film, one of Ma's major speeches comes after Tom has killed the deputy who killed Casy. Tom wants to run away, but Ma wants him to stay and help her with the family. She begins the speech with the statement "They's a whole lot I don't understan'" and then bemoans the loss of land and traditions that bound the family together. Darwell's Ma is both nostalgic, her eyes cast on faraway sights, and pleading, she needs Tom to stay and help her.[16] Her pleas are effective. Tom does stay, and they go on to a better situation, the Weedpatch camp. The same speech in the novel has a different context. First of all, Ma is questioning Tom about Casy's death. She wants to know how and why it happened and what Casy said. The significance of Casy's Christ-like final words, "You don' know what you're a-doin'," is not lost on Ma. She repeats the words and exclaims, "I wisht Granma could a heard" (535).

In the novel, after Ma delivers the speech about the family "crackin' up," she is shown acting decisively to assure both Tom's safety and to protect, as best she can, the health of the other members of the family. Ma has a clear sense of priorities. She makes Pa buy milk for Winfield, though the rest of the family must eat mush for dinner. Winfield has collapsed, suffering from an acute case of the "skitters." When Rose of Sharon complains that she needs milk, Ma responds, "I know, but you're still on your feet. This here little fella's down." Nonetheless, she manages to sneak a little of the milk to Rose of Sharon later. Again, when the group has a family council about what to do about Tom, it is Ma who decides they will leave the camp they are in, sneaking Tom out between the mattresses. Pa complains, "Seems like the man ain't got no say no more. She's jus' a heller. Come time we get settled down, I'm a-gonna smack her" (546). Ma barely acknowledges his challenge, responding "Come that time, you can," as she orders Al to get the truck ready and Pa and Uncle John to put the mattresses in.

They accomplish their goal of hiding Tom, but rather than going to a better place, the Joads end up sharing a boxcar with another family. Tom is hidden in a cave and it is Ma who, fearing for his safety after Ruthie's indiscreet remarks about him, tells him he must go away. Rather than the movie's passive and plaintive "Ain't you gonna tell me goodbye, Tommy?," the novel presents Ma moving "majestically" through the camp, down the stream, and up an embankment to deliver Tom some food and tell him he must go. This Ma is anything but resigned and passive. She tells Tom to come close so she can feel his face to know how his scars are healing. She tells him, "I wanta touch ya again, Tom. I wanta remember, even if it's on'y my fingers that remember. You got to go away, Tom." She then gives him some money that she has been "squirrelin'" away. When he demurs, her response is a good illustration of how effectively Ma can manipulate people. She tells Tom that he has no right to cause her pain. Tom knows he is beaten and tells her, "You ain't playin' fair" (570).

In the film, although much of Tom's speech about being part of a great big soul and following Casy's lead in the separation scene follows Steinbeck's dialogue exactly, the differences in context and in Ma's dialogue effectively diminish her character. No longer is she the actor; she is responding to Tom's decisions. Her astuteness is not evidenced. And the intensity of her feelings for Tom are changed from a desire to memorize the feel of him with her fingers to asking for a good-bye kiss with the feeble excuse, "We ain't the kissin' kind, but...." The end of the scene finds her weeping softly, an appropriate behavior for Ford's stereotyped mother. Steinbeck's Ma responds in an opposite manner. Her eyes are wet and burning, "but she did not cry." Instead she returns to the boxcar to face still more adversity.

There follows yet another scene in which Ma articulates her authority. Mr. Wainwright asks Pa to speak to Al so as to forestall any shame that might come on their family by Aggie becoming pregnant. Ma speaks up, assuring Mr. Wainwright not only that Pa will talk to Al, but that if he will not, she will. When she realizes how she has embarrassed Pa, she apologizes. Pa's response indicates how deeply disheartened he has become. No longer able to manage even an impotent threat to get out a stick, he says, "Funny! Women takin' over the fambly. Woman sayin' well do this here, an well go there. An I don' even care" (377–78). This is then followed by Ma's "woman is all one flow like a river" speech in which she assures Pa that though people are changing a little, they will go right on.

In the novel Ma's encouragement is not buttressed by subsequent scenes. The engagement between Al and Aggie Wainwright means that Al will be lost to the family group. Rose of Sharon's baby is born dead. And to cap off their troubles, the family is flooded out of their boxcar home. Steinbeck's closing scene is only faintly reassuring. That reassurance is embodied in the behavior of mother and daughter, particularly in Rose of Sharon's nurturing gesture. Though she is weak, wet, and undernourished, Rose of Sharon inherits her mother's mantle and acts as an agent for the preservation of life.

The film Joads are not nearly so beaten. When, in the last scene, they head out to find work, they are leaving a situation in which the people have shown that they can take care of themselves. The clean and orderly government camp is a haven where even the powerful hand of the law is not allowed entrance. Using their own resources, the men in camp preserve the peace and prevent a riot. Though Tom must leave, the family situation is not as dire as in the novel. Pa, Uncle John, and Al all seem fit and raring to go. The only one down is Rose of Sharon. There is no occasion for her to rise to and therefore Ma's thematic sentiment that "Woman can change better'n a man" is not borne out by the behavior of the women in the film. Rose of Sharon does not change, nor does she bear up to the hardships as well as the men. Ma changes very little. She is nurturing and optimistic from beginning to end.

If at one level the Joads represent the human family, then Ma and Rose of Sharon embody the role of women in that context. They are Mother and Daughter, Demeter and Persephone, the eternal feminine that duplicates itself and thus provides continuity and promise for the future. The truncation of Rose of Sharon's role in the movie removes this aspect of the significance of feminine renewal. While the film Ma remains a figure of hope, her passivity and lack of assertion leave the film's audience with a reinforcement of the traditional stereotype of the sweet, but long-suffering mother, a woman very unlike Steinbeck's strong, forceful, invincible Ma Joad.

Steinbeck's early novels, with their terse, dramatically developed plots, lend themselves well to the film medium. His scenes can often be lifted directly from the page to the screen. And the best screenwriters did just that. It is possible that an actress such as Beulah Bondi could have translated both the physical and spiritual strength of Steinbeck's Ma Joad. With her in the role, the jack handle scene might have been retained. But production decisions prevented this possibility and we are left with a fine, but flawed, film. John Ford's *The Grapes of Wrath* has many excellences. Still, as the story of humanity, the story of family, it grossly underplays the role of half the human race. One is left disappointed by the devitalization and diminishment of Ma Joad, one of the American novel's most admirable and engaging heroines. The women in the film are soft, sweet, passive, and long-suffering—nurturers, but not leaders in the struggle for survival. Steinbeck's women, though few in number, are strong in significance. They are tough as well as tender, feisty, and assertive. Though often helpless against overwhelming odds, they do more than mouth platitudes. At the end of Steinbeck's *The Grapes of Wrath* it is Ma Joad and Rose of Sharon who serve as both the symbols and the actors in human survival.

NOTES

1. Besides the Academy Award *The Grapes of Wrath* won for its director and for Jane Darwell as best supporting actress, the movie appears on various other "best" lists. The American Film Institute voted it one of the ten best American films of all time. John Gassner includes it in his *Twenty Best Film Plays*.

2. Robert E. Morsberger, "Steinbeck's Films," Second International Steinbeck Congress, 3 August 1984.

3. Letter to Elizabeth Otis, 15 December 1939, in *Steinbeck: A Life in Letters*, ed. Elaine Steinbeck and Robert Wallsten, 195 (New York, Viking Press, 1975).

4. Joseph R. Millichap calls *Of Mice and Men* and *The Grapes of Wrath* the best film adaptations of Steinbeck's works although he acknowledges "the ultimate failure to translate the full meaning of Steinbeck's novel to the screen." About Ma Joad, his understatement is that Jane Darwell is "a bit less fierce than Steinbeck's Ma," noting that if Ford had not chosen to excise the jack handle scene it might have provided a nice balance to the "sentimentalizing of Jane Darwell's film role" (*Steinbeck and Film* [New York: Frederick Ungar Publishing Co., 1983], 45). Russell Campbell thinks that Ma's sentimental idealization is a result of Ford's view of the Okies as "simple folk" and that by excising the jack handle scene Darwell's character is consistently presented as passively resigned to the vagaries of fate rather than fiercely resistant ("tramping Out the Vintage:

Sour Grapes, in *The Modern American Novel and the Movies*, ed. Gerald Peary and Roger Shatzkin, 114–15 [New York: Frederick Ungar Publishing Co., 1978]). Andrew Sarris argues that "Ford's own feelings are so powerfully patriarchal that when Grandpa dies, something in the movie seems to die with him." The inference, then, is that perhaps Ford's strong patriarchal feelings may account for the softening of Ma's part (*The John Ford Movie Mystery* [Bloomington: Indiana University Press, 1975], 98). Peter Roffman and Jim Purdy think that in keeping with Johnson's and Ford's highlighting of "Steinbeck's optimistic belief in the indestructibility of mankind" as opposed to "his many references to the need for mass action, Ma's role in the film is to counter Tom's radicalism. In the novel, Ma shares some of Tom's political sense; in the movie she just calls for all to sit back and wait for the good times to come back (*The Hollywood Social Problem Film* [Bloomington: Indiana University Press, 1981], 126).

5. Steinbeck says that there are five layers to the book and that the reader can participate to the level of his or her depth or hollowness. Letter to Pascal Covici, 16 January 1939, in *Steinbeck: A Life in Letters*, 178.

6. John Steinbeck, *The Grapes of Wrath* (New York: The Viking Press, 1939). All references to the novel will be in the text and refer to this edition. All references to the movie will also be in the text and are taken from the film script as published in *Twenty Best Film Plays*, ed. John Gassner and Dudley Nichols, 333–78 (New York: Crown Publishers, 1943).

7. Tetsumaro Hayashi, "Steinbeck's Women in *The Grapes of Wrath*: A New Perspective," *Kyushu American Literature* 18 (October 1977): 4.

8. Leonard Lutwack, *Heroic Fiction: The Epic Tradition and American Novels of the Twentieth Century* (Carbondale and Edwardsville: Southern Illinois University Press, 1971), 54.

9. Warren Motley, "From Patriarchy to Matriarchy: Ma Joad's Role in *The Grapes of Wrath*," *American Literature* 54 (October, 1982): 397–98.

10. Andrew Sarris says it is no accident that this scene is dominated by Charley Grapewin's Grandpa while scenes between Jane Darwell's Ma and Russell Simpson's Pa are dominated by Darwell (*John Ford Movie Mystery*, 97).

11. Campbell, Modern American Novel and the Movies, 109.

12. John Baxter, "The Grapes of Wrath, in *The International Dictionary of Films and Filmmakers: Volume 1*, ed. Christopher Lyon, 185 (Chicago: St. James Press, 1985).

13. Motley, "From Patriarchy to Matriarchy," 397.

14. Sarris, *John Ford Movie* Mystery, 97.

15. See my *The Indestructible Woman in Faulkner, Hemingway, and Steinbeck* (Ann Arbor: UMI Research Press, 1986), for a fuller explication of Rose of Sharon's role in the novel.

16. Warren French is so unsympathetic and out of patience with Jane Darwell's Ma that his description of this scene reads, "the camera jumps nervously about as Ma *rattles* [emphasis mine] on about her need for help" (*Filmguide to "The Grapes of Wrath"* [Bloomington: Indiana University Press, 1973], 51).

NELLIE Y. McKAY

"Happy[?]-Wife-and-Motherdom"[1]:
The Portrayal of Ma Joad in
John Steinbeck's The Grapes of Wrath

Women's social roles in western culture are central concerns in contemporary feminist criticism. The discourse focuses on the idea that our society is organized around male-dominated sex-gender systems that admit two genders, that privilege heterosexual relationships, and that embrace a sexual division of labor in which wife and mother are the primary functions of women.[2] In such works as *Of Woman Born* by Adrienne Rich,[3] *Man's World, Woman's Place* by Elizabeth Janeway,[4] *The Reproduction of Motherhood: Psychoanalysis and the Sociology of Gender* by Nancy Chodorow,[5] and *Contemporary Feminist Thought* by Hester Eisenstein,[6] critics argue that, in spite of prevailing social dogma to the contrary, the biological functions of childbearing and lactation (motherhood), and the cultural one of nurturing (mothering) are divisible. Whereas one is restricted to women, the other need not be. Parenting, in place of mothering, is not biologically determined, and there is no proof that men are less capable of nurturing children than women, or that children would suffer adverse effects if women were not their primary caretakers. However, female oppression under patriarchy dictates an institution in which the heterosexual family is at the center of the social system; woman, wife, motherhood, and mothering are synonymous; and sex-role stereotyping separates the social expectations of women from those of

From *New Essays on* The Grapes of Wrath, David Wyatt, ed. © 1990 by Cambridge University Press.

men. From this institution, "Happy-Wife-and-Motherdom" assumes woman's ideal social, emotional, and psychological state.

The success of such sex-role stereotyping depends on establishing socially acceptable clusters of behavioral attitudes that define male and female gender identities differently from the biological (sex-based) identities of women and men. To function properly, these behaviors require social placement on a hierarchical scale of dominant versus submissive, strong versus weak, independent versus dependent, in favor of men.[7] Consequently, women are conditioned toward passivity while men are rewarded for more aggressive behavior. For women, the expressive traits (affection, obedience, sympathy, and nurturing) are hailed and rewarded as "normal" behavior; men are expected to be aggressive, tenacious, ambitious, and responsible. Objecting to psychological impositions that render women subordinate to men, Elizabeth Janeway, among others, speaks out against social scientists like Freud and Eric Erickson who, in defense of the status quo, made it their business to substitute "*prescription*" for "*description*," as they tried to explain how women ought to be, rather than how they are.[8] She argues that there is no scientific basis for the male-constructed definition of women's nature, and that opinions on the biological aspects of women's inabilities to perform as well as men in some areas, and vice versa, are not facts, but are, rather, social mythology based on beliefs and practices that shape social life according to a particular set of values.[9] This social mythology of women's nature enables men to define the "natural" capabilities of women in ways that make women socially and economically dependent on men.

The image of woman/wife/mother with children as the "core of domestic organization is implicit in patriarchal sex-gender systems."[10] Traditionally, men perform in the public sphere, while women's place is in the home, where they loom large and powerful, although, in the larger world, they remain under the control of husbands and fathers. Nor are women innocent in the development of these systems. Several feminist critics now argue that sex-role differentiation originated partly in male propaganda, and partly because women found certain of its elements sufficiently attractive willingly to give up intellectual, economic, and political power in exchange for private power in the domestic sphere. As women/wives/mothers, they are able to hold sway over the lives of their children, and to manipulate their husbands in the sexual arena.[11] This arrangement frees men from domestic responsibilities and permits them to focus their lives primarily in the public sphere: the masculine world of social and political control that determines the lives of men and women. The husband/father assumes the socially approved masculine responsibility to make important decisions and provide monetarily for his family, while the wife/mother agrees to accept a variety of unspecified familial obligations, including constant attunement to the needs of her husband and children. His support is expected to be largely material; hers, emotional. Nor are the rewards equal. By society's standards, his contributions to the family are perceived greater; hers are lesser. He articulates his family and gives it a place in the larger world; she is bound by that articulation.[12]

Until recently, literary representations of women, especially by men, subscribed almost exclusively to the ideology of locating women's place in the domestic world. Women who moved outside of their designated boundaries in search of authority over their own lives were stigmatized as unfeminine, bad mothers and wives, and social deviants. The most well-known positive image in the category of the good woman is the Earth Mother, who, engaged in selfless mothering, dedicates her entire being to the welfare of her husband and children. In *The Lay of the Land*, Annette Kolodny reminds us of how powerful the representation of a symbiotic relationship between femaleness and the land (the earth) is in the national consciousness. The desire for harmony between "man" and nature, based on an experience of the land as woman/mother—the female principle of "receptivity, repose, and integral satisfaction," is one of our most cherished American fantasies, she tells us.[13] In her analysis of seventeenth- and eighteenth-century writings by early settlers in America, Kolodny writes that the members of this group carried with them a yearning for paradise, and perceived the New World as a "maternal 'garden,' receiving and nurturing human children."[14] Furthermore, she asserts that for these settlers there was

> a *need* to experience the land as a nurturing, giving maternal breast.... Beautiful, indeed, that wilderness appeared—but also dark, uncharted, and prowled by howling beasts.... Mother was ready to civilize it ... [to make] the American continent ... the birthplace of a new culture ... with new and improved human possibilities ... in fact as well as metaphor, a womb of generation and a provider of sustenance.[15]

This equation of the American land with woman's biological attributes did much to foster the widespread use of literary images of women as one with the "natural" propensities of a productive nurturing earth, and to erase, psychologically, the differences between the biological and the social functions of women.

Fully immersed in this tradition, men, male vision, and the relationships of men to each other and to the rest of the world dominate the works of John Steinbeck, whereas women, without whom the men would have no world, have no independent identity of their own. The social and economic conditions in the lower working-class milieu in which many of these women appear can easily give rise to what on the surface seems to represent a very different relationship to the social structure from that of women in other strata. On the contrary, the ideology that woman's place is rooted in her interests in others, preferably those of husbands and children, remains the same. Steinbeck's women seldom need seek the right to work outside of their homes, or to choose careers equal to those of men. They have no connections to the "gentle-companions" female identity or to the ideology of femininity that became popular in the nineteenth century. Work, as hard as that of farm men, or lower class men struggling for survival outside of the agrarian economy, occupies a great deal of their time. In the words of Tom Joad, "Women's always tar'd, ... that's just the way women is, 'cept at meetin' once an' again."[16] They are always tired because they are always attending to the needs of everyone but themselves. Even domestic violence against these women is socially acceptable within the group.[17] Only race privilege protects them from the barbarous abuse of others outside of their community that women of color in similar situations experience. Yet, the most they can achieve and hold onto with social dignity is the supportive nurturing role of woman's place in a man's world.

The centrality of women to the action of *The Grapes of Wrath* is clear from the beginning as well. For one thing, not only among the Joads, the main characters in this novel, but in all the families in crisis, the children look to the women for answers to their immediate survival: "What are we going to do, Ma? Where are we going to go?" (47) the anonymous children ask. In male-dominated sex-gender systems, children depend on their mothers for parenting, and their stability rests mainly on the consistency and reliability with which women meet their needs. There is no question that in this model the woman/wife/mother makes the most important contributions to family stability. This chapter does not challenge Steinbeck's understanding of the value of women's roles in the existing social order. I attempt, however, to place his vision of those roles within the framework of an American consciousness that has long been nourished by gender myths that associated women with nature, and thus primarily with the biological and cultural functions of motherhood and mothering, whereas men occupy a separate masculine space that affords them independence and autonomy. By adopting Robert Briffault's theory that matriarchy is a cohesive, nonsexually dominating system,[18] Steinbeck assures us that the family can survive by returning to an earlier stage of collective, nonauthoritarian security while the larger society moves towards a socialistic economy. As he sees it, in times of grave familial or community need, a strong, wise woman like Ma Joad has the opportunity (or perhaps the duty) to assert herself and still maintain her role as selfless nurturer of the group. In this respect, she is leader and follower, wise and ignorant, and simple and complex, simultaneously.[19] In short, she is the woman for all seasons, the nonintrusive, indestructible "citadel" on whom everyone else can depend.

This idealistic view of womanhood is especially interesting because, although there are qualities in Steinbeck's work that identify him with the sentimental and romantic traditions, as a writer with sympathies toward socialism he also saw many aspects of American life in the light of harsh realism. His reaction to the plight of the Oklahoma farmers in this novel moved him to a dramatic revision of the frontier patriarchal myth of individual, white-male success through unlimited access to America's abundant and inexhaustible expanses of land. He begins with the equivalent of a wide-lens camera view that portrays the once-lush land grown tired and almost unyielding from overuse, and then follows that up with vivid descriptions of farmers being brutally dispossessed by capitalist greed from the place they thought belonged to them. His instincts are also keen in the matter of character development; unanticipated circumstances alter the worldview that many of the people in the novel previously held, and their changes are logical. As they suffer, the Joads, in particular the mother and her son Tom (the other Joad men never develop as fully), gradually shed their naïveté and achieve a sound political consciousness of class and economic oppression. This is a difficult education for them, but one which they eventually accept. Through it all, without the unshakable strength and wisdom of the mother, who must at times assert her will to fill the vacuum of her husband's incapability, nothing of the family, as they define it, would survive. Still, she never achieves an identity of her own, or recognizes the political reality of women's roles within a male-dominated system. She is never an individual in her own right. Even when she becomes fully aware of class discrimination and understands that the boundaries of the biological family are much too narrow a structure from which to challenge the system they struggle against, she continues to fill the social space of the invincible woman/wife/mother.

Critics identify two distinct narrative views of women in Steinbeck's writings. In one, in novels such as *To a God Unknown* (1933) and *The Grapes of Wrath* (1939), the image is positive and one-dimensional, with female significance almost completely associated with the maternal roles that Kolodny and others decry. In the other, for example *Tortilla Flat* (1935), *Of Mice and Men* (1937), *East of Eden* (1952), and several of the short stories in *The Long Valley* (1938), the portraiture is socially negative. Whores, hustlers, tramps, or madams are the outstanding roles that define the majority of these women. More graphically stated by one critic, these women "seem compelled to choose between homemaking and whoredom."[20] Interestingly, in spite of their questionable behavior, women within this group are often described as "big-breasted, big-hipped, and warm," thus implying the maternal types.[21] In his post-1943 fiction, after he moved to New York City, sophisticated women characters who are jealous, vain, and cunning—the opposite of the women in his earlier works—appear (as negative portrayals) in Steinbeck's work. Furthermore, Steinbeck's "positive" women are impressively "enduring," but never in their own self-interests. Their value resides in the manner in which they are able to sustain their nurturing and reproductive capabilities for the benefit of the group. As Mimi Reisel Gladstein notes,

> they act as the nurturing and reproductive machinery of the group. Their optimistic significance lies, not in their individual spiritual triumph, but in their function as perpetuators of the species. They are not judged by any biblical or traditional sense of morality.[22]

In conjunction with their ability to endure and to perpetuate the species, they are also the bearers of "knowledge—both of their husbands and of men generally," knowledge which enables them to "come ... [closer than men] to an understanding of the intricacies of human nature and the profundities of life in general."[23]

Since its publication in 1939, *The Grapes of Wrath*, one of Steinbeck's most celebrated works, has been the subject of a variety of controversial appraisals. Seen by some as "an attempted prose epic, a summation of national experience at a given time,"[24] others belabor its ideological and technical flaws. The disagreements it continues to raise speak well for the need to continue to evaluate its many structural and thematic strands.

The novel opens on a note that explodes the American pastoral of the seventeenth and eighteenth centuries that Kolodny describes in her work. The lush and fertile lands that explorers in Virginia and the Carolinas saw give way to the Oklahoma Dust Bowl, where "... dawn came, but no day. In the gray sky a red sun appeared, a dim red circle that gave a little light, like dusk; and as that day advanced, the dusk slipped toward darkness, and the wind cried and whimpered over the fallen corn" (5). The impotence and confusion of a bewildered group of displaced people replace the assuredness and confidence of the nation's early settlers. In this world where nature is gone awry, and human control lies in the hands of men greedy for wealth and in possession of new technology that enhances their advantages, the men, women, and children who have, until now, lived on the land are helpless against an unspeakable chaos.

Feeling completely out of control in a situation they cannot comprehend, the men stand in silence by their fences or sit in the doorways of the houses they will soon leave, space that echoes loudly with their impotent unspoken rage, for they are without power or influence to determine their destinies. Even more outrageous for them is their profound sense of alienation. Armed with rifles, and willing to fight for what they consider rightfully theirs, there is no one for them to take action against. They can only stare helplessly at the machines that demolish their way of life. They do not understand why they no longer have social value outside of their disintegrating group, and they do not know how to measure human worth in terms of abstract economic principles. "One man on a tractor can take the place of twelve or fourteen families," the representatives of the owner men explain to the uncomprehending displaced farmers. That some of their own people assist the invaders leaves them more befuddled.

> "What are you doing this kind of work for—against your own people?"

a farmer asks the tractor-driver son of an old acquaintance. The man replies:

> [for] "three dollars a day.... I got a wife and kids. We got to eat ... and it comes everyday."
> "But for three dollars a day fifteen or twenty families can't eat at all,"

the farmer rebuts, and continues:

> "nearly a hundred people have to go out and wander on the roads for your three dollars a day. Is that right?" ... And the driver says, "Can't think of that. Got to think of my own kids. Three dollars a day, and it comes in every day. Times are changing, mister, don't you know? Can't make a living on the land unless you've got two, five, ten thousand acres and a tractor. Crop land isn't for little guys like us anymore.... You try to get three dollars a day some place. That's the only way." (50)

The quality of the frustration and level of the ineffectiveness that the men feel is displayed in the actions of Grampa, the patriarch of the Joad clan. He fires a futile shot at the advancing tractor, but succeeds only in "blow[ing] the headlights off that cat', ... [while] she come on just the same" (62). The march of technology and the small farmers' distress go hand in hand.

Deprived of traditional assertive masculine roles, for the most part, the helpless, silent men seldom move; only their hands are engaged—uselessly— "busy," with sticks and little rocks as they survey the ruined crops, their ruined homes, their ruined way of life, "thinking—figuring," and finding no solution to the disintegration rapidly enveloping them. Nor do the women/wives/mothers precipitously intrude on their shame. They are wise in the ways of mothering their men; of understanding the depth of their hurt and confusion, and in knowing that at times their greatest contribution to the healing of the others' psychic wounds lies in their supportive silence. "They knew that a man so hurt and so perplexed may turn in anger, even on people he loves. They left the men alone to figure and to wonder in the dust" (7). Secretly, unobtrusively, because they are good women, they study the faces of their men to know if this time they would "break." Also furtively, the children watch the faces of the men and the women. When the men's faces changed from "bemused perplexity" to anger and resistance, although they still did not know what they would do, the women and children knew they were "safe"—for "no misfortune was too great to bear if their men were whole" (7).

In the face of such disaster, enforced idleness is the lot of men. Their work comes to a halt. The women, however, remain busy, for the housewife's traditional work, from which society claims she derives energy, purpose, and fulfillment, goes on. In addition, as conditions worsen and the men further internalize impotence, the women know they will be responsible for making the crucial decisions to lead their families through the adjustment period ahead. Critic Joan Hedrick explains the dynamics of the division of labor in sex-gender-differentiated systems this way, rather than as women's "nature":

> Though there are no crops to be harvested, there are clothes to mend, cornmeal to stir, side-meat to cut up for dinner. In a time of unemployment, women embody continuity, not out of some mythic identity as the Great Mother, but simply because their work, being in the private sphere of the family, has not been taken away....[25]

According to critics Richard Astro and Warren Motley, Steinbeck's philosophy of women was deeply influenced by his readings of Robert Briffault's *The Mothers: The Matriarchal Theory of Social Origins* (1931), a work they include in a group that "strove to heal the ... post-Darwinian split between scientific thinking and ethical experience."[26] Although Briffault saw matriarchy (historically antecedent to patriarchy) as a primitive and regressive order, he felt it described a "relationship based on cooperation rather than power," and fostered an "equalitarian" society to which "authority" and "domination" were foreign. As Motley sees it, Steinbeck did not believe that matriarchy was regressive, but he was convinced that the shock of dispossession undermined the patriarchal authority (based on male economic dominance) of the Joad men and the other farmers to such an extent that they were forced to turn back to matriarchy, the more positive social organization force, epitomized by Ma Joad's "high calm," "superhuman understanding," and selfless concern for her family, as the hope for a better future.[27] Matriarchy, divested of the threat of authority and domination over men, was a system that suited Steinbeck's purpose in this novel.

The Grapes of Wrath delineates the tragedy of an agrarian family in a world in which capitalist greed and the demands of rapidly advancing technology supersede human needs and extenuating financial circumstances. Different in their attitudes from other white groups who seek the American Dream in social and economic mobility, the hard-working Joads, once tenant farmers, now reduced to sharecropper status, lived contentedly on the land in a community of like others, for three generations. They asked little of anyone outside of their world. Solid Americans, as they understand that term, they wanted only to live and let live. For instance, oblivious to the implications of his racial politics, the tenant man proudly explains his family's contributions to the pioneer history of white America. His grandfather arrived in frontier Oklahoma territory in his youth, when his worldly possessions amounted to salt, pepper, and a rifle. But before long, he successfully staked out a claim for his progeny:

> Grampa took up the land, and he had to kill the Indians and drive them away. And Pa was born here, and he killed weeds and snakes.... An we [the third succeeding generation] was born here.... And Pa had to borrow money. The bank owned the land then, but we stayed and got a little bit of what we raised. (45)

Unfortunately, the irony of their helplessness in confrontation with the power of the banks, with the absent, large land owners, and with the great crawling machines versus the fate of the Indians (to the farmer, of no greater concern than the comparison he makes of them to snakes or weeds) completely escapes the present generation. The subsequent education in

class politics might have come sooner and been less psychologically
devastating to the Joads and their friends if they had been able to recognize
the parallels between racial and economic hegemony.

Three characters drive the action in *The Grapes of Wrath*: Jim Casy, a
country preacher turned political activist; Tom Joad, the eldest son, ex-
convict, and moral conscience of the family; and the indestructible Ma Joad,
who holds center stage. At times she assumes mythic proportions, but her
portraiture is also realistic and she acts with wisdom. Impressionistically, she
is firmly planted in the earth, but she is more dependable than the land,
which could not withstand the buffeting of nature or the persistent demands
of small farmers or the evil encroachment of technology and corporate
power. Her position is established at the beginning of the novel:

> Ma was heavy, but not fat; thick with child-bearing and work ...
> her strong bare feet moved quickly and deftly over the floor....
> Her full face was not soft; it was controlled, kindly. *Her hazel eyes
> seemed to have experienced all possible tragedy and to have mounted
> pain and suffering like steps into a big calm and superhuman
> understanding. She seemed to know, to accept, to welcome her position,
> the citadel of the family.* (99–100—italics mine)

Unless she admitted hurt or fear or joy, the family did not know those
emotions; and better than joy they loved her calm. They could depend on
her "imperturbability." When Tom, Jr., returns from prison to find no
homestead, the house pushed off its foundations, fences gone, and other
signs of living vanished, his first thought is "They're gone—or Ma's dead"
(56). He knows that under no circumstances would she permit the place to
fall into such ruin if she were there. His is not a casual observation, but a
statement fraught with anxiety. As Nancy Chodorow points out, in the sex-
gender system, the absent mother is always the source of discomfiture for her
children. Tom Joad closely associates the physical deterioration of his home
with a missing mother, a signal for him of the catastrophe of which he is yet
unaware.[28]

There is no question that Steinbeck had, as Howard Levant stresses,
"profound respect" and "serious intentions" for the materials in *The Grapes
of Wrath*. His sympathies are with a group of people who, though politically
and economically unaggressive by other traditional American standards,
represented an important core in the national life.[29] His portrayal of the
misfortunes and downfall of this family constitutes a severe critique of a
modern economic system that not only devalues human lives on the basis of
class but, in so doing, that violates the principles of the relationship between

hard work and reward and the sanctity of white family life on which the country was founded. In light of the brutal social and economic changes, and the disruptions of white family stability, there is no doubt that Steinbeck saw strong women from traditional working-class backgrounds as instrumental in a more humane transformation of the social structure. Of necessity, women are essential to any novel in which the conventional family plays a significant role. Here, he gives the same significance to the destruction of a family-centered way of life that one group had shaped and perpetated for generations as he does to the economic factors that precipitated such a dire situation. Furthermore, through female characters in *The Grapes of Wrath*, Steinbeck's sensitivities to the values of female sensibilities demonstrate a point of view that supports the idea of humanitarian, large-scale changes that would make America, as a nation, more responsive to larger social needs.

In this respect, in spite of the grim reality of the lives of the Joads and their neighbors, *The Grapes of Wrath* is optimistic in favor of massive social change. We can trace this optimism from the beginning of the book, in which, unlike traditional plots of the naturalistic novels of its day, events unfold through the consciousness of the characters in such a way as to permit them to envision themselves exercising free will and exerting influence on their social world. In addition, as a result of his economic politics, Steinbeck reinforces the idea that the situation is not the dilemma of an isolated family, but of an entire group of people of a particular class. If sufficiently politicized, they can and will act. The novel chronicles the misfortunes and political education of the Joad family, but they represent the group from which they come, and share the feelings of their like-others. For example, also at the beginning, an unnamed farmer, recognizing his individual impotence in the face of capitalism and the technological monster, protests: "We've got a bad thing made by man, and by God that's something *we* can change" (52—italics mine). While neither he nor his fellow farmers can comprehend the full meaning of that statement at the time, the end of the novel suggests that those who survive will come to realize that group action can have an effect on the monstrous ideology that threatens their existence. But first they must survive; and the women are at the center of making that survival possible.

The first mention of Ma Joad in the novel occurs when Tom, recently released from jail after serving four of a seven-year sentence for killing a man in self-defense, returns to the homestead to find it in ruin. During his absence, he had almost no contact with his family, for, as Tom observes to his friend Casy: "they wasn't people to write" (57). Two years earlier, however, his mother sent him a Christmas card, and, the following year, the grandmother did the same. His mother's appears to have been appropriate;

his grandmother's, a card with a "tree an' shiny stuff [that] looks like snow," with an embarrassing message in "po'try," was not:

> Merry Christmus, purty child,
> Jesus meek an' Jesus mild,
> Underneath the Christmus tree
> There's a gif' for you from me. (35)

Tom recalls the teasing of his cellmates who saw the card. Subsequently, they call him "Jesus Meek."

Given the living situation within the Joad community—the hard work and frustration over the yield of the land and the absence of genteel rituals, especially in such hard times—the fact that both women sent Christmas cards to the incarcerated young man is testimony to the quality of their commitment to mothering. Granma's card, however, is not appropriate for the young man confined involuntarily among men for whom only masculine symbols and behavior are acceptable. Nevertheless, Tom does not hold this against her. He understands and accepts her impulse and her motive. He believes she liked the card for its shiny exterior and that she never read the message, perhaps because, having lost her glasses several years before, she could not see to read. Symbolically, Granma may have good intentions, but she lacks the perception to fill successfully the present or future needs of her family. Later, when both grandparents die en route to California, the family realizes that they were too old to make the transition from one way of life to another. On the other hand, although there is no mention of the nature of Ma Joad's card, we can assume that it was not a cause of embarrassment for her son. She is the woman of wisdom who knows how to use her talents to comfort her family in its moments of greatest distress. The differences in the two Christmas cards set the stage for understanding that Ma Joad is the woman who will be the significant force in the life of the family in the difficult times ahead.

Critics of Steinbeck's women often note that the first time we come face to face with Ma Joad she is engaged in the most symbolic act of mothering—feeding her family. I add that the second time we see her, she is washing clothes with her arms, up to her elbows, in soapsuds, and the third time, she is trying to dress the cantankerous grandfather who is by now incapable of caring for his own basic needs. Occurring in quick succession on a busy morning, these are the housewife's most important tasks: feeding the family, keeping them clean, and tending to the needs of those too young or too old to do so for themselves. In these earliest scenes with Ma Joad, the family is making its final preparations for the journey to California, and women's work not only goes on almost uninterruptedly, but increases in intensity. The adults, though full of apprehensions, have high hopes that steady work and a return to stability await them at the end of the trip. They have seen handbills calling for laborers to come to California to reap the harvests of a rich and fruitful land. They believe the handbills, for who would go to the expense of printing misrepresentations of the situation?

Although at all times the Joads have very little or almost no money; and, while in Oklahoma, no realistic appraisal of how long the trip to California will take in their dilapidated vehicle; and, in California, no assurances of how soon they will find work or a place to settle or know the nature of their future; an interesting aspect of Ma Joad's mothering psychology surfaces in different locations. On one hand, through most of the novel, she insists that her considerations are mainly for her family; on the other, she is willing to share the little food she has, to nurture whoever else is in need and comes along her way. We see this for the first time in Oklahoma, on first meeting her. Tom and his friend Casy arrive just as she completes the breakfast preparations on the day before the long, uncertain journey begins. Before she recognizes who they are, she invites them to partake of her board. Most notably, evidence of her largesse occurs again under more stressful circumstances, when she feeds a group of hungry children in California, although there is not sufficient food even for her family.

Another extension of Ma Joad's mothering precipitates her into a new and unaccustomed position of power within the family when she insists that Casy, with no family of his own, but who wishes to travel with them, be taken along. This is her first opportunity to assert herself outside of her housewife's role, to claim leadership in important decision making, whereas previously only the men officiated. Casy travels with the Joads only because Ma Joad overrides the objections of her husband, whose concerns for their space needs, and the small amount of money and little food they have, lead him to think it unwise to take an extra person, especially an outsider to the family, on the trip. Questioned on the matter, Ma replies:

> It ain't kin we? It's will we? ... As far as 'kin,' we can't do nothin',
> not go to California or nothin'; but as far as 'will,' why, we'll do
> what we will. (139)

When the conversation ends, Casy has been accepted and she has gained new authority. She accepts this unpretentiously and with an absence of arrogance that will accompany her actions each time she finds it necessary to assert her will in the weeks and months ahead. And always, she asserts herself only for the good of the family. Two incidents that illustrate the group's understanding and acceptance of her wisdom and good judgment are especially noteworthy in this context. One occurs when the car breaks down during the journey and she refuses to agree to split up the family in order to hasten the arrival of some of its members in California. When her husband insists that separating is their better alternative, she openly defies him and, armed with a jack handle, challenges him to "whup" her first to gain her obedience to his will (230).[30] The second incident takes place in California, when, after weeks of the groups' unsuccessful search for work and a decent place to settle down, she chides the men for capitulating to despair. "You ain't got the right to get discouraged," she tells them, "this here fambly's goin' under. You jus' ain't got the right" (479).

But these situations, in which Ma's voice carries, also illustrate the tensions between men and women, in sex-gender-role systems, when women move into space traditionally designated to men. Each time Ma asserts her leadership she meets with Pa's resentment, for, regardless of her motives, he perceives that she usurps his authority. In the first instance, when Casy is accepted into the group, "Pa turned his back, and his spirit was raw from the whipping" her ascendancy represented to him (140). She, mindful of her role, leaves the family council and goes back to the house, to women's place, and women's work. But nothing takes place in her absence, the family waits for her return before continuing with their plans, "for she was powerful in the group" (140). During the trip (when Ma challenges Pa to "whup" her), after several suspenseful minutes, as the rest of the group watch his hands, the fists never form, and, in an effort to salvage his hurt pride, he can only say: "one person with their mind made up can shove a lot of folks aroun'!" (230). But again she is the victor and the "eyes of the whole family shifted back to Ma. She was the power. She had taken control" (231). Finally, in California, when Ma has her way once more in spite of Pa's opposition, and the family will move from a well-kept camp that had been a temporary respite from the traumas of the journey and their stay in Hooverville, but that placed them in an area in which they could find no work,

> Pa sniffled. "Seems like times is changed," he said sarcastically. "Time was when a man said what we'd do. Seems like women is tellin' now. Seems like it's purty near time to get out a stick." (481)

But he makes no attempt to beat her, for she quickly reminds him that men have the "right" to beat their women only when they (the men) are adequately performing their masculine roles.

"You get your stick Pa," she said. "Times when they's food an' a place to set, then maybe you can use your stick an' keep your skin whole. But you ain't a-doin' your job, either a-thinkin' or a-workin'. If you was, why, you could use your stick, an' women folks'd sniffle their nose an' creep-mouse aroun'. But you jus' get you a stick now an' you ain't lickin' no woman; you're a fightin', 'cause I got a stick all laid out too." (481)

In each of the instances mentioned here, once the decision is made and Ma's wise decision carries, she returns to women's place and/or displays stereotypical women's emotions. After her first confrontation with Pa over Casy, she hastens to tend the pot of "boiling side-meat and beet greens" to feed her family. Following the second, after she has challenged Pa to a fight and wins, she looks at the bar of iron and her hand trembles as she drops it on the ground. Finally, when she rouses the family from despair, she immediately resumes washing the breakfast dishes, "plunging" her hands into the bucket of water. And, to emphasize her selflessness, as her angry husband leaves the scene, she registers pride in her achievement, but not for herself. "He's all right," she notes to Tom. "He ain't beat. He's like as not to take a smack at me." Then she explains the aim of her "sassiness."

Take a man, he can get worried an' worried, an' it eats out his liver, an' purty soon he'll jus' lay down and die with his heart et out. But if you can take an' make 'im mad, why, he'll be awright. Pa, he didn't say nothin', but he's mad now. He'll show me now. He's awright. (481)

Only once does Ma come face to face with the issue of gender roles, and the possibilities of recognizing women's oppression within the conventions of the patriarchal society, and that is in her early relationships with Casy, when, in her psychological embrace of him, he is no longer a stranger, or even a friend, he becomes one of the male members of the family. He thanks her for her decision to let him accompany them to California by offering to "salt down" the meat they will carry with them. To this offer, she is quick to point out that the task is "women's work" that need not concern him. It is interesting that the only crack in the ideology of a gender-based division of labor to occur in the novel is in Casy's reply to Ma, and his subsequent actions: "It's all work.... They's too much to do to split it up to men's and women's work.... Leave me salt the meat" (146). Although she permits him to do it, apparently, she learns nothing from the encounter, for it never becomes a part of her thinking. On the other hand, Casy's consciousness of the politics of class is in formation before we meet him in the novel and he is the only character in the book to realize that women are oppressed by the division of labor based on the differentiation of sex-gender roles.

If the wisdom that Steinbeck attributes to women directs Ma to step outside of her traditional role in times of crisis, as noted above, her actions immediately after also make it clear that she is just as willing to retreat to wifehood and motherdom. In this, she supports Steinbeck's championing of Briffault's theory that, in matriarchy, women do not seek to have authority over men. In her case, not even equality of place is sought, only the right to lead, for the good of the group, when her man is incapable of doing so. And Steinbeck suggests why women are better equipped to lead in time of great social stress: They are closer to nature and to the natural rhythms of the earth. When family morale is at its lowest point, Ma continues to nurture confidence: "Man, he lives in jerks—" she says, "baby born an' a man dies, an' that's a jerk—gets a farm an' loses his farm, an' that's a jerk." But women are different. They continue on in spite of the difficulties. "Woman, its all one flow, like a stream, little eddies, little waterfalls, but the river, it goes right on. Woman looks at it like that" (577). In times of crisis, Steinbeck suggests, the survival of the family and, by extension, the social order, depends on the wisdom and strength of the mother, whose interests are always those of her husband and children.

The long trek from Oklahoma to California provides many instances that demonstrate Ma's selfless nurturing, her wisdom, her leadership abilities, and, above all, her centeredness in the family. An important illustration of the latter occurs at the time of the death of the grandmother on the long night in which the family makes an incredibly precarious desert crossing into California. Lying with the dead old woman all night to conceal this partially unforeseen mishap from the rest of the group, Ma Joad's only thought during the ordeal is: "The fambly hadda get acrost" (312). Alone with her secret of the true state of the old woman's condition, her considerations for the other members of the family, in this case particularly for the future of the younger children and for her daughter's unborn child, take precedence over the tremendous emotional cost to herself. Her determination to protect the family is almost ferocious, as she stands up to the officials at the agricultural inspection station on the California border to prevent them from discovering the dead woman by making a thorough check of the contents of the truck.

> Ma climbed heavily down from the truck. Her face was swollen and her eyes were hard. "Look, mister. We got a sick ol' lady. We

got to get her to a doctor. We can't wait." She seemed to fight
with hysteria. "You can't make us wait." (308)

Her apparent distress over the welfare of the old woman's health is
convincing. One inspector perfunctorily waves the beam of his flashlight into
the interior of the vehicle, and decides to let them pass. "I couldn' hold 'em"
he tells his companion. "Maybe it was a bluff," the other replied, to which
the first responded: "Oh, Jesus, no! You should of seen that ol' woman's face.
That wasn't no bluff" (308). Ma is so intent on keeping the death a secret,
even from the rest of the group as long as their overall situation remains
threatening, that, when they arrive in the next town, she assures Tom that
Granma is "awright—awright," and she implores him to "drive on. We got
to get acrost" (308). She absorbs the trauma of the death in herself, and only
after they have arrived safely on the other side of the desert does she give the
information to the others. Even then she refuses the human touch that would
unleash her own emotional vulnerability. The revelation of this act to protect
the family is one of the most powerful scenes in the novel. The members of
the family, already almost fully dependent on her emotional stamina, look at
her "with a little terror at her strength" (312). Son Tom moves toward her in
speechless admiration and attempts to put his hand on her shoulder to
comfort her. "'Don' touch me,' she said. 'I'll hol' up if you don' touch me.
That'd get me'" (312). And Casy, the newest member of the family, can only
say: "there's a woman so great with love—she scares me" (313).

In Steinbeck's vision of a different and more humane society than
capitalistic greed spawned, he also believed that efforts like Ma Joad's, to
hold the family together in the way she always knew it (individualism as a
viable social dynamic), were doomed to failure. Although she is unconscious
of it at the time, her initial embrace of Casy is a step toward a redefinition of
family, and, by the time the Joads arrive in California, other developments
have already changed the situation. Both Grampa and Granma are dead.
Soon after, son Noah, feeling himself a burden on the meager resources at
hand, wanders away. In addition, Casy is murdered for union activities; Al,
whose mechanical genius was invaluable during the trip, is ready to marry
and leave; Connie, Rose of Sharon's husband, deserts, and her baby is
stillborn; and Tom, in an effort to avenge Casy's death, becomes a fugitive
from the law and decides to become a union organizer, to carry on Casy's
work. Through these events, first Tom, and then Ma, especially through
Tom's final conversation with her, achieve an education in the politics of class
oppression, and realize that the system that diminishes one family to the
point of its physical and moral disintegration can only be destroyed through
the cooperative efforts of those of the oppressed group. "Use' ta be the

fambly was fust. It ain't so now. It's anybody," Ma is forced to admit toward the end of the novel (606).

But, although the structure of the traditional family changes to meet the needs of a changing society, in this novel at least, Steinbeck sees "happy-wife-and-motherdom" as the central role for women, even for those with other significant contributions to make to the world at large. Ma Joad's education in the possibilities of class action do not extend to an awareness of women's lives and identities beyond the domestic sphere, other than that which has a direct relationship on the survival of the family. The conclusion of the novel revises the boundaries of that family. In this scene, unable physically to supply milk from her own breasts to save the old man's life, she initiates her daughter into the sisterhood of "mothering the world," of perpetuating what Nancy Chodorow calls "The Reproduction of Mothering." Ma Joad is the epitome of the Earth Mother. Critics note that Steinbeck need give her no first name, for she is the paradigmatic mother, and this is the single interest of her life. The seventeenth- and eighteenth-century metaphor of the fecund, virgin American land (women) gives way to that of the middle-aged mother (earth), "thick with child-bearing and work," but Steinbeck holds onto the stereotypical parallels between woman and nature. In our typical understanding of that word, Ma may not be happy in her role, but "her face ... [is] controlled and kindly" and she fully accepts her place. Having "experienced all possible tragedy and ... mounted pain and suffering like steps into a high calm," she fulfills her highest calling in the realm of wife and motherdom.

NOTES

1. I borrow from a phrase in Elizabeth Janeway's *Man's World, Woman's Place* (New York: William Morrow & Company, 1971), p. 151.

2. See Nancy Chodorow, *The Reproduction of Mothering: Psychoanalysis and the Sociology of Gender* (Berkeley: The University of California Press, 1978), p. 9.

3. Adrienne Rich, *Of Woman Born* (New York: W. W. Norton and Company, 1976).

4. See Note 1.

5. Nancy Chodorow, *The Reproduction of Motherhood: Psychoanalysis and the Sociology of Gender* (Berkeley: The University of California Press, 1978).

6. Hester Eisenstein, *Contemporary Feminist Thought* (Boston: G. K. Hall, 1983).

7. Eisenstein, p. 7. This is a point of view also expressed by almost all feminist critics.

8. Janeway, p. 13.

9. Ibid.

10. Chodorow, p. 9.

11. Janeway, pp. 192–208.

12. Chodorow, p. 179.

13. Annette Kolodny, *The Lay of the Land: Metaphor as Experience and History in American Life and Letters* (Chapel Hill: University of North California Press, 1975), p. 4.

14. Kolodny, pp. 5–9.

15. Ibid., p. 9.

16. John Steinbeck, *The Grapes of Wrath*, Peter Lisca, ed. (New York: Viking, 1972), p. 147. Subsequent references to this work are taken from this text.

17. See the scenes in which Ma Joad explains the conditions under which wives will allow themselves to be beaten without fighting back: pp. 230, 479.

18. Robert Briffault, *The Mothers: The Matriarchal Theory of Social Origins* (New York: Macmillan, 1931). Cited from Warren Motley, "From Patriarchy to Matriarchy: Ma Joad's Role in *The Grapes of Wrath*, *American Literature*, Vol. 54, No. 3, October 1982, pp. 397–411.

19. Mimi Reisel Gladstein, *The Indestructible Woman in Faulkner, Hemingway, and Steinbeck* (Ann Arbor, MI: University of Michigan Research Press, 1986), p. 79.

20. Peter Lisca, *The Wide World of John Steinbeck* (New Brunswick, NJ: Rutgers University Press, 1958), pp. 206–7. Quoted from Sandra Beatty, "A Study of Female Characterization in Steinbeck's Fiction," in Tetsumaro Hayashi, *Steinbeck's Women: Essays in Criticism* (Muncie, IN: The Steinbeck Society of America, 1979), p. 1.

21. Even though this is the prevailing opinion among critics of Steinbeck's women, I repeat it here to emphasize my basic agreement with this reading of the female characters. Steinbeck, like many male authors, sees a close link between woman as mother, nature, and the American land.

22. Gladstein, p. 76.

23. Sandra Falkenberg, "A Study of Female Characterization in Steinbeck's Fiction," in *Steinbeck Quarterly*, Vol. 8(2), Spring 1975, pp. 50–6.

24. Howard Levant, "The Fully Matured Art: *The Grapes of Wrath*," in *Modern Critical Views* edited and with an introduction by Harold Bloom (New York: Chelsea House Publishers, 1987), p. 35.

25. Joan Hedrick, "Mother Earth and Earth Mother: The Recasting of Myth in Steinbeck's *Grapes of Wrath*," in The Grapes of Wrath: *A Collection of Critical Essays*, Robert Con Davis, ed. (Englewood Cliffs, NJ: G. K. Hall, 1982), p. 138.

26. Motley, p. 398.

27. Ibid., p. 405.

28. Chodorow, pp. 60–1.

29. See Kolodny, pp. 26–28 for an account of the high regard men like Thomas Jefferson had for the small farmer. In spite of the benefits of large-scale farming, he advocated the independent, family-size farm, and believed that those who tilled the earth gained "substantial and genuine virtue."

30. Ma Joad's challenge to her husband is that she be "whupped," not beaten. A woman may be beaten if her husband thinks she deserves it, and she accepts it without resistance. To be whipped indicates that she will fight back, and that he must win the fight in order to claim that he has whipped her.

STEPHEN RAILTON

Pilgrims' Politics:
Steinbeck's Art of Conversion

The Grapes of Wrath is a novel about things that grow—corn, peaches, cotton, and grapes of wrath. From the start Steinbeck identifies his vision of human history with organic, biological processes. A recurrent image is established in the first chapter, when the drought and wind in Oklahoma combine to uproot and topple the stalks of corn. In Chapter 29, the last of Steinbeck's wide-angle interchapters, it is the rain and flooding in California that "cut out the roots of cottonwoods and [bring] down the trees" (589). Tragically, even human lives are caught in this pattern of being pulled up from the soil. Farmers are made migrants. Forced to sell and burn all of their pasts that won't fit onto a homemade flatbed truck, they too are uprooted, torn from their identities. Right alongside this pattern, however, Steinbeck establishes a second one: that of seed being carried to new ground, new roots being put down. This image is announced in Chapter 3. The turtle who serves as the agent of movement in that chapter has attracted a lot of commentary from the novel's critics, but Steinbeck's main interest is not in the turtle. Chapter 3 is organized around seeds, all "possessed of the anlage of movement" (20). The turtle simply continues on its way, but by involuntarily carrying one "wild oat head" across the road, and accidentally dragging dirt over the "three spearhead seeds" that drop from it and stick in

---

From *New Essays on* The Grapes of Wrath, David Wyatt, ed. © 1990 by Cambridge University Press.

the ground (22), the mere movement of the turtle becomes part of the process of change and growth.

The Grapes of Wrath is a novel about an old system dying, and a new one beginning to take root. Movement, to Steinbeck, including the movement of history, works like the "West Wind" in Shelley's ode. It is "Destroyer and preserver" both; it scatters "the leaves dead" and carries forward "The winged seeds." The system that is dying we can call American capitalism, the roots of which had always been the promises of individual opportunity and of private property as the reward for taking risks and working hard. Steinbeck makes it more difficult to name the new system that is emerging from the violent ferment of the old system's decay. It is certainly socialistic, yet a goal of the novel is to suggest that a socialized democracy is as quintessentially American as the individualistic dream it will replace. "Paine, Marx, Jefferson, Lenin" he writes in Chapter 14 (206)—this list would confound a historian, but it is meant to reassure the American reader by linking socialism with our own revolutionary tradition. That was one reason for his enthusiasm about the title his wife found for the novel. He wanted the whole of Julia Ward Howe's fighting song printed as a sort of preface, because, he wrote his editor at Viking.

> The fascist crowd will try to sabotage this book because it is revolutionary. They try to give it the communist angle. However, The Battle Hymn is American and intensely so.... So if both words and music are there the book is keyed into the American scene from the beginning. (L [*Steinbeck: A Life in Letters*] 174)

At the same time, by tying his novel of history to the rhythms and laws of nature, the growth of seeds, the fermenting of grapes, Steinbeck tries to suggest that this coming American revolution is inevitable, organically decreed. The western states sense "the beginning change" with the nervousness of "horses before a thunder storm" (204); on the road west, separate families "*grew to be* units of the camps" (265; my italics).

These repeated biological locutions allow the novelist to assume the role of a Darwinian prophet, reading the political future instead of the natural past. Revolution is made to seem as inexorably sure as evolution. The novel is simply recording the process. Yet this quasi-scientific stance, while it helps account for the authority with which Steinbeck's prose tells his story, belies the real engagement of the book. Critics have accused Steinbeck of being wrong, because the drastic social change he apparently predicted never took place. But he knew better than that. If he had himself believed the stance his narrative adopts, he would have written a much less brilliant book, for the novel owes its power to Steinbeck's urgent but painstaking intention to enact the revolution he apparently foresees. Even his assumption of change is part of his strategy for creating it. And Steinbeck knew what he was up against. Despite his desire to make his vision seem "American and intensely so," he undertakes the task of radically redefining the most fundamental values of American society. The novel uproots as much as the forces of either nature or capitalism do, though far more subtly. And, ultimately, there is hardly anything natural about the kind of change—"as in the whole universe only man can change" (267)—that Steinbeck is anxious to work. *Supernatural* probably describes it more accurately. Nor is *change* the right word for it, although it's the one Steinbeck regularly uses. *The Grapes of Wrath* is a novel about conversion.

You and I, the novel's readers, are the converts whom he is after. Working a profound revolution in our sensibilities is his rhetorical task. His chief narrative task, however, is to recount the story of the Joads' conversions. Thematically, Route 66 and the various state highways in California that the Joads travel along all run parallel to the road to Damascus that Saul takes in Acts, or to the Way taken by Bunyan's Christian in *Pilgrim's Progress*. The problem with the way most readers want to see that turtle in Chapter 3 as an emblem of the Joads is precisely that it denies their movement any inward significance. Steinbeck finds much to admire in the Joads and the class of "the people" whom they represent, including the fierce will to survive and keep going which they share with that turtle, but he explicitly makes the capacity for spiritual regeneration the essence of humanity. That humans can redefine the meaning of our lives is what makes us "unlike any other thing organic or inorganic in the universe" (204). Conversion—to turn around, to turn together—is a metaphysical movement. This is the route on which Steinbeck sets the Joads. For, as much as he finds to admire in them, he also knows that before American society can be saved from its sins, "the people" will have to change, too.

Thus there is a tension between the novel's rhetorical and its narrative tasks. Steinbeck is writing about the migrant families, not for them; their lives have no margin, either of income or leisure, for reading novels. He is writing for the vast middle class that forms the audience for best-selling fiction, and one of his goals is to educate those readers out of their prejudices against people like the Joads. As soon as they reach California, the Joads are confronted by the epithet "Okie," and the attitude that lies behind it: "'Them goddamn Okies got no sense and no feeling. They ain't human.... They ain't a hell of a lot better than gorillas'" (301). As victims of such prejudice, and of the economic exploitation that it serves to rationalize, the migrants are treated with nothing but respect by the novel. Steinbeck takes pains not to prettify their earthiness, but the whole book is a testimony to their immeasurable human worth. By bringing his readers inside the life of an "Okie" family, and keeping them there for so many hundreds of pages, Steinbeck writes as an advocate to the migrants' claims on America's understanding, compassion, and concern. That he does this largely by letting the Joads' lives and characters speak for themselves is one of the novel's great achievements.

As his letters from the winter of 1938 reveal, Steinbeck's decision to write the novel was precipitated by his own firsthand encounter with the thousands of dispossessed families who were starving in the valleys of California. At first he could only see the migrants as victims: "I want to put a tag of shame on the greedy bastards who are responsible for this" (L 161), by which he meant "the fascist group of utilities and banks and huge growers" (L 158). There is no mistaking the element of moral indignation in the novel he started that spring; although they never appear directly in it, the novel treats the large landowners as unequivocally, allegorically evil. But he had gotten beyond his first reaction to the plight of the migrants by deepening his insight into the causes of their exploitation. Although it can be misread as one, *The Grapes of Wrath* is not a morality play in which the virtues of the people contend with the viciousness of the "huge growers." The source of the economic injustices that drought and Depression magnified so drastically is in the values that the Joads themselves initially share with their oppressors in California.

Perhaps the truest thing about the novel is its refusal to sentimentalize the life in the Midwest from which the Joads and the other families they meet have been dispossessed. When their dream of a golden future out West is destroyed by the brutal realities of migrant life in California, the past they left at the other end of Route 66 appeals to them as the paradise they have been driven from. When the novel winds up at the Hooper Ranch, the place seems as infernal as Simon Legree's plantation in *Uncle Tom's Cabin*. The armed guards, the filthy conditions, the edge of outright starvation on which Hooper Ranches, Inc., is content to keep the pickers—Steinbeck does want to expose this as one of the darkest places of the earth. At no point in the novel do the Joads feel further from "home," but Steinbeck also wants us to see how much Hooper's farm in California has in common with the Joad farm in Oklahoma that Tom had been trying to get back to at the beginning.

There is, for instance, a wire fence around both farms. The Joads didn't really need a fence, Tom tells Casy, but "'Pa kinda liked her there. Said it give him a feelin' that forty was forty'" (39). And Pa got the wire by taking advantage of his own brother. That is Steinbeck's point; that is what both fences delimit. We hear just enough about the Joads' earlier life in Oklahoma to recognize that they lived on their forty acres with essentially the same narrowly selfish values as Hooper on his much larger orchard. The Sooners took their land by force from the Indians, just as the large owners in California took theirs from the Mexicans. In both places, what prevailed was the "right" of the strongest—or say, the greediest. The Joads even stole the house they are evicted from. Grampa hangs onto the pillow he stole from Albert Rance with the same fierceness that the owners display in defense of their ill-gotten profits. Steinbeck's antagonist in the novel is not the group of large owners, but rather the idea of ownership itself. It is at the Hooper Ranch that Ma, on the verge of despair, grows most sentimental about the past:

> They was the time when we was on the lan'. They was a boundary to us then. Ol' folks died off, an' little fellas come, an' we was always one thing—we was the fambly—kinda whole and clear. (536)

Given what the Joads have been through since leaving home, it is impossible not to sympathize with her nostalgia. But finally, for Steinbeck, any kind of boundary—whether it's drawn around forty acres or forty thousand, around a family or a class—is wrong. And it is "the quality of owning" that builds boundaries, that "freezes you forever into 'I,' and cuts you off forever from the 'we'" (206).

Yet if owning separates, dispossession becomes the basis for a new unity. If one set of values is being uprooted, that prepares the ground for another to develop. On the one hand, the westward journey of the Joads is a moving record of losses: their home and past, Grampa and Granma's deaths, Noah and Connie's desertions. The sufferings inflicted on the family bear witness not only to their strength of character, but also to the evils of the social and economic status quo. Their hapless pursuit of happiness indicts and exposes the America they move across. Steinbeck forces his reader to suffer even more steadily. Ma has a sudden moment of insight on the road west when she "seemed to know" that the family's great expectations were "all a dream" (225), but, for the first half of the novel at least, the Joads are sustained by their dreams. The reader is denied any such imaginative freedom. While most narratives are organized around some kind of suspense about what will happen next, *The Grapes of Wrath* is structured as a series of inevitabilities. Each of the book's wide-angle chapters precedes the Joads, and in them we see the tenant farmers being tractored off before Tom comes home to an empty house, or the new proletariat being exploited before the Joads even begin to look for work, or the rain flooding the migrant camps before the Joads try to battle the rising water. Again and again what will happen next is made narratively inescapable. "I've done my damndest to rip a reader's nerves to rags," Steinbeck wrote about the novel (L 178). It is a good technique for a protest novel. The narrative enacts its own kind of oppression, and, by arousing in its readers a desire to fight this sense of inevitability, it works strategically to arouse us toward action to change the status quo.

On the other hand, however, the journey of the Joads is also an inward one. And there the same pattern of losses is what converts their movement into a pilgrimage toward the prospect of a new consciousness. As in Bunyan's book, homelessness and suffering become the occasion of spiritual growth. In several of the interchapters Steinbeck describes this process: "The families, which had been units of which the boundaries were a house at night, a farm by day, changed their boundaries" (267). They expand their boundaries. Having lost their land, the migrants' minds are no longer "bound with acres" (268); their new lives, their very losses, lead them toward the potentially redemptive discovery of their interrelatedness, their membership in a vastly extended family—the "we." In the novel's main narrative, Steinbeck dramatizes this process; near the very end, Ma sums up the new way she has learned to define her life: "'Use' ta be the fambly was fust. It ain't so now. It's anybody'" (606).

As an interpretive gloss on the meaning of her pilgrimage, however, Ma's pronouncement is much too pat. Simply quoting it denies Steinbeck the credit he deserves as both a novelist and a visionary. Again as in Bunyan's book, Steinbeck's faith is neither simple nor naive. Ruthie and Winfield, the youngest Joads, remind us how innately selfish human nature is. In his representation of their naked, nagging need for place and power, Steinbeck looks unflinchingly at the fact that "mine" is always among the first words an infant speaks. Similarly, Grampa and Granma are too old to learn to redefine themselves. The disruptions, the losses by which the others' assumptions are broken up, in the same way that a field has to be broken before new seed can be put into it, kill them both. Even with the other Joads, Steinbeck admits a lot of skepticism about whether they can be converted. Although Pa has become a victim of the capitalist system, it seems unlikely that he could ever abandon the economics of self-interest. As Tom tells Casy on the other side of the fence around the Hooper Ranch, it wouldn't do any good to tell Pa about the strike Casy is trying to organize: "'He'd say it wasn't none of his business.... Think Pa's gonna give up his meat on account a other fellas?'" (524).

Steinbeck here allows Tom, in his blunt vernacular voice, to ask the novel's most urgent question. The American Dream of individual opportunity has clearly betrayed "the people," but can they plant themselves on a different set of instincts? Can they redefine their boundaries? When he looks at the horrors of the migrants' plight, he knows that the answer is— They must. When he writes in the interchapters as an analyst of American society, the answer is—They will. But the narrative of the Joad family deals with specific people, not analytical abstractions. And their story, while it leads to the birth of the new "Manself" that Steinbeck sees as the only hope for a failed nation, tells a different story. Its emphasis is on how long and hard, and finally private, is the labor by which that New Man will be delivered into the world. Shortly after beginning the novel, Steinbeck wrote his agent that "The new book is going well." But then he added, "Too fast. I'm having to hold it down. I don't want it to go so fast for fear the tempo will be fast and this is a plodding, crawling book" (L 167). One reason for the book's length is Steinbeck's appreciation of the almost insurmountable obstacles that lie on the path between "I" and "we." And time alone cannot accomplish the birth of a new sensibility. It will also require a kind of violence. As Casy replies to Tom in their exchange about Pa, "'I guess that's right. Have to take a beatin' 'fore he'll know'" (524). Even that turtle in Chapter 3 gets hit by a truck before the seeds it carries fall into the ground.

The threat of violence hangs over the land Steinbeck is surveying from the outset, when the evicted sharecroppers wonder whom they can shoot to save their farms. In Howe's hymn, of course, "the grapes of wrath" are immediately followed by that "terrible swift sword," and in those places where Steinbeck's prose rises to its most oratorical pitch, it seems to predict a second American civil war with all the righteousness of an Old Testament prophet: "three hundred thousand—if they ever move under a leader—the end. Three hundred thousand, hungry and miserable; if they ever know themselves, the land will be theirs and all the gas, all the rifles in the world won't stop them" (325). Yet such passages never ring quite true. They seem to be another of the rhetorical strategies by which Steinbeck is trying to work on the sensibilities of his readers: To their sympathy for the dispossessed he adds this appeal to their fear of what driven people might resort to. Organized, militant action is not at the center of Steinbeck's program for apocalyptic change. His concern is with consciousness. That is where the most meaningful revolution must occur. Even physical violence matters chiefly as a means to spiritual change.

It is because Steinbeck's emphasis is on inward experience that Jim Casy, a supernumerary as far as most of the book's action is concerned, is central to its plot. Casy's presence is what allows Steinbeck to dramatize his concern with consciousness. At the beginning, Steinbeck gives him a head start on the Joads. They are looking to start over in California; although they have lost their home and land, they still hang on to their belief in the American Dream. Casy, however, is looking to start anew. He has already lost the faith in the Christian values that had given meaning to his life, and is self-consciously questing for a new belief, a new cause to serve. He remains a preacher—long after he has rejected the title, the narrative continues to refer to him as "Reverend Jim Casy" and "the preacher"—but cannot find the Word he should announce. In much the same passivity as the novel's reader, he watches and absorbs the meaning of the Joad's attempt to carry their lives and ambitions westward. His first, indeed his only decisive action in the narrative itself is precipitated by an act of violence. In the Bakersfield Hooverville, a migrant named Floyd hits a deputy sheriff to avoid being arrested for the "crime" of telling the truth; when the deputy pulls his gun, Tom trips him; when he starts shooting recklessly into the camp, Casy knocks him out—it is worth noting the details because this same sequence will recur at the Hooper Ranch. In describing this action, Steinbeck's prose departs from its usual syntactic straightforwardness to signal its significance: "and then, suddenly, from the group of men, the Reverend Casy stepped" (361). His kicking the deputy in the neck is presented as an instinctual reflex, and his actions, here, and subsequently when he gives himself up to the deputy to save Floyd and Tom, speak a lot louder than any words he uses, but Reverend Casy has at last found a cause to serve.

That cause can be defined as the "group of men" he steps from, but it is also here that Casy disappears from the narrative for 150 pages. In this case Steinbeck refuses to allow his story to get ahead of itself. The exemplary significance of Casy's self-sacrifice is barely registered by the Joads, who still feel they have their own lives to live. And Casy himself cannot conceptualize the meaning of his involuntary action, or the values of the new faith he commits his life to, until later. When he reappears at the Hoover Ranch, he tries to explain it to Tom:

> "Here's me, been a-goin' into the wilderness like Jesus to try to
> find out somepin. Almost got her sometimes, too. But it's in the
> jail house I really got her." (521)

What he got in jail could be called an insight into the moral logic of socialism: that the greatest evil is human need, and that the only salvation lies in collective effort. Although the novel is deliberately vague about how Casy came to be at the Hooper Ranch, and what his role is in the strike there, we could see his new identity in strictly political terms: Like the strike organizers Steinbeck had written about in *In Dubious Battle*, Casy has committed himself to the cause of Communist revolution. As a fundamentalist preacher in Oklahoma, he had aroused and exhorted crowds to feel the operation of grace, and save their individual souls; as a left-wing strike organizer in California, he is teaching the migrants to organize and act in the interests of their class. But, at this crucial point, the novel complicates its message by keeping its focus on spiritual rather than political concerns. The individual soul retains its privileged position. For Casy's actions at the Hooper Ranch speak much less resonantly than his words, and the revolutionary change they bring about occurs inwardly.

Steinbeck brings Casy back into the narrative at this point to complete Tom Joad's conversion. Tom is the novel's central pilgrim. The book begins with his attempt to return "home." This works a nice inversion on *Pilgrim's Progress*, for Bunyan's Christian must choose to leave home before he can begin the path that leads to salvation. Tom has no choice; economic and natural forces have already exiled him from "home" before he can get there. In both works, however, the quest ultimately is for "home." For Bunyan, of course, the spirit's true home is in eternity, while all the action of Steinbeck's novel is set in this world. It is through this world that Tom moves to find a new home; it is still in this world that he finds it. But it is nonetheless a spiritual dwelling place that he finds. Tom chooses to leave his family at the end of his pilgrimage; almost the last thing he says before disappearing from the story is that Ma need not worry about where to find him:

> "Well, maybe like Casy says, a fella ain't got a soul of his own, but on'y a piece of a big one—an' then—"
> "Then what, Tom?"
> "Then it don't matter. Then I'll be all aroun' in the dark. I'll be ever'where—wherever you look." (572)

Wherever the people are—that is Tom's new home. All the boundaries around his self have dissolved. In this communion with the world soul, Tom finds a freedom that merely being paroled from prison could never provide, and a meaning that living for himself or for his family could never have bestowed upon his acts. By losing himself—to use the phrase that would have been equally familiar to Bunyan's readers and Casy's revivalist congregations—he has found himself.

As Tom's last conversation with Ma repeatedly acknowledges, Casy was the agent of his conversion. It is Casy's words ("like Casy says") and Casy's mystical presence ("Seems like I can see him sometimes" [572]) that show Tom the way that leads to his being's true home. But this conversion is only accomplished painfully, through another act of violence that indicates how much of Tom's old self must be destroyed before the exemplary New Man that he embodies can be born. Twice in Tom's last conversation with "the preacher," Casy asks him if he can't "see" the revelation that Casy has seen in the jail house, and that he is trying to realize at the Hooper Ranch. "No," Tom replies both times (521, 522), not because he is stupid, but because he has always lived within the boundaries of self-interest. As Casy had predicted about Pa, Tom, too, has to take a beating before he can know. Within a few minutes of this discussion, Tom is literally clubbed in the face. The more important "beating," however, occurs in the realm of Tom's spirit. In a scene that mirrors the moment of Casy's conversion at the Hooverville, Tom witnesses Casy's death at the hands of the "deputies" who have come to break the strike. It is out of the violent trauma of this act of witnessing that Tom's new self begins to emerge.

Steinbeck, using a club of his own, makes it impossible for the reader (who is also witnessing this violence) to overlook the scriptural power of Casy's life and death. His likenesses to Christ are established at the start, when a man with the initials "J. C." departs for California with twelve Joads. Not only does Casy die as a martyr: twice he tells the men who are about to kill him that they know not what they do (cf. 527). As if these cues were not enough, immediately after he dies one of the vigilantes says, "'Jesus, George. I think you killed him'" (527). And, as if even this were not enough, Ma has Tom repeat Casy's last words, then repeats them herself:

> "That's what he said—'You don' know what you're doin"?"
> "Yeah!"
> Ma said, "I wisht Granma could a heard." (535)

The most devoutly Christian of the Joads, Granma presumably would have taken the most pleasure from the preacher's appropriation of the Word. But, for all this, Steinbeck insists that we understand Casy's death and its implications in ways that Granma never could, unless she were willing to throw off her old self as well. For if it is easy to note how Christlike Casy is, especially in death, it is crucial to note how un-Christian, anti-Christian are the values to which his death converts Tom.

As others have noted, *The Grapes of Wrath* contains many echoes of and allusions to the Bible. Yet the novel never wavers on the point that Casy's rejection of Christianity makes at the very start. Throughout the book Steinbeck returns to Christianity only to attack it. He exposes and condemns the several "Jesus-lovers" whom the Joads meet, the Salvation Army as a Christian relief agency, the preachers who teach Christlike submission to Caesar. One of the ways that Ma is made to change in the course of her pilgrimage is by replacing her acquired faith in God and the next world with the belief in the people and in this life that she gradually learns from Casy. Who shall inherit the earth is among the book's most urgent questions, but Steinbeck has no patience with the idea that it shall be the meek. In his last talk with Ma, Tom's vernacular sums up the novel's displacement of Christianity, citing scripture to the end that Steinbeck has consistently had in mind:

> "most of the preachin' is about the poor we shall have always with us, an' if you got nothing', why, jus' fol' your hands an' to hell with it, you gonna git ice cream on gol' plates when you're dead. An' then this here Preacher says two get a better reward for their work." (571)

This "Preacher" is Solomon, whose words in Ecclesiastes Steinbeck converts into a socialist manifesto. Much like Melville in "The Try-Works" chapter of *Moby-Dick*, Steinbeck is using "unchristian Solomon's wisdom" to carry his readers beyond the New Testament to a new revelation. Christianity itself is another evil that must be uprooted. And Casy's death not only completes his apotheosis by being paired with Christ's; it also violently repudiates the legacy of the Crucifixion. The strike breakers may not know what they're doing, but Casy doesn't ask anyone to forgive them for that reason. His death may be a martyrdom, but Tom's immediate, instinctive reaction to it is neither to love his enemies nor to turn the other cheek, but to murder the man who killed Casy.

It is surprising how little notice Tom's act of violence has gotten from the novel's commentators. In a sense, Tom's crime here is a more enlightened act than the murder he had gone to prison for before the novel begins. There he had killed to defend himself. Here he kills to avenge and defend an idea—the idea that Casy and the strike at Hooper's represent. His readiness to fight and kill for this larger concept is a measure of the spiritual distance he has traveled in the course of his pilgrimage. Like Casy's stepping forth at Bakersfield to knock out the deputy, Tom's involuntary action indicates his preparedness to take the final leap into the kingdom of spirit he attains at the end. But still, Tom's act is a brutal murder. He hits "George" four times in the head with a pick handle. Steinbeck hardly expected it to pass unnoticed. "Think I'll print a forward," he wrote about the novel, "warning sensitive people to let it alone" (L 168). He may even have been comparing himself as a writer to Tom's savage reaction when he added: "It pulls no punches at all and may get us all into trouble."

Once we have noticed all this, however, it is by no means easy to know what to make of it. While he was writing *The Grapes of Wrath*, Steinbeck apparently needed to disguise even from himself how skillfully the novel works to convert rather than confront the sensibilities of his audience. "I am sure it will not be a popular book" he wrote (L 172), not long before it zoomed to the top of the best-seller lists. He was writing a "revolutionary" novel fueled by his own wrath at the moral and economic horrors of contemporary America; such a work had to be "an outrageous book" (L 172). Yet his deeper need was to reach "the large numbers of readers" (L 172) he expected to outrage. His very ambitions as a prophet of social change depended on being read by the widest possible audience. His handling of Tom's murderous action epitomizes his own divided intentions. Tom's action aggressively defies the laws of both society and the New Testament. At the same time, Steinbeck makes it incredibly easy for his reader to accept Tom's act. Immediately afterward, he retreats to the shack on the ranch, and as soon as possible he confesses his crime to the whole family. When he and his mother are left alone, he goes over the event again, and Ma—who for 500 pages has stood for love and compassion—Ma unhesitatingly absolves him of any wrongdoing: "'I can't read no fault on you'" (535). By returning the "murderer" to the bosom of his family, and having him shriven by his own mother, Steinbeck domesticates his deed. In one respect, he disarms it of its radical power. In another, though, he uses it to further his task of radicalizing his audience's sensibilities: The reader who remains sympathetic to Tom has already been made, subliminally, an outlaw from the values of American society and the New Testament. Our willingness to harbor Tom, to continue to identify him as the book's moral hero, is a measure of *our* preparedness for conversion to a new vision of the truth.

We could explain Steinbeck's use of biblical typology along the same lines, as a purely rhetorical strategy. "Large numbers of readers" could not be expected to endorse militant socialism. Instead, Steinbeck shrewdly insinuates his revolutionary vision by presenting it in the familiar guise of Christianity. Just as Casy's quest carries him from the fundamentalist's Bible to a Marxist reading of Ecclesiastes, so Steinbeck's choice of Casy as the narrative agent of revelation allows the novel to find a middle ground between the conventional American's old allegiances and Steinbeck's newer testament. There would be nothing inherently wrong with such a device. Every novel of purpose must make some compromises with its audience if it wants to reach and move them. Yet explaining Steinbeck's affinity for the Bible this way would never get to the heart of his novel. His use of Christianity is more than strategic. For the private, inward operation of grace is as fundamental to his vision as it is to St. Paul's or Bunyan's.

To the doctrinaire socialist, meaning is found in collective action. Steinbeck offers his version of that ideal in his descriptions of the government camp at Weedpatch where the Joads stay for a month after being driven out of the Hooverville. The camp has a wire fence around it, too, but it only matters when the forces of capitalism try to destroy the communal harmony of the camp. The novel presents life in the camp as a Utopian but practicable antithesis to the selfishness that rules on both the Joad farm and the Hooper Ranch. In the camp happiness is pursued by owning things jointly, sharing responsibilities, making decisions by democratically elected committees. The camp's weekly square dances provide the book's most attractive image of a communal society: The music belongs to no one individual; the dancers obey the calls in unison and joy. It is not an accident that the Growers' Association and its hired reactionaries try to discredit the camp by disrupting a dance. That episode allows Steinbeck starkly to polarize the two worlds, within the camp and without: There's harmony and expression inside, violence and exploitation outside. He may in fact have meant for this portrayal of men and women acting collectively to occupy the center of the book's moral ground. But, if so, he complicates his own values by reintroducing Casy into the narrative, and shifting the drama back inside Tom's consciousness. He also betrays his misgivings about collective action as redemptive in the book's only other extended account of it. This occurs in the final chapter, when Pa convinces another group of migrants to work together to build a dam to save their campsites from the rising floodwater. Not only do their efforts fail; although they work frantically through the night with as much unison as those square dancers, their shared labor brings them no closer to true unity, no nearer to the "we," than they had been before. To recognize and act collectively in the interests of the group, it seems, is not enough. Indeed, since the men remain divided and bitter after the failure of their dam, it seems that collective action in itself is meaningless.

Instead, what the novel presents as most meaningful are Casy's and Tom's conversions: the purpose and inner peace that each man finds, not in acting with others, but in "feeling" or "seeing" his oneness with all. Casy, presumably, is acting at Hooper's to organize the strike—but it is telling that the novel has no interest in elaborating such a role. Tom at the end does tell Ma what he aims to *do*: "'What Casy done,' he said" (571)—but again, what that means is left extremely vague, although Tom goes on to talk in eloquent detail about what he will *be* as the disembodied spirit of the people. The novel's two most important events, if we can call them events, actually occur in private—to Casy in jail, and to Tom while he's hiding out after killing the vigilante. Still more striking is the fact that both these "events" occur entirely outside the narrative. It is offstage, in solitude, alone with his own consciousness that each man somehow arrives at the new faith that Steinbeck is preaching to us, becomes the New Man who can redeem the waste land.

Thus Steinbeck offers an essentially religious and mystical solution to the economic and political problems that inspired him to write the novel in the first place. For when we compare the rapturous accents of Tom's last speech with Ma to Pa's futile efforts to organize the migrants to battle circumstances together, we're left with the conclusion that people merely working together cannot succeed—while one person who has experienced unity with the "big soul," whatever he or she does, cannot fail. Despite the narrative's persistent attention to external forces—natural, historical, economic, social—it ultimately points to what its own representation excludes, to an inward "act" of consciousness or spirit, as the only place the revolution can begin. And once Tom has been brought "home" to this sense of selflessness, it seems that the revolution is effectively over as well.

Of course, Tom's climactic scene with Ma, although it does bring the novel's central pilgrimage into Steinbeck's version of the Celestial City, is not the end of the story. Tom's apotheosis is followed by two additional moments of conversion, both of which are brought on by another kind of violence: the death in birth of the baby that Rose of Sharon has been carrying through the novel. Death in birth, in keeping with the pattern of uprooting and planting, destruction and new growth, leads to birth out of death. The first conversion is Uncle John's, and it occurs when he goes out into the rain to bury the stillborn infant. Up until this moment, John has been crippled by the guilt he has felt since his wife's death many years ago. But now, having been pushed around by the American economic system and knocked down by the floodwaters, John reaches a higher state of consciousness. With the wrath of an inspired Biblical prophet, he sends the dead baby down the flood as a judgment and curse on the society that produced it. In the swirling waters he has been cleansed of more than his guilt; he's been freed entirely from his fundamentalist Christian's sense of sinfulness; he's been politically radicalized. It is not he who is damned, but the nation.

Like Tom's unforgiving reaction to Casy's death, John's conversion from guilt to wrath is Steinbeck's way of insisting that his faith is a newer testament. To be saved, the nation needs to be converted, yet it will have to leave Christianity as well as capitalism behind. The novel's very last scene tries to build a bridge between the realm of spirit, where individuals find their home, and the world of action, where men and women can help each other; it redresses the imbalance of Tom's story, where the emphasis had been almost entirely on faith, by adding to that a doctrine of works. Thematically the novel's last scene is perfect. It is the moment of Rose of Sharon's conversion. Out of the violent loss of her baby (which she has "witnessed" with her whole body) comes a new, self-less sense of self. When she breastfeeds the starving stranger who would otherwise die, a new, boundary-less definition of family is born. Rose of Sharon's act is devoutly socialistic: from each according to ability, to each according to need. At the same time, the novel's last word on this scene, which is also the novel's last word, is "mysteriously"—a word that has no place in Marx's or Lenin's vocabulary. The scene's implications are as much religious as political. Iconographically, like Casy's death, this tableau of a man lying in a woman's lap both recalls and subverts the familiar imagery of Christianity. By calling our ultimate act of attention in the novel to the look of "mysterious" satisfaction on Rose of Sharon's face, Steinbeck keeps this scene in line with his focus on the private, inward, ineffable moment of conversion. Yet here we also see how that inner change can lead to redemptive action. The barn in which this scene takes place is not only "away in a manger"; it is also halfway between the social but bureaucratic world of the government camp and the spiritual but solitary state that Tom found while hiding out in the bushes. And what happens in this barn triumphantly completes the novel's most pervasive pattern: One family has been uprooted and destroyed; out of those ruins, another, a new one, takes root. Manself can change, and by change can triumph over the most devastating circumstances.

For all its thematic aptness, however, this ending has been widely condemned. I can certainly understand why adolescent readers, especially young women, are uncomfortable with the picture of a teenage girl suckling a middle-aged, anonymous man. We can see Steinbeck's divided attitude toward his readers at work in this scene too: He gives them an ending that is essentially happy, but also disturbing. I frankly find it harder to see why adult critics have singled out this particular scene to object to. Rose of Sharon's conversion does not occur more suddenly than Tom's or John's—or, for that matter, than Saul's on the road to Damascus. The scene is unquestionably sentimental, but Steinbeck's most dramatic effects are invariably melodramatic—Ma sitting with Granma's corpse across the desert, Casy's death, Tom's valedictory eloquence, the anathema John pronounces with a dead baby in his arms. The novel could hardly have the impact it does on most readers without these unlikely, outsized gestures. For that matter, almost all novels of protest try to pluck the reader's heartstrings, and homelessness and hunger in a land of plenty is an inarguably legitimate cause in which to appeal to people's emotions. Steinbeck's editors at Viking were the first readers to object to the ending. Refusing to change a word of it, he defended it on the grounds of "balance" (L 178). I find it a strange but powerful tribute to Steinbeck's faith in selflessness as the one means by which men and women can transcend their circumstances in a world that is otherwise so harshly and unjustly determined. I think it would be less powerful if it were any less strange.

In any case, whether the novel's last scene is esthetically successful is probably not the most important question to ask. Having seen the starving migrants in the valleys of California, and determined to write a novel in response to that human fact, Steinbeck was shocked out of his modern assumption that art mattered more than life. At the end of a letter from the winter of 1938, recording in horrified detail his own reaction as a witness to the sufferings of the migrant families, he wrote: "Funny how mean and little books become in the face of such tragedies" (L 159). He wrote the novel in the belief to which the trauma of seeing the homeless, wretched families had converted him: that American society had to change, quickly and profoundly. This then leads to the largest question raised by the novel's several endings. Is conversion the same as revolution? Can the re-creation of society be achieved by an individual's private, inner, spiritual redefinition of the self?

That Steinbeck believed it could is the most "intensely American" aspect of the novel. "Paine, Marx, Jefferson, Lenin"—those names are relevant to his vision, but the tradition to which *The Grapes of Wrath* belongs is best identified with a different list: Winthrop, Edwards, Emerson, Whitman. Steinbeck's emphasis on inner change as the basis of social salvation has its roots in the Puritan belief that the New Jerusalem is identical with the congregation of converted saints, and in the Transcendentalists' credo that, as Emerson put it, "The problem of restoring to the world original and eternal beauty is solved by the redemption of the soul." Harriet Beecher Stowe, as the author of *Uncle Tom's Cabin*, has to occupy an especially prominent place on that list. Her great protest novel is also organized around movement as both a means to expose social evil and as the pilgrimage of the spirit toward home. And when Stowe, in her last chapter, sought to answer the many aroused readers who had written to ask her what they could *do* to solve the terrible problem of slavery, her response was, "they can see to it that *they feel right*." It is in this ground that the seeds of Steinbeck's revolution must also grow. Tom and Rose of Sharon at last feel right when they have redefined themselves as one with the people around them. Steinbeck oppresses and exhorts, threatens and inspires, shocks and moves us to bring us each, individually, to the same point of communion.

Ultimately, of course, people's feelings are all that any novelist has to work with. Even if Steinbeck had gone on to specify exactly what Tom will do to realize the vision of human unity that he has attained, Tom could never act in the real world. He can only act on the reader, as Casy's example acted on him. Hiding out in the bushes or reading *The Grapes of Wrath* both occur in private. Any change that the novel might make in American society will have to happen first in the consciousness of its readers. But this doesn't answer the question raised by Steinbeck's politics of consciousness. The origins of the evils that the novel decries are, as many of the interchapters insist, social and economic. They result from patterns of ownership, margins of profit, lack of security, and the other characteristics of a capitalistic system with a dispossessed proletariat to exploit. Can anything but a social revolution change that system? *Pilgrim's Progress*, like the sermons Casy preached before losing his original faith, is about getting to heaven; that kind of salvation depends upon inner change. But Steinbeck wants to save the nation from its sins. Babies like Rose of Sharon's are dying because of social inequalities and economic injustices. Can the private, spiritual birth of a New Man or a New Woman—the unrecorded "event" that the novel leaves at the center of its narrative and its vision—affect that?

DAVID N. CASSUTO

Turning Wine into Water:
Water as Privileged Signifier in
The Grapes of Wrath

For the past century in the American Southwest, water's scarcity and its obvious utility have made it both a vital commodity and a powerful cultural symbol. In The Grapes of Wrath, Steinbeck is keenly aware that to control water is to control the land. Powerful banking and farming interests in both Oklahoma and California dominated the land because they determined water use. Water and its absence therefore assume symbolic weight throughout the novel, informing its very structure and meaning. Steinbeck dismantles both the frontier myth of open land and the edenic promise of abundant yield through hard work.

Eastward I go only by force; but westward I go free.

—Henry David Thoreau

The Old Testament describes wilderness as "a thirsty ground where there was no water." When the Lord wished to punish, He threatened to "turn the rivers into islands and dry up the pools and ... command the clouds that they rain no rain upon it." When granting redemption in Isaiah, God promises instead that "waters shall break forth in the wilderness and streams in the desert" and that "the desert and dry land shall be glad" (Deut. 8:7, 15; Isaiah 5:6, 35:1, 6, 43:20). The Garden of Eden provided the antithesis of desert wilderness, a place where water flowed freely and bounty of all sorts lay ready to spring out of the ground. This is the legacy that spawned what Henry

---

From *Steinbeck and the Environment: Interdisciplinary Approaches*, Susan F. Beegel, Susan Shillinglaw, Wesley N. Tiffney, Jr., ed. © 1997 by The University of Alabama Press. Originally published in *Papers on Language and Literature* 29, 1 (Winter 1993). © 1993 by the Board of Trustees, Southern Illinois University.

Nash Smith termed the "myth of the garden" in the American West. At the dawn of the common era, John offered Jesus his baptism in the river Jordan. Two millennia later, Casy baptized Tom Joad in an irrigation ditch.

I will argue that *The Grapes of Wrath* represents an indictment of the American myth of the garden and its accompanying myth of the frontier. The lever with which Steinbeck pries apart and ultimately dismantles these fictions is a critique of the agricultural practices that created the Dust Bowl and then metamorphosed into a new set of norms that continued to victimize both the land and its inhabitants. Both nineteenth-century homesteading (based on the Homestead Act of 1862) and agribusiness, its twentieth-century descendant (born from the failure of the Homestead Act), relied on the (mis)use of water to accomplish their respective goals. And both policies resulted in ecological disaster.

The Plains were called upon to supply grain for the international war effort in 1914 and to feed a hungry nation whose population continued to multiply exponentially. Throughout the nation, industrialization held sway as the isolationism of the nineteenth century gave way to the globalism of the twentieth. These transitions required great expenditures of resources, and, in the grain belt, the resource most in demand was water. As farmers poured their short-term profits back into land and seed, their fates depended ever more on the availability of water. When the climatic pendulum swung back toward aridity, Plains farmers had to declare hydrological bankruptcy, though neither they nor the federal government would abandon the myth of the garden. As the government scrambled to dam rivers and force water into the desert, farmers clung fast to their vision of uncountable abundance amid a green world.

Water was a commodity, symbol of wealth and expanding capabilities. Admitting its unattainability involved acknowledging the limited productive capabilities of the land. Such an admission also meant conceding the limitations of the nation and its people, a prospect that remained anathema to a culture steeped in the dominant myths. Myra Jehlen notes that "the conviction that farming brought reason and nature together (since man and nature had the same reasons) inspired cultivation ... but made it particularly difficult, in fact, contradictory to contemplate basic changes in agrarian policy" (73). Instead of abandoning the American dream, the dream itself underwent an ideological shift. The myth of the garden remained intact, but its form evolved from an Edenic Xanadu to a neo-Baconian Atlantis that no longer awaited manna from heaven but wrested it instead from the grips of Nature.

Water's primacy as both commodity and signifier in the Southwest arose through a combination of its scarcity and utility. Its privileged place in the biotic schema predates its commodification by the state and corporate apparatus, but the two forces are by now inseparable in the history and mythology of the American West. The social and environmental conditions in the Southwest made water an ideal unit of exchange, and this led to its concurrent fetishization. As Gregory Jay characterizes commodity fetishism, "Capitalism structures symbolic exchange so as to elicit desire, manipulate its character, and teach it to find sublimity in prescribed objects" (167). Since water is necessary to human biology, in an arid region a dominant state apparatus would need to expend relatively little effort to transform water into a commodity whose scarcity would privilege it as well as its controllers. Once established as a commodity, any item of exchange value acquires symbolic value, connoting power and wealth and thereby enhancing the prestige of its possessor. In this sense, water becomes not just a measure of economic value but a culturally powerful symbol as well.

The class stratification depicted in *The Grapes of Wrath* arose from corporate control over the region's most precious resource. The region's aridity, however, made water an *absent* signifier. Both in the novel and in the desert itself, water's conspicuous absence is what makes it so powerful. The flooding that climaxes the novel is thematically situated to provide maximum counterpoint to the drought that originally forced the Joads to migrate west. Disenfranchised and dehumanized, the Joads can only curse the rising floodwaters even as they once prayed for a deluge to feed their parched crops.

The cycle of alienation appears complete; people whose humanity was once integrally tied to the land and the weather now care nothing for the growing season or the health of the earth. Their survival has come to depend on shelter from the elements rather than the elements themselves. They have become components of the factory-farming process, economically distant from their bourgeois oppressors but closely tied to the industrial ethos that rewards the subjugation of nature. The primary difference between the growers and the migrants now lies in their respective relationships with the privileged signifier. The growers—owners of the irrigation channels, centrifugal pumps, and watertight mansions—control it, while the Okies, starving and drenched, are at its mercy.

In *The Grapes of Wrath*, Steinbeck presents an archetypal Plains family caught in the modernization of the American dream. Forced to adapt to the realities of a closed frontier and a desert in the country's midsection, Americans retrofit their dominant myths to encompass corporate capitalism and, in so doing, accept water's scarcity and preeminence as commodity in the western region. This shift in ideology completed the antiquation of the Joads' way of life. Ecological realities had long ago proven their lifestyle quixotic, but it took the formidable alliance of the Dust Bowl and corporate agribusiness to dislodge the Okies from their land and homes. Later in his life, Steinbeck returned to criticize the America-as-Eden myth by writing *East of Eden*, a novel whose very title suggests alienation from paradise. It is in *The Grapes of Wrath*, however, that he is most concerned with the hydrological causes for that estrangement.

Steinbeck acknowledges water's primacy in the West by documenting the social ramifications of the ideology that permits its monopolization and waste. At the same time, his abiding affection for the yeoman agricultural ideal forms a strong undercurrent throughout the novel. Donald Worster believes that this nostalgia comes at the expense of a coherent critique of the water-based oligarchy primarily responsible for the ecological demise of the Southwest and its accompanying human suffering (Worster, *Rivers of Empire* 1985, 229). While Worster's criticism has substantial merit, it fails to address the symbolic power attached to water that pervades the novel. From the drought in Oklahoma to Noah's refusal to leave the river in Arizona to the raging floodwaters that climax the text, Steinbeck weaves water into the novel's structure as well as virtually every thematically significant event in the novel.

This tendency to privilege water, either by absence or surfeit, appears frequently in the Steinbeck canon. *Of Mice and Men*, for example, opens and closes on the banks of a river; *The Log from the Sea of Cortez*, showing a fascination with tide pools, offers the clearest presentation of Steinbeck's ecophilosophy; and *The Wayward Bus*, like *The Grapes of Wrath*, uses floodwaters in the desert to spur its characters to action and the acquisition of wisdom. That in *The Grapes of Wrath* Steinbeck chose to stress his affection for the yeoman tradition rather than explicitly condemn modern hydraulic society does not detract from the book's acknowledged success in subverting that same hydraulic apparatus. The reactions of the state and federal governments to the book's publication as well as that of the oligarchy-controlled media clearly demonstrate the novel's effectiveness. Vehement condemnations of the book and its author followed shortly after its publication in 1939 and continued for years afterward. That the most vociferous denunciations came from the water barons and their political allies demonstrates that, contrary to Worster's contention, Steinbeck did indeed understand the politics of water use and that his novel attacked it successfully.[1]

I

Water's dominance in the cultural and agricultural hierarchy of the arid region is neither new nor surprising. Not just in the Hebrew Bible but throughout history, the habitability of any region has traditionally been determined by the availability and accessibility of its water. The Spanish explorers who first traversed the Southwest deemed it an inhospitable wasteland, unfit for human settlement except by those savages already content to scrape an existence from the unforgiving rock. American trailblazers including Lewis and Clark and Zebulon Pike held little hope that the arid region could sustain American settlements (Reisner 1986, 20). Such criticism, however, quickly disappeared in the storm of patriotism that surged through the new United States. Parallel visions of world dominance and transcendental bonding with nature created a unique blend of ideologies that sought simultaneously to sustain an extractive economy and an unspoiled, untrammeled frontier. Not till near the turn of the twentieth century did the inexorable collision of these visions loom close enough to draw the notice of the nation's policymakers. The resulting tension between ecosystemic requirements and the modes of production caused a "transformation in consciousness and legitimating worldviews," a phenomenon Carolyn Merchant has termed an "ecological revolution" (5).

American history shows that people traditionally settled the Plains during periods of high rainfall. When the rains subsided to typical levels, people retreated or pressed on. But by the 1920s, the frontier was closed and Americans had bought solidly into the notion that technology and God would see to it that the Great Plains became the agricultural capital of the world. Unable to accept that meeting the grain demands of a global market economy in a region where annual rainfall fluctuated between seven and twenty inches made little ecological sense, Dust Bowl residents lashed out at the weather, believing it caused their woes. There was not enough water, they complained; the weather had failed them. Such an argument is analogous to blaming the mint for not making people enough money. I do not mean to belittle the very real human tragedy of the Dust Bowl or to deny the nobility of many of those who suffered through it. Nevertheless, the Dust Bowl's ecosystemic catastrophe was both avoidable and remediable except that neither option was palatable to the region's residents (Worster 1979, 28). It is precisely this sort of stubborn adherence to traditional values while implementing ecologically pernicious agricultural methods that brought on the "dirty thirties."

Early in the novel, Steinbeck establishes the fundamental conflict between the yeoman farmer and the land and then diagrams the imperialist maneuverings of corporate agribusiness:

> Grampa took up the land, and he had to kill the Indians and
> drive them away. And Pa was born here, and he killed weeds and

snakes. Then a bad year came and he had to borrow a little
money. An' we was born here ... our children born here. And Pa
had to borrow money. The bank owned the land then.... Sure
cried the tenant men, but it's our land. We measured it and broke
it up. We were even born on it, and we got killed on it, died on
it. Even if it's no good, it's still ours.... That makes ownership,
not a paper with numbers on it. (*TGOW* [*The Grapes of Wrath*]
34–35)

The above passage reveals several of the guiding principles governing life in
the Plains. First, the term "bad year" refers to inadequate rainfall and an
accompanying water shortage, a cyclical reality of Plains life that formed one
of the bases for the collapse of the yeoman lifestyle. Second, right of
ownership was established through displacing the native peoples. That act in
and of itself constituted (in the farmer's eyes) a right of title. Last, birthing
and dying on the land created a blood right of succession that no financial
transaction could negate. And most important, working the land formed the
litmus test of possession. The quotation reveals the teller's sadness that the
laws of the country conflict with the laws of the land. The agrarian ideology
held that only those who work and love the land can truly own it: "If a man
owns a little property, that property is him, it's part of him and it's like him.
If he owns property only so he can walk on it and handle it and be sad when
it isn't doing well, and feel fine when the rain falls on it, that property is
him.... Even if he isn't successful he's big with his property" (39). Such
feelings descend directly from the dual myths of the frontier and the garden.
The frontier myth posited that land in the West was uninhabited by anybody
with legal rights and that the strength of the nation lay in its boundless and
unsettled western frontier.[2] The myth of the garden held that the land would
yield bountiful harvests to any American willing to work it. Rain would fall
in direct proportion to the farmer's needs. Any failure in these natural laws
was necessarily transitory and had no lasting relevance. This supposed law of
nature was disproven by the Okies' experiences in both Oklahoma and
California. After a prolonged drought revealed the unsustainability of their
farming methods and drove them from their homes, the wet/dry cycle in
California nearly caused their demise.

Not only did meteorological laws conflict with the yeoman belief
system, the Okies also found their way of life colliding with the policies of a
nation committed to corporate capitalism. While for agrarians land
constituted a part of themselves and their culture—something for which the
term "market value" lacked a referent—banks and corporations translated it
into assets on a balance sheet. Where the Joads spoke of "bad years," account

managers acknowledged the reality of sparse rainfall and a semiarid climate. Historical climatic patterns decreed that "bad years" for rainfall were the norm for the Plains, a fact that made tenant farmers a poor investment. For banks, it became a matter of short-term profit at any cost. Years of drought and over-reliance on nutrient-draining cash crops had left the land ecologically devastated. Those keeping accounts looked to squeeze out every vestige of production before abandoning it for more lucrative investments: "But you'll kill the land with cotton. We know. We've got to take cotton quick before the land dies. Then we'll sell the land. Lots of families in the East would like to own a piece of land" (34). The sight of faceless corporate "monsters" intentionally destroying the land's fertility moved the tenants to violence. Yet the Joads and their neighbors had often planted cotton and were at present sharecropping in a frenzy so as to build up a stake to take west: "The whole bunch of us chopped cotton, even Grampa" (90). The differences between the Okies and the banks lay more in scale and philosophy than methodology and eventual result. Both sides participated in the capitalist mechanism, but the banks had better adapted to thrive within it.

Mining the land of nutrients and leaving it for dead demonstrate a new, production-oriented allegiance to the frontier myth. Treating the nation's breadbasket as an expendable resource necessarily assumes an infinite resource reservoir from which to replace it. Short-term profiteering, by its very nature, posits that the future will take care of itself. Such a position depends on a telos of inexhaustible plenty, a concept central to the frontier and garden myths. This pattern of behavior again shows that the onset of the Industrial Age and accompanying supremacy of corporate capitalism did not eradicate the dominant myths but simply adapted them to twentieth-century exigencies. Richard Slotkin offers an intriguing explanation for this transition. He argues that the systems of myth and ideology that developed in this country depended on a positive association with physical migration that revolved around two geographical poles: the "Metropolis" and the "Frontier." The Metropolis must have a negative association or no one would want to leave, while the Frontier needs to offer riches enough to satisfy all of our dreams. Emigrants suffer in the wilderness while temporarily regressing to a more primitive state. The results, though, more than compensate for the ephemeral loss of civilization's comforts: "The completed American was therefore one who remade his fortune and his character by an emigration, a setting forth for newer and richer lands; by isolation and regression to a more primitive manner of life; and by establishing his political position" (Slotkin 1985, 35).

This discussion offers striking parallels to the Joads' saga. Slotkin's analysis takes the city, or the "Metropolis," as the emigrant's point of departure, but we can substitute the Dust Bowl region without interfering with the argument. Since the trappings of the Industrial Revolution came late to the Plains, the region lacked the large, mechanized urban areas that pose such an effective antipode to the wilderness frontier. Instead, mechanization and factory farming—both consequences of industrialization—provided the major impetus that drove families like the Joads from their homes. In the Dust Bowl, wage slavery and the specter of starvation resulting from technological and economic displacement offered the negative contrast to the frontier. Not present was the traditional coupling of those factors with the dense population centers that characterized urban industry. The Okies' choices, in Steinbeck's view, were either to drive a tractor through their neighbors' homes while raping the land with machinery and cash crops or to leave.

When they attempted to settle in California, the geographical border of the once limitless frontier, they found themselves wage slaves on a privatized corporate fiefdom. Once more the Okies suffered primitive, dehumanizing conditions while attempting to exercise their supposedly inalienable human rights. The growers' cartel, however, had disenfranchised them even before they arrived, forcing them into a nomadic existence designed to destroy the homesteading instinct so central to the Frontier Myth.

Despite uncountable acres lying fallow, no land was available for the Okies, a reality Steinbeck often demonstrates (*TGOW* 225). Their dreams of subsistence farming were fundamentally incompatible with the market economy that allowed a select few to grow vastly wealthy from the toil of disenfranchised adherents to the old American dream. What ultimately kills Casy and exiles Tom is—just as in Slotkin's paradigm—an urgent desire to participate in the political process. They do not succeed, for the moment, because the growers' control over water rights allows them complete dominion over the local government and media. I will discuss this phenomenon at greater length later in the essay. Its relevance here stems from water's role in the third major cause for the Okies' westward migration: inadequate irrigation and a perceived drought.

II

Steinbeck's humanistic bent impelled him to focus on the human side of the agricultural morass that drove the Okies west. The underlying motivation for both the Okies' behavior and that of the agribusiness concerns, however, can ultimately be analyzed in hydrological terms. Rainfall in the Southwest in the 1930s fell well within historical norms; cycles of drought are more common than periods of heavy rain. Drought did not cause the Dust Bowl—a more accurate description of the region's troubles should instead focus on the Depression and local agricultural mismanagement. The Depression, though, did not seriously affect the Great Plains until the onset of the Dust Bowl. If local farmers had been able to continue planting and harvesting cash crops at the rate they had in the 1920s, the Plains might have escaped the worst of the Depression. Unfortunately, by the end of the decade, they had borrowed heavily and expanded their acreage to maximize annual yields. When the crops failed and the "black blizzards" came, the national plague of poverty and joblessness infected the Plains states as well.

By the 1930s, Plains farmers had plowed under virtually all the region's grasslands. Without sod and other vegetation to hold the topsoil in place, the land became extremely vulnerable to ecological disturbance. When the drought hit, the land had no natural defenses with which to keep its topsoil intact. The resulting dust storms stripped the land bare. Yet if the region had retained its indigenous vegetation, the drought would have had little long-term effect on the land. Profit-oriented agriculture and ecological ignorance turned a cyclical shortfall of water into a disaster.

High-yield monoculture is a dubious ecological proposition even in humid regions, but in the Southwest such methods become disastrous (Worster 1979, 13). When Grampa Joad cleared the land and put it to plow, he hoped to fulfill the traditional yeoman ideal. Barring precipitation shortfalls, the average homestead proved more than adequate for subsistence farming. The region could not, however, sustain the rigors of a capitalist-based agriculture, a task that the metamorphosis of the American dream soon demanded. Steinbeck condemns what he sees as a dissolution of the values so cherished by the people who settled the region. Reverence for the land became obsolete with the ascension of factory farming.

> The driver sat in his iron seat and he was proud of the straight lines he did not will, proud of the tractor he did not own or love, proud of the power he could not control. And when that crop grew, and was harvested, no man had crumbled a hot clod in his fingers and let the earth sift past his fingertips. No man had touched the seed, or lusted for the growth. Men ate what they had not raised, had no connection with the bread. The land bore under iron, and under iron gradually died. (*TGOW* 38)

Steinbeck mourned this change in values but could offer no viable solutions. Even as they cursed the technology that drove them west, the Okies traveled in cars bought through the trade of their mules and watched with sadness as tractors did their work in a fraction of the time. The Okies formed the pivot for the western land's transition from earth mother to degraded resource. As the yeoman ideal gave way to the wages of capitalism, the Okies adapted their methods to meet the parameters of a market-based economy. Even as they clung tenaciously to their preindustrial, terrestrial reverence, they grudgingly accepted the new dominance of the capitalist shift. Muley Graves, unable to relinquish his ties to the land, cannot go with his family when they move west. Rooted to the place where he was born, Muley rages against the dual inequity of bad land and evil bankers: "'Cause what'd they take when they tractored the folks off the lan'? What'd they get so their margin a profit was safe? ... God knows the lan' ain't no good.... But them sons-a-bitches at their desks, they just chopped folks in two.... Place where folks live is them folks. They ain't whole, out lonely on the road in a piled-up car. Them sons-a-bitches killed them" (*TGOW* 55).

For Muley, the link with the land still stained with his father's blood is stronger than his ties to wife and family. He cannot leave even as he acknowledges that he is a living anachronism ("You fellas think I'm touched?"). Sadly, Muley's protestations held little weight with a population caught up in the quasi-divine status allowed them by technological advance. It did not matter if the land was poor because human ingenuity could and would transform it. No longer need the land yield forth its bounty; it will instead be mined and harvested. Modern agriculture provided the means to merge Henry Adams's classic juxtaposition of the dynamo and the virgin. Through this synthesis, the earth ceased to be a virgin and became a wife.[3] Similar phenomena occur often both in the American landscape and in the literary corpus. The masculine, aggressive machine assaults and reshapes the idyllic, feminine landscape (Leo Marx 1976, 29).

As farmers were forced more and more to mistreat their holdings, they degraded the land further to sexual plaything and chattel. This ideological evolution progressed naturally from the dominant myths.[4] As industrialism began to dominate the West, the accompanying mindset fit a unique niche in the American dream of rugged individualism and merit-based achievement.

Bacon, anticipating the Industrial Revolution, advocated reclaiming Eden through industry and science; a century later, Americans embraced the challenge as their destiny.[5] Westerners could reclaim the garden, but doing so involved literally "reclaiming" their place in paradise through diligence and industry. Men would finish what Nature had begun. Eden, ideologues hastened to point out, was after all an irrigated garden. Adam fell; Americans will stand tall. The Reclamation Act of 1902 established the Bureau of Reclamation, intending to fulfill Powell's credo of "rescuing" and "redeeming" the land from its arid state. The true meaning of the word "reclamation" lost all significance in the technological assault on the region's hydrology. The verb "to reclaim" infers prior ownership; the people seeking to irrigate the desert could make no such claim. Nevertheless, whatever needed to be done would be done to get water to the land and restore it to its imagined, bountiful state.[6] Any water that ran into the sea without serving some agricultural purpose was "wasted," a Providential oversight correctable through human diligence.

Denying the hydrological realities of the Southwest while modernizing the dominant mythology permitted Westerners to reject the implication that all is not within the grasp of any perspicacious American. Henry Luce's *Time* magazine trumpeted the rediscovered limitlessness that irrigation technology brought to the frontier: "Irrigation experts are now convinced that the rapidly growing U.S. can expand indefinitely within its present boundaries" (qtd. in Worster, *Rivers of Empire* 1985, 266). This quotation is pregnant with the contradictions inherent in the American and specifically western dream of infinite abundance. The notion of indefinite expansion within acknowledged boundaries is fundamentally self-contradictory. Attributing this ability to accomplish the impossible to the calculations of irrigation experts beautifully underscores the incongruities within western water policy. Western land barons relied on irrigation to accomplish the impossible and ignored or destroyed anyone or anything that interfered with their pursuit of that grail. The Joads and their contemporaries were ill equipped for the ramifications of the growers' zeal. They clung fast to traditional yeoman values even while participating in the market economy. Caught between two worlds, they could not linger in Oklahoma and set out instead for the land where corporate growers had remanufactured the traditional Myth of the Garden to entice exodusters westward.

As they traversed the migrant highway, the Joads met many who, like themselves, had readily believed the leaflets spread by agents of the California growers. "Why, I seen han'bills how they need folks to pick fruit, an' good wages.... An' with them good wages, maybe a fella can get hisself a piece a land an' work out for extra cash. Why, hell, in a couple a years I bet a fella could have a place of his own" (*TGOW* 160). That the Great Plains could no longer sustain the yeoman ideal did not necessarily spell the death of the American dream for a dispossessed people, barely literate and ready to jump at any hope of salvation. The California growers' cartel, already enmeshed in a cycle of wage slavery, remained convinced that additional workers could only lengthen their profit margins. They recruited Dust Bowl refugees with promises of a vast, temperate paradise wherein they might re-create the homesteads they had been forced to leave.

This new myth of the garden presented an even more seductive exterior than the Plains by adapting the Jeffersonian ideal to a region where husbandry was allegedly secondary to the munificence of nature. Grampa, before becoming overwhelmed by his attachment to the land on which he had cleared and raised his family, fantasized about bathing in a washtub full of grapes where he would "scrooge aroun' an' let the juice run down my pants" (100). But this vision of unchecked abundance was less a cultural phenomenon than a calculated product of the growers' propaganda mills. The agribusiness consortia dangled visions of their own wealth and massive landholdings before the Okies in order to fuel their (the cartel's) hegemony. And the irony of that vision, as Steinbeck depicts it, is that the growers were as alienated from their land wealth as they forced the Okies to be: "And it came about that the owners no longer worked their farms ... they forgot the land, the smell and the feel of it, and remembered only that they owned it.... And the owners not only did not work the farms any more, many of them had never seen the farms they owned" (TGOW 257).

The California growers had become immensely wealthy and powerful as the result of an uneasy but mutually profitable alliance with the Bureau of Reclamation.[7] Having already incarnated themselves in the image of the new garden that depended heavily on the tools of the technocracy to subdue the land, they looked to consolidate their holdings by enacting the Social Darwinism that fueled their telos of industry. They had managed to consolidate the dual definitions of "garden" into one highly profitable vision of production and wealth. No longer could "garden" signify either a region of natural, providential splendor or an area of human-created agrarian abundance (Leo Marx 1976, 85); the Edenic garden propounded by Gilpin and his nineteenth-century allies was completely replaced by its opposing Baconian definition of a human-engineered paradise achieved through work and intellect. Humans—specifically men—had invented the tools necessary to subjugate nature. Those tools had brought water to the desert via centrifugal pumping and, more important, through the diversion of rivers.

By shaping the perceived objectivity of science to fit the needs of western agriculture, an elite group's control over the dissemination of knowledge led to dominion over the region's geography (Foucault 1980, 69). The men whose schemes created this technological garden stood to profit most from its enactment, and it was they who formed the powerful growers' cartel that enslaved the migrants. Those who controlled the water controlled the entire regional economy, and that domination bled into every other facet of life.

Californian agribusiness's command over nature required large temporary workforces, while the capitalist regime demanded that this transient labor force be paid very little. The growers had traditionally indentured immigrants and other disenfranchised groups because little public outcry arose from their mistreatment. Still, the arrival of the Okies, a large, skilled, English-speaking labor force whose migrant status left them bereft of any governmental protection, appeared to be a tremendous windfall to the growers' cartel. In the novel, however, the latent power of the oppressed becomes the looming threat to the water-based oligarchy as the Okies come to embody Marx's concept of alienated labor (Karl Marx 1964, 69). Their corporate oppressors force them to work ever harder and faster in order to eke out subsistence, yet each hour worked and each piece of fruit harvested bring them that much closer to unemployment and starvation. They must further compete against each other by underbidding fellow workers in a futile attempt to participate in an exclusionary economic system. Conversely, growers must dehumanize the workers, degrading them as they do the land so that their acts of subjugation can be perpetrated on objects beneath contempt.[8] In *In Dubious Battle*, Steinbeck treats the worker/grower relationship as a matter strictly related to class struggle. In *The Grapes of Wrath*, he elevates it to the realm of epistemology, viewing the schism between workers and land barons as symptomatic of the larger issue of human alienation from the earth and as a catalyst for the synthesis of humans and their surroundings into the all-encompassing organismic one (Benson, *True Adventures* 1990, 268–69). "Three hundred thousand, hungry and miserable; if ever they know themselves, the land will be theirs.... And the great owners, who had become through their holdings both more and less than men, ran to their destruction, and used every means that in the long run would destroy them" (*TGOW* 263).

The cycle of poverty imposed on the Okies contained a seasonal period of starvation during the rainy season. Water again, this time through superabundance, became the immediate threat to the Okies' survival. When Rosasharn goes into labor, the men outside labor frantically to erect a dam to keep the boxcar shelters dry. Water, priceless commodity and building block of life, endangers the birthing process and threatens to starve an entire class of people. Both attempts—the birth and the dam—are unsuccessful. As the floodwaters force the Joads to flee, Uncle John is assigned the task of burying the stillborn child. Rather than do so, he coopts the water, using it and the dead child to spread his message of despair and defiance: "Go down an' tell 'em. Go down in the street an' rot an' tell em that way. That's the way you can talk.... Go on down now an' lay in the street. Maybe they'll know then" (494). Driven from Oklahoma, where widespread refusal to acknowledge water's scarcity resulted in an unsustainable way of life, the Okies found themselves in a new region with an already intact and sophisticated capitalist infrastructure with water at its plinth. As a disenfranchised and powerless class, the migrants had no opportunity to gain control over water rights and consequently could not participate in the dominant discourse. John's act represented an ephemeral yet powerful appropriation of the preeminent unit of capital. Using water to convey a message of worker defiance strikes at the heart of the power structure: if the Okies were to gain actual control over the region's water, the growers' cartel would collapse. Legions of migrants could then seize power and redistribute the land according to need and fairness.

The dual hopes for the migrants, according to Steinbeck, are class alliance and worker control over the tools of domination. When Tom takes over the task of organizing the Okies from the martyred Casy, the class struggle takes a symbolic step forward. When Uncle John seizes control over the waters that enslave his people and threaten their lives, he takes another major step toward toppling the ruling class. Shortly after Uncle John's act of defiance, Rosasharn's gift of her maternal milk to another starving Okie demonstrates that both Tom's and John's acts will eventually bear fruit. Sheltered from the water by a barn, itself a potent symbol of the yeoman agricultural ideal, Rosasharn, by offering her breast to a fellow migrant, demonstrates the class cohesion that will ultimately topple the ruling class. While her stillborn infant rots in the town below, Rosasharn breastfeeds an old man whose advanced state of starvation has caused him to regress to a prelingual state. Her act and the old man's condition represent the succoring of the infant movement toward social change. Each act, while primarily symbolic, is also genuinely subversive. In these small acts of defiance and hope, suggests Steinbeck, lie the restoration of traditional ties between people and between people and the land. So despite their socialization into a culture in which water is both hoarded and feared, the Okies have not completely acquiesced to their role in the factory-farm mechanism. They retain their dreams of an idyllic land where the family farm reigns supreme and water and land are distributed according to need and connectedness to the land rather than according to amassed corporate capital and political dominance.

In the final analysis, however, the migrant dream of resurgent family farms reclaiming their place as the preeminent agricultural ideal cannot work in the arid lands. Water reclamation projects, because of their expense and complexity, require the participation of an elite, educated class. The projects therefore become political pawns. The family farmer, allied with a subsistence ideology and unwilling to exploit the land past its carrying capacity, cannot compete with wealthy, powerful corporate interests. For this reason, the novel, though hopeful, does not offer any quantifiable hope.

Worster identifies this lack of an attainable goal as the novel's major failing. Decrying the system of land distribution without explicitly condemning the accompanying hydrological autocracy leads to the specious conclusion that simply putting the land in the hands of the migrants will solve the region's agrarian morass. In a section of *Rivers of Empire* titled "The Grapes of Wealth," Worster argues: "Nowhere in *The Grapes of Wrath* does Steinbeck draw attention to the elaborate hydraulic apparatus that has been required to create the California garden.... Grapes, carrots, cotton and the like are the products, it would seem, of spontaneous nature, not the contrivances of advanced water engineering and the social organization it has required" (229). Because Steinbeck failed to acknowledge the inherent oligarchic nature of irrigation-based societies, he creates the false impression that equitable land distribution and a classless society will return the region to ecological stability. Historically, there are no precedents for this vision being realizable. In fact, returning the family farm to the arid region without altering the national capitalist infrastructure will, given the Plains example, cause devastating ecological harm.

Worster's critique does raise the problematic issue of Steinbeck's unrepentant affection for the family farm but does not, as I mentioned earlier, address the powerful critique of hydraulic society implicit in the novel's structure.[9] That he used water throughout the novel as an absent signifier suggests that Steinbeck was well aware of its power and complicity in the region's power hierarchy. When, at the novel's end, Steinbeck suddenly introduces water as a tangible presence and powerful symbolic force, it empowers the migrants by demonstrating their class cohesion and latent strength. Structuring the novel in this manner permitted Steinbeck to criticize the extant hydraulic society more effectively than he could through overt polemics. Indeed, the novel's reception, both locally and nationally, bears witness to its powerful subversive nature, a fact that underscores the most crucial flaw in Worster's argument. If the novel caused both the government and the nation at large to reevaluate federal irrigation subsidies for corporate growers, clearly it must have effectively criticized the inequity and corruption infusing California's water-appropriation schema.

The migrants' struggle became a national cause célèbre, and the novel's verisimilitude was debated at the highest levels of government.[10] The Hearst-Chandler-Copley yellow press pilloried the novel and its author throughout California. Only after a *Life* magazine exposé and Eleanor Roosevelt's endorsement of the book's veracity did the tide of public opinion begin to turn in Steinbeck's favor.[11] The rage and furor from agribusiness conglomerates and their allies arose because *The Grapes of Wrath* shook the very foundations of the water-based oligarchy. Worster himself acknowledges this:

> Up to the very end of the decade, both the Bureau [of Reclamation] and the Department of the Interior were placidly moving forward ... avoiding any cause for alarm on the part of the growers in California ... What changed all of that undoubtedly was ... the publication in 1939 of *The Grapes of Wrath*.... Suddenly, it became rather difficult for a liberal government in Washington to give subsidized, unrestricted water to groups like the reactionary Associated Farmers, to underwrite their labor policies and their concentration of wealth. (Worster, *Rivers of Empire* 1985, 245)

Nevertheless, despite a temporary surge in popular and governmental concern, neither the novel nor the reform movement it generated achieved any lasting change in western water policy. Pork barrel appropriations bills continued to subsidize corporate growers, who continued to couch their greed within the rubric of a technologically controlled Eden that they believed should form the destiny of the West. The migrants' struggle faded into the background with the outbreak of World War II. U.S. entry into the conflict stoked the fires of nationalism, and the nation turned to the West once again to fuel the American war machine. The Okies benefitted from the wartime surge in production, finding work in munitions factories and other war-related industries. Relieved, the growers turned once again to immigrant labor, a class of people they could be relatively certain of keeping disenfranchised and powerless. The cycle of exploitation thus resumed after only a brief hiatus. Public interest in the issue peaked again two decades later when Cesar Chavez briefly managed to organize the Migrant Farm Workers Union into an effective national lobby.

Only in the 1990s, after a prolonged drought and numerous aborted attempts at reform, has the Californian agricultural machine seemingly run dry. Faced with a severe, unremitting drought and a recession-locked nation unwilling to finance any more quixotic reclamation projects, the growers in California now face a complete embargo on federally supplied water (Reinhold, *New York Times* 1992). Years of drought and insupportable agriculture in an arid land are seemingly on the verge of accomplishing what no individual person could accomplish alone: decanonization of the myth of the garden and its accompanying myth of the frontier. These two myths, dominant since the birth of the nation, eventually ran headlong into the realities of a closed frontier and a finite hydrology. Steven Goldstein, spokesman for interior secretary Manuel Lujan, aptly summed up the situation when announcing the curtailment of further water subsidy, saying: "We recognize ... what a hardship this will be. But we cannot make it rain" (Reinhold, *New York Times* 1992).

NOTES

1. One of the most effective techniques used by the press to discredit the novel involved letters to the editor from supposed "Okies" protesting that the conditions depicted in the novel did not really exist. The letters told of friendly treatment by the growers, clean living conditions, and enough work for everybody. The papers also spread rumors of Okies wanting to kill Steinbeck for telling lies about them. Little information defending Steinbeck's version of events reached the public at large until a number of other exposés (most notably Carey McWilliams's *Factories in the Field*) were released and photographs documenting the migrants' conditions gained widespread notoriety.

2. Frederick Jackson Turner's essay "The Significance of the Frontier in American History" (1892) (see Turner 1947) posited that the existence of the frontier allowed the nation's economy to expand constantly and thus allowed capitalism to dominate. His thesis was widely accepted until the middle of this century and is discernible in the literature as well as the governmental policies of the period.

3. In *To a God Unknown*, Steinbeck openly acknowledges the sexual bond between men and the land. After Joseph literally makes love to the earth, the narrator matter-of-factly notes that "for a moment, the land had been his wife" (11). In *The Grapes of Wrath*, which postdates *To a God Unknown* by a decade, Steinbeck again acknowledges the sexual link—this time in the form of rape: "Behind the harrows, the long seeders—twelve curved iron penes erected in the foundry, orgasms set by gears, raping methodically, raping without passion" (37).

4. Kolodny argues that the progressive deterioration in cultural reverence for the land was an unavoidable by-product of viewing it as feminine while seeking to settle it: "Implicit in the metaphor of the land-as-woman was both the regressive pull of maternal containment *and* the seductive invitation to sexual assertion: if the Mother demands passivity, and threatens regression, the Virgin apparently invites sexual assertion and awaits impregnation" (67).

5. Jehlen argues convincingly that the uniquely American bond with the land and nature makes anything Americans choose to do necessarily right and natural: "The settlers' implementation of the continent's permanent contours and conditions ... places the emerging social structures ... in the realm of nature. Those who assist the emergence of those structures, moreover, wield the power of nature itself" (57). One of the ways Americans cast the conquest of the land within the current political climate was by classifying irrigation programs as a struggle between the forces of good and the forces of godless communists dedicated to subverting the American way of life. Robert Kerr, former governor of Oklahoma and head of the Senate's Select Committee on Water Resources, rhetorically asks: "Can a pagan Communist nation ... make more efficient use of soil and water resources than the most advanced and enlightened nation in the world? Can ruthless atheists mobilize and harness their treasure of God-given wealth to defeat and stifle freedom-loving peoples everywhere?" (Kerr 1960, 323–24).

6. Worster offers this account of the Plains mentality during the mid-1930s: "'You gave us beer,' they told Roosevelt, 'now give us water.' ... 'Every draw, arryo [*sic*], and

canyon that could be turned into a lake or lagoon,' wrote a clothing store manager, 'should be turned into one by dams and directed ditches & draws until there are millions of them thru these mid-western states.' A Texas stockman wanted to use natural gas to pump flood waters from the Mississippi River to the Plains.... An old soldier from Denver penciled his ideas on ruled tablet paper: stage sham battles with 40,000 Civilian Conservation Corp boys and $20 million worth of ammunition—the noise would be sure to stir up some rain.... 'Try it,' he finished, 'if it works send me a check for $5000 for services rendered'" (1979, 39).

7. California's water wars are far too complex to treat in this essay. Many excellent studies on the subject exist, and I have made extensive use of several, including Worster's *Rivers of Empire* and Reisner's *Cadillac Desert*. For a well-researched, highly critical history of the Bureau of Reclamation, see Berkman and Viscusi's *Damming the West*.

8. The women/nature, men/civilization duality linked women to the land, and so they shared in its degradation. By viewing the landscape as feminine, the patriarchy was traditionally able to construct the cultural paradigm both of women and of the land in an image that suited its perpetuation. Damming rivers and mining aquifers in an attempt to reconstruct the landscape to fit a masculine ideal is analogous to girdling and reshaping women to fit the masculine concept of beauty. See Warren and Cheney, "Ecological Feminism and Ecosystem Ecology," and Catherine Roach, "Loving Your Mother: On the Woman-Nature Relation."

9. Louis Owens contends that Steinbeck does not romanticize the agrarian ideal. The novel's harsh depiction of Okie tenant farmers mitigates any endorsement of family farms and Jeffersonian agrarianism while demonstrating Steinbeck's awareness of their ecological impracticality: "By carefully and precisely placing the tenants within the historical pattern that has led to the destruction of the land, Steinbeck is making it obvious that agrarianism alone is insufficient. In fact, the ideal of the independent small farmer, the Jeffersonian image of the heroic individualist wresting an isolated living from the soil is firmly scuttled in *The Grapes of Wrath*" (54).

10. Congressman Lyle Boren of Oklahoma declared *The Grapes of Wrath* to be "a lie, a black, infernal creation of a twisted, distorted mind" (qtd. in *WD*, xxiv). Steinbeck also became the target of a whispering campaign by the Associated Farmers, including one rumor that Steinbeck was a Jew acting on behalf of a Zionist-Communist conspiracy to undermine the economy (Benson 1984, 420).

11. After visiting a series of migrant camps in 1940, Mrs. Roosevelt told reporters, "I have never believed *The Grapes of Wrath* was exaggerated" (qtd. in Benson 1990, 402).

BRIAN E. RAILSBACK

The Darwinian Grapes of Wrath

"I often bless all novelists."
—Charles Darwin, *The Autobiography of Charles Darwin*, 1892

A study of Charles Darwin and the art of John Steinbeck must, like any expedition through the novelist's life work, finally arrive at his masterpiece, *The Grapes of Wrath*. In no other book is Steinbeck's dramatization of Darwin's theory more clear; the novel resonates with the naturalist's ideas. Through Steinbeck's narrative technique, from the parts (i.e., the characters in the Joad chapters) to the whole (the intercalary chapters), we are presented with a holistic view of the migrant worker developed through Steinbeck's own inductive method. This epic novel demonstrates the range of Darwin's theory, including the essential aspects of evolution: the struggle for existence and the process of natural selection. The migrant workers move across the land as a species, uprooted from one niche and forced to gain a foothold in another. Their struggle is intensified by capitalism's perversion of natural competition, but this only makes the survivors that much tougher. Because of their inability to see the whole picture, the bankers and members of the Farmers Association diminish themselves by their oppressive tactics while the surviving migrant workers become increasingly tougher, more resourceful, and more sympathetic. Ultimately, seeing Darwin's ideas in *The Grapes of Wrath* enables us to perceive some hope for the Joads and others

From the *Critical Ressponse to John Steinbeck's the Grapes of Wrath*, Barbara A. Heavilin, ed. ©2000 by Barbara A. Heavilin. Originally published in *Parallel Expeditions: Charles Darwin and the Art of John Steinbeck*. © 1995 by The University of Idaho Press.

like them—here is Steinbeck's manifesto of progress, based on biological laws rather than political ideology. Despite the dismal scene that concludes the book, we come to a better understanding of what Ma Joad already knows, that "the people" will keep on coming.

Steinbeck embarked on an expedition of his own from 1934 to 1938 to gather information that would ultimately lead to his great novel. Jackson L. Benson's biography of Steinbeck provides a very complete and accurate account of the novelist's research, and, in direct reference to *The Grapes of Wrath* itself, Robert DeMott's introduction and notes for *Working Days* provide further illumination and detail.

Benson writes that Steinbeck, who "seems to have remembered in detail nearly everything he saw or heard," entered the world of migrant labor in California when he interviewed two starving, fugitive strike organizers in Seaside in early 1934 (*True Adventures* 291). Steinbeck gathered more information from James Harkins, an organizer who helped in the Imperial Valley strike (1934) and the Salinas lettuce strike (1936). Eventually strike organizers began to frequent the Steinbeck's cottage in Pacific Grove and discuss their "holy mission": "Since you were either for them or against them—there was no compromise—[Steinbeck] did more listening than talking" (294). Steinbeck also met the famous social reformer and muckraker, Lincoln Steffens, who was spending his last years in a house in nearby Carmel. Benson writes that Steffens and Steinbeck agreed on "the importance and value of observing and discovering" (295). Steinbeck, as early as the summer of 1934, had himself gone out to see the migrant labor camps in the Salinas area. All of the information he gathered, along with very detailed information from a union leader, Cicil McKiddy, eventually became a part of *In Dubious Battle*. Significantly, the book does not follow anyone's party line but rather works out many of Steinbeck's and Ed Ricketts's biological views.

Serious research for *The Grapes of Wrath* began with Steinbeck's assignment for *The San Francisco News* to write a series of articles about migrant farm labor in California, which necessitated observing conditions at various labor camps. He saw firsthand the destitution of migrant families in these government camps and spontaneous Hoovervilles. As Benson and DeMott show, a tremendous influence on Steinbeck as he prepared to write *The Grapes of Wrath* was Tom Collins, the manager of "Weedpatch," the government Sanitary Camp at Arvin (he is the "Tom" that the book is partly dedicated to). Collins was something of a social scientist who made meticulous reports and gathered statistics about the migrant's life which Steinbeck used extensively in *The Grapes of Wrath* (Benson, *True Adventures* 343–44). Even at home near Salinas, Steinbeck found more information to gather, as incidents of vigilantism were occurring as a result of the strike of 1936 (346). In 1937 Steinbeck took another, longer tour of migrant camps with Collins, and in February of 1938, Steinbeck went to the flooded areas of Visalia where, as he wrote to his agent, "Four thousand families, drowned out of their tents are really starving to death" (368). As DeMott writes, "What he witnessed there became the backdrop for the final scenes of *The Grapes of Wrath*" (*Working Days* 134).

When the author began to write up his observations into a novel, his first bitterly satirical attempt, "L'Affaire Lettuceberg," failed because he was too close to the subject. Like Darwin's *Origin*, *The Grapes of Wrath* is a gathering of observations fused by a hypothesis, in this case a biological consideration of cycles in land ownership. Of course, unlike *Origin*, it is fictionalized, and, above all else, a work of art. Still Steinbeck's method in putting together the novel resembles an inductive, scientific one. Anything less, in the hands of some other writer, might have been another political satire like the "L'Affaire Lettuceberg."

From the first pages of *The Grapes of Wrath*, Steinbeck's biological, holistic view is evident. The novel presents a large picture in which humans are only a small part; in the great natural scheme of sky and land, of rain, wind, and dust, they suffer with the teams of horses and the dying corn all life forms are helpless in this huge canvas of natural machinations. And there are beasts at the door; not more than a night after the people leave Oklahoma enter new occupants who were always waiting outside: weasels, cats, bats, and mice (*Grapes* 126–127).

People are further associated with the natural world by being rendered in animal metaphors, either by their own language or the narrator's. In chapter 8, we meet the Joad family and hear that Ma fears Tom will be like Pretty Boy Floyd ("They shot at him like a varmint ... man' then they run him like a coyote, an' him a-snappin' an' a-snarlin', mean as a lobo"); that Grampa once tortured Granma "as children torture bugs"; that Grampa had hoped the "jailbird" Tom would "come a-bustin' outa jail like a bull through a corral fence"; and that somewhere Al is "a-billygoatin' aroun' the country. Tom cattin' hisself to death" (82–89).

The narrator's famous image of the land turtle is the most extensive metaphor for the migrant worker. In chapter 3, the tough, wizened turtle navigates the road, pushing ahead with "hands" rather than front claws. Tom picks up the turtle and Casy observes, "Nobody can't keep a turtle though.... at least one day they get out and away they go off somewheres. It's like me." (21). When Tom releases it, a cat attacks it to no avail, and the turtle goes in the same direction that the Joads will: southwest. The connection is made even stronger when, in chapter 16, a description of the flight of the Joads and the Wilsons across the Panhandle is juxtaposed with the image of the land turtles which crawled through the dust" (178). Steinbeck's extensive use of personification and anthropomorphism underscores his view of *Homo sapiens* as just another species.

This recognition leads to the same collision with traditional religion that Darwin's theory encountered in Victorian England, by directly challenging the idea that the human is above the animals, a being made in God's own image. In an eerie scene, Steinbeck powerfully demonstrates the self-delusion of a group of "Jehovites" who pray in a tent for Granma. Aspiring to be superior to the natural world, they are more beast-like than those they call sinners: "One woman's voice went up and up in a wailing cry, wild and fierce, like the cry of a beast; and a deeper woman's voice rose up beside it, a baying voice, and a man's voice traveled up the scale in the howl of a wolf. The exhortation stopped, and only the feral howling came from the tent" (233). Like meetings Casy devised as a preacher, in which excited men and women went from the meeting place to the bushes to make love, traditional religion is only another veneer over animal nature.

Certainly the world Steinbeck portrays in *The Grapes of Wrath* demonstrates what Darwin, Ricketts, and he believed: humans are subject to the laws of ecology. That the Darwinian principles of competition and selection are an essential part of the novel is no surprise. The Joads and Wilsons are part of a movement of migrants, acting as a species turned out of a niche by natural and unnatural forces. The migrants go to a richer niche that would appear to have plenty of room for them, but many of them die, overwhelmed by competition and repression. Yet the survivors display an astounding ability to adapt. They come to California, a vigorous new species quite terrifying to the natives who, despite the crushing power of a brutal economic system which they control, act from a growing sense of insecurity. "They weathered the thing," Steinbeck writes of the migrant workers, "and they can weather much more for their blood is strong. [T]his new race is here to stay and heed must be taken of it" (*Gypsies* 22).

The process of evolution that leads to the creation of "this new race" is patently Darwinian. With drought upon the land and the dissolution of the tenant system, the farmer can no longer live in the region—forcing the migration west. In *The Origin of Species*, Darwin observes that if an open country undergoes some great change, "new forms would certainly immigrate, and this would likewise seriously disturb the relations of some of the former inhabitants" (Appleman 55; see also 97). From the first day of the Joads' migration, a process of selection begins; those who can adapt to the new way of life survive. Although a tough man, Grampa proves too rooted in the old land to adapt to the new, and his death, as Casy knows, is inevitable:

"Grampa didn' die tonight. He died the minute you took 'im off the place" (*Grapes* 160). Muley cannot leave either, and his future is doubtful; ironically, Noah, who himself will wander off alone into oblivion, tells Muley, "You gonna die out in the fiel' some day" (121). Granma cannot recover from the death of Grampa and loses touch with reality and eventually life. The Wilsons also fail, despite help from the Joads; Ivy lacks the essential mechanical knowledge of cars to succeed, and Sairy is too physically weak to survive.

Because of the migrants' relentless trek, during which they are driven by the harshness of the weather, by poverty, and by cruelty, the ones who arrive in California already are transformed. As intercalary chapter 17 shows, the group has adapted to the new way of life on the road: "They were not farm men anymore, but migrant men" (215). The new breed pours into California "restless as ants, scurrying to find work to do." But "the owners hated them because the owners had heard from their grandfathers how easy it is to steal land from a soft man if you are fierce and hungry and armed" (256–57). Ma Joad typifies the strong blood that Steinbeck refers to, for she adapts to each new situation, meeting difficulties with whatever ferocity or compassion is needed, constantly working to keep the family together and push them forward. Toward the end of the novel, Ma gives her famous speech about the people, and certainly she has come to understand what survival of the fittest means: "We ain't gonna die out. People is goin' on— changin' a little, maybe, but goin' right on ... some die, but the rest is tougher" (467–68).

A Darwinian interpretation of *The Grapes of Wrath* reveals the novel's most terrible irony: the owners' perversion of the natural process only hastens their own destruction. In states such as Oklahoma, the bank—the "monster"—must be fed at the expense of the tenant system, thus losing something precious: "The man who is more than his chemistry ... that man who is more than his elements knows the land that is more than its analysis" (126). And the tenacity of these people, their potential, is drawn to another land. The Farmers Association of California sends out handbills to attract a surplus of labor, intensifying the competition for jobs so that the migrant laborers will work for almost nothing. But the owners are unconscious of the other part of the equation, that increased competition only toughens the survivors, as Darwin notes: "In the survival of favored individuals and races, during the constantly recurrent Struggle for Existence, we see a powerful and ever-acting form of Selection" (Appleman, *Origin* 115). The novel's omniscient narrator recalls "the little screaming fact evident throughout history, of which the owners remain ignorant: 'repression works only to strengthen and knit the repressed'" (*Grapes* 262).

Steinbeck recognizes the untenable position of the owners in California. "Having built the repressive attitude toward the labor they need to survive, the directors were terrified of the things they have created" (*Gypsies* 36). As the economic system blindly pushes people out of the plains states and just as blindly entices them to California with the intention of inhumane exploitation, it proves a system of men who fail to see the whole. Often the owners win, and some workers are hungry enough to betray their own kind, such as the migrants hired to move in and break up the dance at Weedpatch. But at the end of chapter 19, the omniscient voice describes how in their suffering people come together, as the migrants gather coins to bury a dead infant; soon they will see beyond themselves and the illusion of their religion. "And the association of owners knew that some day the praying would stop. And there's the end" (*Grapes* 263).

The narrator describes the sense of coming change in more ominous tones at the end of chapter 25: "[I]n the eyes of the hungry there is a growing wrath. In the souls of the people the grapes of wrath are filling and growing heavy, growing heavy for the vintage" (385). The narrator presents the whole view, which characters like Casy and Tom eventually see but the owners remain blind to as they continue to create a breed that will be their undoing. "For while California has been successful in its use of migrant labor," Steinbeck writes, "it is gradually building a human structure which will certainly change the State, and may, if handled with the inhumanity and stupidity that have characterized the past, destroy the present system of agricultural economics" (*Gypsies* 25). This is the dynamic that Steinbeck describes in *The Log* after visiting Espiritu Santo Island, where in certain areas only one or two species dominate an ecosystem. He parallels the territorial habits of these animals with humans. While the "dominant human" grows weak from too much security, "[t]he lean and hungry grow strong.... Having nothing to lose and all to gain, these selected hungry and rapacious ones develop attack rather than defense techniques ... so that one day the dominant man is eliminated and the strong and hungry wanderer takes his place" (97).

In the thinking of Darwin and Steinbeck, the California landowners' "inhumanity" is their keen lack of sympathy and their "stupidity" is the reason for that lack, the inability to see the whole. As Casy tells his assassin just before the death blow, "You don't know what you're a-doin" (*Grapes* 426). His last words appropriately echo Christ's, for in killing the leader of a cause, one leaves tougher disciples, such as Tom Joad.

From his knowledge of the whole, of past and present, and of humanity's true place in the scheme of nature, Charles Darwin nears the end of *The Descent of Man* with the interesting realization that he would rather be a "heroic little monkey" than the human "savage who delights to torture his enemies ... knows no decency, and is haunted by the grossest superstitions" (Appleman 208). It is not the kind of statement that anyone with illusions about the inherent superiority of human beings would wish to hear. Darwin's view is certainly played out in *The Grapes of Wrath*, as we encounter a group of the most civilized people practicing many of the atrocities that delight Darwin's savage. They lack sympathy and therefore will lose their humanity and probably their existence as a group. In contrast, the migrant workers show a sense of compassion for their fellows that binds them together and can eventually insure their existence in a hostile environment, for the cooperation that grows out of sympathy is the greatest threat to the owner, as Steinbeck foresees: "And from this first 'we' there grows a still more dangerous thing: 'I have a little food' plus 'I have none.' If from this problem the sum is 'We have a little food, the thing is on its way, the movement has direction.... If you who own the things people must have could understand this, you might preserve yourself'" (*Grapes* 165–66). Steinbeck goes on to warn that "the quality of owning freezes you forever into 'I', and cuts you off forever for the 'we'" (166). Clearly, the owners do not understand this reality.

The other great irony of the novel is that, through a Darwinian process of adaptation and evolution, the dehumanizing conditions created by the owners only make the migrant workers more human. This process can be seen in nearly every chapter, as migrants share money, food, transportation, work, and ultimately their anger, as they briefly unite in a strike that is defeated by an influx of hungry workers who do not yet see the big picture. But as the suffering continues and more Casys are martyred and more Toms are created, the people will eventually move forward. As Casy tells Tom, "ever' time they's a little step forward, she may slip back a little, but she never slips clear back" (425). Casy's words resonate with the narrator's definition of what man is in chapter 14: "This you may say of man ... man stumbles forward, painfully, mistakenly sometimes. Having stepped forward, he may slip back, but only a half step, never the full step back" (164). Owners, comfortable and rich, are frozen in their "I" mentality, the surviving migrants move forward; they are vigorous and continue to evolve into their "we" mentality. This process is the essence of Steinbeck's scientific, Darwinian belief in a progression for humankind based on biological principles generally and struggle in particular. This is why, by the time he wrote *America and Americans* in 1966, he worries most of all that the country has lost its survival drive.

This particular kind of evolution is best illustrated through the development of Tom Joad, perhaps Steinbeck's most complete hero.

Although Ma, too, shows a tremendous capacity for adaptation and sympathy, her sense of "we" does not extend much beyond the family unit, and while Casy certainly comes to see the whole picture and extends his sympathy to all oppressed laborers, the greatest change occurs in Tom, whose near-animal introversion becomes an almost spiritual extroversion during his family's struggle to survive. This change in character has been noted by several critics. Lisca calls Tom's conversion one from the personal/material to the ethical/spiritual ("Grapes" 98). Charles Shively believes that Tom's widening horizon reflects the influence on Steinbeck of American holistic philosopher Josiah Royce (there is no evidence the novelist had heard of Royce before 1948, however [see DeMott's *Steinbeck's Reading* 96, 169]). And Leonard Lutwack sees Tom's conversion through Biblical imagery, from his "baptism" when he kills Casy's assailant by a stream to his "resurrection from the tomb" while he speaks to his mother in the cave (70–71).

Tom has received so much attention from critics probably because he is Steinbeck's most dynamic character. At the beginning of the novel, Tom—like Grampa, Al, Ruthie, and Winfield—is preoccupied with his own needs. Sitting with Casy and Muley in his parents' wrecked house, Tom has only food on his mind while Casy talks about their pathetic existence: "load turned the meat, and his eyes were inward" (*Grapes* 54). Once the meat is done, Tom seizes it, "scowling like an animal" (57). Casy suddenly is inspired to go with the people on the road, but Joad merely rolls a cigarette and ignores the preacher's speech. Later, Tom rails at a gas station attendant who worries about what is happening to the country, then pauses, noticing for the first time that the attendant's station is near bankruptcy. Tom corrects himself, "I didn't mean to sound off at ya, mister" (139). When Casy questions Tom about the larger picture, about the fact that their group is only a small part of a mass migration, Tom begins to feel the inadequacy of his narrow vision: "I'm jus' puttin' one foot in front a the other. I done it at Mac for four years.... I thought it'd be somepin different when I come out! Couldn't think a nothin' in there, else you go stir happy, an' now can't think a nothin'" (190). Like Ma, keeping the family together becomes a project for Tom; he finds his drunken Uncle John and feels pity for him, and later he sacrifices his natural anger for the good of the family (306, 309).

After Tom sees Casy killed, the change that has been gradually occurring in him becomes complete. He understands the entire structure, for he has been both in the camp with the laborers and outside with the strike leaders. His immediate concern is to flee to protect his family, but to appease Ma he hides in a cave of vines near the Joads' new camp. After Ruthie spills the news that Tom killed Casy's assassin, Ma goes to him in the cave for a final talk. Although he has been reduced to living like an animal, in the darkness of his cave Tom has been thinking about Casy: "He talked a lot. Used to bother me. But now I been thinkin' what he said, an I can remember—all of it" (462). He has come to realize the truth of the "Preacher," a code of survival based on cooperation: "And if one prevail against him, two shall withstand him, and a three-fold cord is not quickly broken" (462). He gives a speech in which he becomes the ultimate expression of sympathy, for he is now less an individual and more the essence of the whole: "I'll be ever'where—wherever you look" (463). He has determined a truth goes beyond even Ma's comprehension, for she says at the end of his speech, "I don' un'erstan" (463). Because of his fierceness, inherited from Ma, he will pose a greater threat to the owners than Casy, who "didn' duck quick enough" (463).

In a work so full of apparently hopeless suffering, the Darwinian view of *The Grapes of Wrath* explains why characters such as Ma or Tom have a sense of victory. The processes of competition and natural selection, artificially heightened by narrow-minded landowners, create a new race with strong blood—a race that can adapt and fight in a way the old one could not. Endowed with a closeness to the land and an increasing sympathy, this new race represents a human being far superior to the old "I" savage. Because of the struggle, people like the Joads become better human beings, cooperating with each other in every crisis. "There is a gradual improvement in the treatment of man by man," Steinbeck wrote in a letter for the *Monthly Record* (a magazine for the Connecticut state prison system) during the period in which *The Grapes of Wrath* was being written. "There are little spots of kindness that burn up like fire and light the whole thing up. But I guess the reason they are so bright is that there are so few of them. However, the ones that do burn up seem to push us ahead a little" (3). Thus, even when famished and facing death herself, Rose of Sharon begins to see past her own selfishness and offers her breast to a starving man. She has reason to smile mysteriously, understanding something larger and greater than her oppressors will ever know.

On the morning of May 15, 1992, Professor Stanley Brodwin of Hofstra University stood in the historic Admiral Coffin School hall on Nantucket Island And gave a lecture titled "The Example of Darwin's Voyage of the Beagle in *The Log from the Sea of Cortez*." His talk was that rare recognition of Darwin's influence upon a book by Steinbeck. Brodwin discussed *The Log* as part of the larger genre of journals of expeditions by such naturalists as Darwin, Alexander von Humboldt, and Edward Forbes. He examined Steinbeck's book on another level among the four Steinbeck professed to be in it: "*The Log* remains a fully romantic work, its theological explorations maintaining a meaningful tension with its search for hard scientific information...."

It was a good day for Steinbeck studies, devoted to the truly deep element in his many-layered vision of humanity. His biological perspective came up again and again. When the conference moved to the Nantucket Marine Laboratory, where participants could examine experiments conducted by Dr. Joseph Grochowski and his associates, they peered into the bubbling tanks of marine life or looked out toward sun-dappled ripples in the harbor and talked of marine biology and the novelists art. Had he been there, John Steinbeck would have been pleased.

References

Benson, Jackson J. *The True Adventures of John Steinbeck, Writer*. New York: Viking, 1984.

Bloom, Harold, ed. *John Steinbeck*. New York: Chelsea House, 1987.

Brodwin, Stanley. "The Example of Darwin's Voyage of the Beagle in *The Log from the Sea of Cortez*." Steinbeck and the Environment Conference. Nantucket, 15 May 1992 (unpublished).

Darwin, Charles. *The Autobiography of Charles Darwin and Selected Letters*. Ed. Francis Darwin, 1892. New York: Dover Publications, 1958.

———. *The Origin of Species and The Descent of Man*. Darwin. Ed. Phillip Appleman, New York: Norton, 1979.

DeMott, Robert. Steinbeck's Reading: A Catalogue of Books Owned and Borrowed. New York: Garland, 1984.

French, Warren. "How Green Was John Steinbeck?" Steinbeck and the Environment Conference. Nantucket, 16 May 1992 (unpublished).

Lutwack, Leonard. "*The Grapes of Wrath* as Heroic Fiction." *The Grapes of Wrath: A Collection of Critical Essays*. Ed. Robert Con Davis. Englewood Cliffs, NJ: Prentice-Hall, 1982, 63–75.

Steinbeck, John. "About Ed Ricketts." *The Log from the Sea of Cortez*, 1951. New York: Penguin, 1975. vii–lxiv.

———. *America and Americans*. New York: Viking, 1966.

———. *The Grapes of Wrath*. 1939. New York: Penguin, 1976.

———. *The Harvest Gypsies*. 1936. Berkeley: Heyday Books, 1988.

———. *In Dubious Battle*. 1936. New York: Penguin, 1979.

———. *The Log from the Sea of Cortez*. 1951. New York: Penguin, 1975.

———. *Sweet Thursday*. 1954. New York: Penguin, 1986.

———. *Working Days: The Journals of The Grapes of Wrath*. Ed. Robert DeMott. New York: Viking Penguin, 1989.

———. The Ghost of Tom Joad: Steinbeck's Legacy in the Songs of Bruce Springsteen.

GAVIN COLOGNE-BROOKES

The Ghost of Tom Joad:
Steinbeck's Legacy in
the Songs of Bruce Springsteen

Like Steinbeck, Bruce Springsteen is a writer with a social conscience. And like Steinbeck's Tom Joad, Springsteen's down-and-out characters evolve from being self-reflective and self-absorbed to being socially conscious. Tom Joad's legacy is readily apparent in Springsteen's album *The Ghost of Tom Joad.*

Just as Elia Kazan's film of *East of Eden* inspired "Adam Raised a Cain" on *Darkness on the Edge of Town* (1978), so Bruce Springsteen cites John Ford's movie of *The Grapes of Wrath* rather than John Steinbeck's novel as the main influence on *The Ghost of Tom Joad* (1995). While Ford once claimed to have "never read the book" (Bluestone 169), Springsteen has clearly been influenced by Steinbeck's actual writing. In fact, he would read from the novel at the top of shows during his Joad tour (Sandford 382). But the adaptability of Steinbeck's vision to other genres remains extraordinary. It's hard to imagine a musician citing, say, a Hemingway or Faulkner novel or even a film adaptation as a primary influence, and not just because such movies have never been classics. Something about Steinbeck's vision crosses boundaries and transcends the mere text. *The Grapes of Wrath* has now traversed three genres. Like the characters themselves, it has meandered from the Oklahoma of noveldom through the arid New Mexican landscape of the movie to Springsteen's California-orientated folk songs of failed

From *Beyond Boundaries: Rereading John Steinbeck*, Susan Shillinglaw and Kevin Hearle, ed. © 2002 by The University of Alabama Press.

dreams in the Promised Land. This essay is specifically about Steinbeck's influence on Springsteen, but to assess this legacy properly is also to appreciate the ways in which genre-hopping illuminates both the meaning and social function of art.

The works of Steinbeck and Springsteen comment on and contribute to our understanding of social forces and injustices, and arguably help foster changes in the way individuals and communities respond. Whether art *really* makes a difference is, of course, a vexed question. In Steinbeck's novel, Al suggests to Uncle John that their struggle to find a better life is about as achievable as "huntin' skunks under water" (435). The phrase echoes Gustave Flaubert's that books are like pyramids: "There's some long-pondered plan" followed by "blocks of stone ... placed one on top of the other, and it's back-breaking, sweaty, time-consuming work. And all to no purpose!" (Barnes 35–36). Both comments imply that art, as a form of questing human endeavor, must have its own reason for being because there's little hope that it will contribute to a better, fairer world. But the fact is that, perhaps partly because of its adaptability to other genres, *The Grapes of Wrath* has had, as works of art go, an unparalleled influence on America's awareness of its own social inequities.

To note that Steinbeck's migrant odyssey is peculiarly adaptable to other genres is nothing new. Bluestone explored this adaptability in his invaluable study of the novel and movie in *Books into Film* in the late 1950s. But Springsteen's album adds a new dimension to our sense of Steinbeck's legacy. Moreover, *The Ghost of Tom Joad* is not an isolated response on Springsteen's part to Steinbeck's moral vision. It is just the most obvious example of a profound, ongoing legacy that evidently began for Springsteen in the late 1970s when he was encouraged by producer Jon Landau and then-girlfriend Lynn Goldsmith "to get more 'arty'" (Sandford 143). Continuing through the 1980s and 1990s into the twenty-first century, it has deepened into a fundamental attitude toward the role of the artist-observer that is wholly evident in such *engagé* songs as "Murder Incorporated," "Streets of Philadelphia," and "American Skin (41 Shots)." Springsteen's songs are no mere passive echoes of a vision filtered through the sentimental tendencies of Hollywood. His specific reference to Steinbeck in *The Ghost of Tom Joad* headlines a *Grapes of Wrath* influence characterized by an increasing tendency to reassert a political radicalism that exists more obviously in the novel than in the film. Brought to the novel via the movie, Springsteen responds both to the style(s) and the content of Steinbeck's novel in ways that restore much of the flavor of the original.

The Ghost of Tom Joad as a title indicates that, like Steinbeck, Springsteen is trying to create art that functions as social commentary. It suggests that the mature Springsteen lays claim to a shared view of artistic endeavor that is closely linked with the historical moment, emphasizing characters in relationships to one another and to their environment, and arguing for collective responsibility rather than individual isolation. For some, like the Hungarian Marxist critic, Georg Lukács, this is the course that art of long-term significance tends to follow. Seeing it as a question of realism versus modernism, he berates the latter for seeing people as by nature solitary, asocial, and unable to enter into relationships with others. In modernism, he argues, history is made "private" and all ties are broken "between historical events and private destinies" (*Contemporary Realism* 20). To seek escape is a modernist "yearning for harmony" that leads to "withdrawal before the contradictory problems thrown up by life.... By seeking inner harmony men cut themselves off from society's struggles" (*Writer and Critic* 89). For Lukács, in significant art the events of characters' lives are integrally connected to history. "The individual event," he argues, is seen to exist "in organic-historical connection with that infinite chain of individual events which in themselves are similarly accidental and in and through whose totality historical necessity always asserts itself" (*Historical Novel* 375).

The Grapes of Wrath is just such an example of artistic engagement. No mainstream modernist, Steinbeck built his novel on public, contextualized incidents in which individual actions affect the lives of families and communities. Even Steinbeck's American landscape is characterized by an attention to detail that fixes it within what Lukács might call its "organic-social connection." "One could easily read *The Grapes of Wrath* and drive along Route 66 today with a full sense of recognition," writes Jay Parini. "Chapter 15, for instance, opens with a vivid evocation of the roadside stands (whose names have, of course, changed)," and "Steinbeck's eye for details like these" helps make it such "a stunning book" (Parini 238). Significantly, this attention to detail is just as notable in Springsteen's *The Ghost of Tom Joad*. Take, for instance, the song "Youngstown." Where a younger Springsteen invariably contented himself with generic references to highways, back streets, cars, rivers and factories, here he documents a specific iron works founded in northeast Ohio in 1803 by James and Dan Heaton. He notes its role as a maker of Union cannon balls in the nineteenth century and tanks and bombs in the twentieth, and he carefully situates one blast furnace worker's story within a cultural, geographical and historical context. By the end of the song he has taken his listeners on a journey from the Monongahela Valley and the Mesabi Iron range to the Appalachian coal mines, and from the Civil War through World War II to Korea and Vietnam. At the same time he has given voice to an American worker as deliberately as

that definitive American cultural witness, Studs Terkel. The legacy of
Steinbeck's work in Springsteen's songs is therefore a matter of both theme
and style. In the whole concept of the songs from sentiments to performance,
Springsteen not only seeks, and finds, the ghost of Tom Joad, but through his
career has become that ghost.

First and foremost there is the thematic legacy, in particular the
relationship between the individual and the community. The songs mark
Springsteen's maturation away from an individual desire to escape, to an
awareness not only of his immediate environment—something evident in
previous albums—but also that his story is part of American history and
culture. Early in his career, Springsteen's travel motif is predominantly about
individual dreams of escape, exemplified by such songs as "Born to Run" and
"Thunder Road." The hero sees his hometown as a restrictive place full of
losers from which he will pull out to find personal success elsewhere. From
this Springsteen moves, via the family ties and reluctant separations evident
in such *River* songs as "Independence Day," to something quite different. His
theme in *The Ghost of Tom Joad* is *enforced* migration and individual
responsibility as part of a wider group. While, between songs like "Johnny 99"
and "Reason to Believe" on the Guthrie-inspired *Nebraska* (1982), hints of
communal responsibility still vie with lonely personal ambition, at no point
in that album does individual escape seem much of an option. By the time of
songs like "Souls of the Departed" on the aptly-titled *Human Touch* (1992),
and through much of *The Ghost of Tom Joad*, the emphasis is even less on
individual escape. Rather, characters try to make connections between one
another, the narratives of their lives and the forces around them.[1] In
"Galveston Bay," for instance, a Vietnam veteran spares a Vietnamese
immigrant who has killed two Texan Klan members in self-defense. As Jim
Cullen puts it, the resolution of the song's racial conflict offers us "the
ultimate definition of brotherhood: love that transcends boundaries" (Cullen
138).[2] Similarly "Sinaloa Cowboys" and "The Line" are songs which raise
questions—again far from the early Springsteen—about how issues to do
with friendship and responsibility relate to family and community issues.

Warren French's analysis of the change in Tom Joad describes much
the same kind of change as is evident in the Springsteen heroes as the singer's
career has evolved. It is, writes French of Joad, from a "selfish, violent
individual concerned only with the survival of his touchy clan into a visionary
operating selflessly in the background as an inspiring influence to his whole
community" (*Fiction Revisited* 76). Springsteen, like Joad, has moved from
merely celebrating the rebel figure, the early Joad, to being just that
"inspiring influence." Again, like Joad, he has ultimately absented himself
from his original community in the process—at least to the extent of owning

a Beverly Hills mansion and becoming "a part-time Californian" (Cullen 191). But that "a fella ain't no good alone" (570) is as relevant to Springsteen's album as it is to Steinbeck's novel. Individuals—and the art that portrays them—mature when they grow out of youthful self-centeredness and see themselves as part of a larger context. The change between Springsteen's youthful and mature visions is put in relief on his 1989 video anthology. Introducing a 1987 live version of "Born to Run"—with all that stuff about towns full of losers the individual has to escape in order to "win"—he is recorded reminding the audience, however dubiously, that "nobody wins unless everybody wins." But still, "this is the beginning," writes Steinbeck, "—from 'I' to 'we'" (206). American myths of individualism strike at the heart of notions of community, and this is evident in both *The Grapes of Wrath* and *The Ghost of Tom Joad*. Those Springsteen fans who prefer the romantic rebel to the emphasis on community may, as Sandford suggests, feel that "he never quite recovered from watching *The Grapes of Wrath* on TV" (Sandford 147). But as Springsteen himself said in 1988, while introducing the acoustic version of "Born to Run" recorded on the same anthology, "I realized that after I'd put all those people in all those cars I was going to have to figure out some place for them to go." "Individual freedom," he came to acknowledge, "when it's not connected to some sort of community or friends or the world outside ends up feeling pretty meaningless."

Indeed, the way Springsteen's statements have changed through his career corroborates the evidence of the songs. In a 1974 interview with Michael Watts, appropriately entitled "Lone Star," he admitted, "the main thing I've always been worried about is me.... I had to write about me all the time," he said, "because in a way you're trying to find out what that 'me' is." His links with Tom Joad, then, are more profound than the fact that, in Watts's words, he used to wear a hat "pulled down low over one ear in the true style of the Depression era" so that he and his crew resembled "young Okies" (Watts 55, 52). In a 1992 interview with David Hepworth, Springsteen again suggests a personal dimension to the journey from "I" to "we" evident in his lyrics. His comments also perhaps explain why he would put geographical distance between himself and his native region. "I'd lived in New Jersey for a very long time and I'd kind of written about a lot of things that had a lot to do—very tight into my *past*, my *past*, my *past* always," he said, "different ghosts you're chasing." Having taken this as far as he could, he was now writing instead about "people trying to connect to each other and that happens everywhere." Connection, as he says about "With Every Wish" on *Human Touch*, means "dealing with a life with consequences." "What does it mean to be a husband?" asks Springsteen rhetorically. "What does it mean to be a father? What does it mean to be a friend to somebody? When you finally get a good look at the world as it is, how do you not give in to cynicism, not give in to despair?" His answer is that you recognize—and this is Springsteen consciously or otherwise quoting the First epistle General of Paul—"a world of love and a world of fear," and that the two go hand in hand. "Perfect love casts out fear," wrote Paul. But of course it doesn't, it just makes fear more palatable.

Such is the thematic aspect of Steinbeck's legacy in the songs of Springsteen. In Lukács's terms, Steinbeck and Springsteen both reject escapism, whether into aesthetic experimentation or private neuroses, in favor of living with, confronting and depicting life's struggles in wider contexts. Out of the world of love and the world of fear comes the world of responsibility. Springsteen's talk of "a world of love and a world of fear" is a confession of life's complex contradictions. Beginning with his own early wrath, he has come to see this class anger in context. This is not to say that he has become a Marxist songwriter. Ironically, he is as enmeshed in the capitalist system as one can imagine, and rich because of it. But the contradictions in his songs and story are by and large to do with the contradictory aspects of American ideals of equality and individualism.

While subject matter is a major source of Steinbeck's influence on Springsteen, it cannot be separated from style and approach. It is here that Springsteen actually reinforces something of the political dimension of *The Grapes of Wrath* arguably muted by the movie adaptation. In his analysis of the book into the film, Bluestone concludes that screenwriter Nunnally Johnson's streamlining of Steinbeck's oscillation between two differing styles—his juxtaposition of documentary naturalism with the Joad narrative—tends to retain the insistence on "family cohesion," "affinity for the land" and "human dignity" (Bluestone 158–59). "The leisurely pace of the novel," he writes, "gives way to a tightly knit sequence of events." But Bluestone notes that this approach also serves to mute and generalize the novel's political radicalism. This is partly because, as one would expect, Steinbeck's seventeen general commentaries find no place in the movie, yet are precisely where we find "the angry interludes, the explicit indictments" that contribute so much to the novel's moral tone (Bluestone 162–63). If part of the withdrawal from political implications exists in the novel itself—for instance with Rose of Sharon's final act of offering her breast milk to a starving man—Bluestone demonstrates how the film invariably uses the novel's "evasive answers" in preference to its "specific accusations" (Bluestone 159–60). "Thus the book, which is an exhortation to action, becomes a film which offers reassurance that no action is required" (Bluestone 167). A novel that is "remembered for its moral anger" becomes a film "remembered for its beauty" (Bluestone 168–69). In certain ways, then, by concentrating on the novel's narrative strengths, the film loses something of the novel's moral strength. It "improves" on the novel as narrative art but only by dropping a vital element of Steinbeck's overall approach.

Given the classic status of the movie version—and the fact that Springsteen chose to cite the film rather than the novel—it is certainly tempting to view Steinbeck's lasting impact in terms of subject matter over style. Some commentators have done this. "There is, finally, something crude about Steinbeck's book," Parini concedes. Rather than a stylist, suggests Parini, "Steinbeck is, foremost, a storyteller" (Parini 275). Harold Bloom, too, intimates that content rather than style accounts for its lasting impact. While there are "no canonical standards worthy of human respect that could exclude *The Grapes of Wrath* from a serious reader's esteem," he writes, it is hard to say "whether a human strength" is in itself "an aesthetic value, in a literary narrative" (*Steinbeck* 5). Steinbeck's style in *The Grapes of Wrath* is fairly rough and ready. His extensive research and a dry-run like "L'Affaire Lettuceberg" notwithstanding, the eventual novel was finally written at speed, the 200,000 words completed in six months, and produced "in the sequence of its publication with minimal revision" (French 193). And perhaps there's some truth in the view that the lasting legacy of much of Steinbeck's work has to do with qualities adaptable to other genres: the understanding of human motivation, the human story.

But if so, this is not the whole truth. For a start, Steinbeck is hardly in danger of being known about rather than read. A random glance at the booking ticket for *The Grapes of Wrath* in my local small-town library revealed that it has been taken out nearly once a month for the past five years. As with Tolstoy in *War and Peace* (which Parini notes might equally be described as in some ways "crude") his actual literary approach, involving both narrative and exposition, can have no equivalent when transferred to the streamlining demands of the screen. Moreover, while the songwriter's art has its own demands and limitations, Steinbeck's legacy in Springsteen's songs certainly goes deeper than the influence of mere subject matter. If "Adam Raised a Cain" provides an early example of Springsteen on his way to being (in the words of *Tom Joad* reviewers) "a musical Steinbeck" (Schoenberg A7) or a "Steinbeck in leather" (Dawidoff) by the time of *Tom Joad*, the legacy had become less superficial than such phrases imply.[3] Quite aside from the similarities between Tom Joad's maturing vision in the novel and Springsteen's through his career, Steinbeck's legacy is also evident in Springsteen's changing approaches, including his choice of musical style, and the juxtaposition of narrative and explicit commentary.

For instance, it's not coincidental that *Tom Joad* is a folk rather than rock album. The translation of Steinbeck's images from novel into song lyric sees Springsteen returning to the origins of storytelling as folk art. Steinbeck's vision is recycled, refined, and updated, but it also reappears in an album that pays homage—in its acoustic intimacy as well as subject matter—to the kind of folk songs alluded to in *The Grapes of Wrath*. Songs like "Youngstown," about alienated labor, or "The New Timer," about an itinerant worker and railrider through Texas, New Mexico, California and back, echo the titles of songs documented in the novel, such as "Ten-Cent Cotton and Forty-Cent Meat" or "I'm Leaving Texas." Meanwhile, Springsteen's sometimes lulling, sometimes eerie rhythms call to mind Steinbeck's ubiquitous campsite guitarist. "And perhaps a man brought out his guitar to the front of his tent," writes Steinbeck. "And he sat on a box to play, and everyone in the camp moved slowly in toward him, drawn toward him," listening to "the deep chords beating, beating, while the melody runs on the strings like little footsteps."

> And now the group was welded to one thing, one unit, so that in the dark the eyes of the people were inward, and their minds played in other times, and their sadness was like rest, like sleep. He sang the "McAlester Blues" and then, to make up for it to the older people, he sang "Jesus Calls Me to His Side." The children drowsed with the music and went into their tents to sleep, and the singing came into their dreams. (272)

This, surely, is the effect Springsteen seeks with *The Ghost of Tom Joad*. It marks a return to music as intimacy—as if around a campfire with only the Joads and Wainwrights to hear—in contrast to his electrified anthems that filled arenas in the 1970s and 1980s. This is also why *The Ghost of Tom Joad* is so markedly warmer and more companionable, for all its dark subject matter, than the album it superficially resembles. The generally bleaker, harder songs of *Nebraska* would not exactly draw in and weld our imagined group of migrants, let alone lull their children to sleep.

Of course, a gulf yawns between Springsteen's position as a rock star, recording songs in a Los Angeles studio for mass consumption, and Woody Guthrie or, say, Joe Hill, who was not just a recorder but a participant, shot in the jailyard in Salt Lake City in 1915.[4] Perhaps there must always be something artificial—something even of postmodernist pastiche—about Springsteen seeking to re-create the fireside intimacy of folk tradition. On the other hand, Springsteen's motivation, and consequent appeal, seem to stem from a genuine commitment to those of his class (especially those who suffered as soldiers in Vietnam or still do as workers in America) that has subsequently branched outward. Seeing the fates of his friends and family in context, he has logically extended this to examine the plights of other beleaguered groups, climbing, in this case, into "the hearts and minds," as Mikal Gilmore puts it, "of a handful of undocumented immigrants" to California (Gilmore 434).

Springsteen, moreover, has learned much from the novel's oscillating use of both "cinematic" narrative and the verbal commentator's (as opposed to the film director's) scope for direct exposition. In a television documentary on Steinbeck, David Thomas recorded Gore Vidal's views on Steinbeck's general legacy. Again the emphasis is on subject matter rather than approach. "He looked at people nobody had ever looked at before and not many people have looked at since," said Vidal, "so I think, as a spirit of a country and of an age, and of his time, he was an honorable recorder." Such sentiments equally apply to Springsteen. That said, Vidal's phrase "honorable recorder" sounds slightly patronizing because it elides the fact that Steinbeck's novel does not simply record the plight of a people but gives it poetic voice through the Joad narrative and indicts the status quo through the alternating expository commentaries. Springsteen does much the same. "Got a lot of sinful idears—but they seem kinda sensible" is a line from *The Grapes of Wrath* (27) that could, as easily, be Springsteen's. But it's not just that Steinspeak and Springspeak grow out of an American vernacular first celebrated in *Huckleberry Finn*. Neither figure is merely "an honorable recorder."

Bluestone's analysis is again useful here. Whereas "the angry interludes, the explicit indictments, the authorial commentary" would have seemed "obtrusive" in the film, they find their "proper filmic equivalents" through direct action, and Steinbeck's narrative style is otherwise highly cinematic (Bluestone 162–63). "Except for the freewheeling omniscience of the interchapters," writes Bluestone, "the novel's prose relies wholly on dialogue and physical action to reveal character. Steinbeck's style is not marked by meditation, it resembles, in this respect, the classic form of the scenario" (Bluestone 163). Such a style "can also serve as precise directions for the actor," with a great many scenes that can "be turned into images of physical reality. Critics who seem surprised at the ease with which Steinbeck's work moves from one medium to another may find their explanation here" (Bluestone 164).

But while Nunnally Johnson's script and Ford's film may be hampered by the demands of the cinema, Springsteen as a songwriter and performer is free of the pressures imposed by the Hollywood system. In various ways, he is able to restore the expository side of Steinbeck's approach, and so the political bite. On the one hand, the songs on *Tom Joad* are full of precisely the same kind of cinematic narrative that Bluestone notes in Steinbeck's style. On the other hand Tom Joad, elevated in the film version to accommodate Henry Fonda and Hollywood's star-vehicle tendency, is again relegated to the role of "ghost" rather than hero as he reprises his oath to the book's strongest character, Ma Joad. In the album he is only one figure on a crowded canvas. Springsteen roams widely across America in a sequence of scenarios that add up to an essayistic indictment of the exploitation of ordinary workers and migrants from the blast furnaces of northeastern Ohio to the plight of Mexican wetbacks.

Also restored is the reference, excised from the film, to police brutality in that speech. If, as Bluestone argues, "the production crew effected alterations which mute the villainy of cops and tradesmen" and "cloud over the novel's political radicalism," Springsteen offers little of the comfort, respite or sentimentalism that arguably colors the movie (Bluestone 167–8). And if there still remains a degree of romanticism in Springsteen's depiction of Joad, romanticism can hardly be a charge leveled at "Balboa Park," about a border drug-runner who dies after a balloon of cocaine bursts in his stomach. Nor has it any place in those especially pointed songs of the 1990s, "Murder Incorporated" and "Streets of Philadelphia," or a song first performed in June 2000, "American Skin (41 Shots)." The latter, to the public dismay of Patrick Lynch, President of the New York City Patrolman's Benevolent Association, does nothing to flinch from detailing the facts of the forty-one shots fired into unarmed Guinean immigrant Amadou Diallo, when police mistook his wallet for a gun. In detailing some of the brutal incidents and aspects of contemporary American life, Springsteen has clearly revealed himself now as an artist whose understanding of Steinbeck's artistic vision goes beyond the mere, incidental influence of a single movie.[5]

Such then is Steinbeck's legacy in the songs of Bruce Springsteen. Both in content and approach, Springsteen's songs reveal some profound debts to Steinbeck's vision, and help to ensure that it continues to impact on American culture, and beyond. But perhaps the most significant debt has to do with a vision of the individual's communal responsibility, and therefore of art's social function. Ultimately Springsteen's return to folk music links with his finding a focus beyond his immediate self and environment: namely the relationship between a variety of individuals and groups and their historical contexts. Springsteen is continuing the tradition of hunting skunks under water. His mature pursuit of connection and community in place of the solipsistic escapism of youth echoes Tom Joad's journey of discovery. It's not a winnable journey except in terms of individuals growing into such recognition within their own lives, but it does shape the art itself. And the kind of art we choose to value, since our choice reflects our outlook, might matter more than we imagine in terms of the kinds of societies we shape. It may be that Steinbeck's legacy is especially important as part of a *collective* legacy. If, as members of a given society, we accept the consensus from Nietzsche and Freud to Wittgenstein and Kuhn that our sense of reality is always some kind of construct, it follows that our view of the function of art may in itself help *create* its function. The individual and collective choice between two kinds of art may, in turn, relate to the individual and collective choice between two kinds of futures. The ghost of Tom Joad may be a specter we, like Springsteen, should heed.

NOTES

1. In 1988, two years before *Human Touch*, Springsteen acknowledged his debt to Guthrie by contributing to *Folkways: A Vision Shared*, a tribute album to Guthrie and his sometime musical partner, Leadbelly.

2. Cullen points out that "Streets of Philadelphia" is a telling landmark in that it was commissioned. Springsteen, suggests Cullen, "may well have regarded tailoring a piece of music for someone else's purposes beneath him at an earlier point in his career" (192).

3. Dale Maharidge, cited by Cullen, is quoted in Tom Schoenberg. Nicholas Dawidoff's cover story is also cited by Cullen.

4. See John Dos Passos "Joe Hill" in *USA*. The same paradox existed for the movie, of course. As Bluestone notes, on one hand you had a reporter "poking fun at the grandiose premiere," attended not only "by glamorous stars adorned in jewels and furs" but "by the representatives of the very banks and land companies that had tractored the Joads off their farms." On the other hand, you had "the industry's discomfort" because the adaptation of Steinbeck's book "came as close as any film in Hollywood's prolific turnout to exposing the contradictions and inequities at the heart of American life" (Bluestone 168).

5. See Sandford 378–79. Springsteen has never been averse to interspersing his songs with exposition. But while this tended to be personal and anecdotal in earlier years, more recently it has reflected his evident sense of himself as an artist in the Steinbeck mold. Sandford records *Los Angeles Times* reporter Mark Arax witnessing Springsteen making "a pitch for the plight of migrant farm-hands" at a Fresno concert. Such exposition did not go down too well in Fresno. "Despite several pleas from the stage, not a single cent was collected for their cause among the audience. A handful of fans even asked for—and were given—their ticket money back. Later, Springsteen wrote the local workers' union a personal cheque."

HAROLD BLOOM

Afterthought

An ambitious writer asks to be judged alongside the strongest of his contemporaries. Try to read William Faulkner's *As I Lay Dying* in conjunction with *The Grapes of Wrath*. Steinbeck is obliterated, as he is by Willa Cather and Theodore Dreiser, Ernest Hemingway and Scott Fitzgerald, Nathanael West and Flannery O'Connor. This saddens me, because I *want* Steinbeck to have been a great writer on the Left. We lack such a figure, though Hemingway attempted to fill the lack in *For Whom the Bell Tolls*, and failed. And yet even his failures remain more readable than Steinbeck's popular successes.

As an American epic, *The Grapes of Wrath* never loses its polemical edge, which is populist rather than Marxist. The late Anthony Burgess, a wise critic and undervalued novelist who remarked that Hemingway was Steinbeck's trouble, noted also that Steinbeck was precisely what he asserted to be, a Jeffersonian Democrat. I myself tend to think of Steinbeck as the Harry Truman of American Novelists: kindly, honorable, pugnacious, and opposed to all forces of exploitation. The shadow of Hemingway hovers over every descriptive passage in *The Grapes of Wrath*. Take "Oklahoma" out of the first sentence of *The Grapes of Wrath* and substitute "the Basque lands," and you could drop the book's first two paragraphs into several contexts in *The Sun Also Rises*. What remains wholly Steinbeck's own in *The Grapes of Wrath*, is the book's stance towards America.

As has been noted frequently by critics, the women of *The Grapes of Wrath* are stronger than the men, except for the prophets Jim Casey and Tom Joad, and yet they are not the devouring women of Hemingway and of Scott Fitzgerald. Why should the best of Steinbeck's women seem less overdetermined than the men, or quite simply, why does Ma Joad have more freedom of the will than he son Tom does? Why are Steinbeck's men more of a social group, their fates settled by economics, when his women are able to manifest an acute individuality? Is Ma Joad's passion for keeping her hard-pressed family together merely an instinctual reflex? Certainly, without her will and drive, Tom Joad would not have had the desire to carry on for the martyred Jim Casy. One could argue that *The Grapes of Wrath* weakens as it approaches its conclusion, and that only Ma Joad keeps this trailing-off from becoming an aesthetic catastrophe. Confused as Steinbeck becomes, mixing allegorical and ironic elements into a previously realistic plot, the consistency of Ma Joad helps the novelist firm up an otherwise wavering structure.

There are other difficulties in trying to reread Steinbeck with any rigor. The Okies of *The Grapes of Wrath* never were: Steinbeck knew Oklahoma about as well as he knew Afghanistan. That might not matter except that Steinbeck's poor whites are contemporary with Faulkner's, and the Joads as a literary creation lack the aesthetic dignity and persuasive substantiality of the Bundrens in *As I Lay Dying*. Floyd Watkins, a quarter-century ago, demonstrated this, as well as the shadow quality of the Joads compared to the rural poor of Eudora Welty and Robert Penn Warren.

You can argue, if you wish, that Steinbeck's Okies are a visionary creation, but then you are likely to find them dwarfed by their cinematic representations in John Ford's *The Grapes of Wrath*, as superior to Steinbeck's novel as Herman Melville's *Moby-Dick* is in comparison to John Huston's filmed travesty of it. It is curious that rereading the novel can be a less rewarding experience than reseeing the film, where the young Henry Fonda's performance as Tom Joad compensates for some of the contradictions built into the character. The achieved pathos of Fonda's acting helps obscure Steinbeck's inability to persuade us that Tom Joad ends with a more fully articulated sense of identity than he possessed at the onset of the story.

Aesthetic defense of *The Grapes of Wrath* is perhaps still barely possible. Steinbeck remains a popular writer, but so is the hopelessly, implacably doctrinaire Ayn Rand, dear to many rightwing readers. There are depths beneath depths in popular fiction: what should one make of John Grisham? I cannot force my way through more than a few pages. It is a sorrow that Steinbeck, a "worthy" writer, as Burgess said, should have fallen into the cosmos of period pieces.

Chronology

1902	John Ernst Steinbeck is born on February 27, in Salinas, California, to John Ernst II and Olive Hamilton Steinbeck.
1919	Graduates from Salinas High School.
1920-25	Attends Stanford and works as laborer intermittently. Publishes first short stories in *The Stanford Spectator.*
1925	Drops out of Stanford and goes to New York. Works as construction laborer and reports for the *American* newspaper.
1926	Returns to California, writes stories and novels.
1929	His first novel, *Cup of Gold*, is published.
1930	Marries Carol Henning and settles in Pacific Grove.
1932	*The Pastures of Heaven*, a novel, is published. Moves to Los Angeles.
1933	*To a God Unknown*, a novel, is published. Returns to Monterey. *The Red Pony* appears in two parts in North American Review.
1934	His mother dies.
1935	*Tortilla Flat* is published. His father dies.
1936	*In Dubious Battle*, a novel, is published. Travels to Mexico.
1937	*Of Mice and Men* is published, chosen for Book-of-the-Month club. Travels to Europe and later from Oklahoma to California with migrants.

1938	*Their Blood Is Strong*, nonfiction, is published. A collection of short stories, *The Long Valley*, is published.
1939	*The Grapes of Wrath* is published. Elected to the National Institute of Arts and Letters.
1940	*The Grapes of Wrath* wins the Pulitzer Prize. *The Forgotten Village*, a documentary, is produced. Goes on research trip with Edward Ricketts to the Sea of Cortez.
1941	*Sea of Cortez* is published with Edward F. Ricketts.
1942	*The Moon is Down* is published. Steinbeck and Carol Henning divorce. Writes the script *Bombs Away* for the U.S. Air Force.
1943	Moves to New York City, marries Gwyndolyn Conger. In Europe covers the war as correspondent for the *New York Herald Tribune*.
1944	Writes script for Alfred Hitchcock's *Lifeboat*. A son, Thom, is born.
1945	*Cannery Row*, a novel, is published. *The Red Pony* is published in four parts.
1946	A second son, John IV, is born.
1947	*The Wayward Bus*, a novel, is published. *The Pearl*, a novella, is published. Travels in Russia with photographer Robert Capa.
1948	*A Russian Journal*, an account of his 1947 tour of Russia, is published. Steinbeck and Gwyndolyn Conger divorce.
1950	*Burning Bright*, a novella, is published. Marries Elaine Anderson Scott. Writes script for *Viva Zapata!*
1951	*The Log from the Sea of Cortez*, the narrative part of *Sea of Cortez*, is published.
1952	*East of Eden* is published.
1954	*Sweet Thursday*, a novel, is published (a sequel to *Cannery Row*).
1957	*The Short Reign of Pippen IV*, a novel, is published.
1958	*Once There Was a War*, a collection of his wartime dispatches, is published.
1960	Steinbeck takes a three-month tour of America with his dog, Charley.
1961	*The Winter of Our Discontent*, his twelfth and final novel, is published.

1962	*Travels with Charley*, the journal of his 1960 tour, is published. Steinbeck is awarded the Nobel Prize for Literature.
1964	Awarded the United States Medal of Freedom and a Press Medal of Freedom.
1966	*American and Americans*, reflections on contemporary America, is published.
1966–67	Reports from Vietnam for *Newsday*.
1968	Dies of severe heart attack in New York City on December 20.

Contributors

HAROLD BLOOM is Sterling Professor of the Humanities at Yale University. He is the author of 30 books, including *Shelley's Mythmaking* (1959), *The Visionary Company* (1961), *Blake's Apocalypse* (1963), *Yeats* (1970), *A Map of Misreading* (1975), *Kabbalah and Criticism* (1975), *Agon: Toward a Theory of Revisionism* (1982), *The American Religion* (1992), *The Western Canon* (1994), and *Omens of Millennium: The Gnosis of Angels, Dreams, and Resurrection* (1996). *The Anxiety of Influence* (1973) sets forth Professor Bloom's provocative theory of the literary relationships between the great writers and their predecessors. His most recent books include *Shakespeare: The Invention of the Human* (1998), a 1998 National Book Award finalist, *How to Read and Why* (2000), *Genius: A Mosaic of One Hundred Exemplary Creative Minds* (2002), *Hamlet: Poem Unlimited* (2003), *Where Shall Wisdom Be Found?* (2004), and *Jesus and Yahweh: The Names Divine* (2005). In 1999, Professor Bloom received the prestigious American Academy of Arts and Letters Gold Medal for Criticism. He has also received the International Prize of Catalonia, the Alfonso Reyes Prize of Mexico, and the Hans Christian Andersen Bicentennial Prize of Denmark.

HOWARD LEVANT is the author of *The Novels of John Steinbeck: A Critical Study*.

PETER LISCA, who died in 2001, taught at the University of North Carolina, University of Washington, and the University of Florida. He was the author of *John Steinbeck, Nature and Myth* and *The Wide World of John Steinbeck*; he was the editor of *The Grapes of Wrath: Text and Criticism*.

WARREN MOTLEY is the author of *The American Abraham (James Fenimore Cooper and the Frontier Patriarch)*.

LOUIS OWENS taught at the University of California at Davis and at Santa Cruz, California State University at Northridge, the University of New Mexico, and was professor of English and Native American Studies and director of Creative Writing at the University of California, Davis, at the time of his death in July 2002. Louis was the author *The Grapes of Wrath: Trouble in the Promised Land* and *John Steinbeck's Re-Vision of America*. He was also a novelist and wrote the acclaimed *Other Destines: Understanding the American Indian Novel*.

MIMI REISEL GLADSTEIN is a professor of English, theatre arts, and women's studies at the University of Texas at El Paso. She is the author of the *Indestructible Woman in Faulkner, Hemingway, and Steinbeck*, and has contributed numerous articles to scholarly anthologies and journals.

NELLIE McKAY is professor of Afro-American studies at the University of Wisconsin. She is co-editor with Henry Louis Gates, Jr. of the *Norton Anthology of African American Literature*; author of *Jean Toomer, The Artist: A Study of His Literary Life and Work*; editor of *Critical Essays on Toni Morrison*; and co-editor of the *Norton Critical Edition of Harriet Jacobs's Incidents in the Life of a Slave Girl*; *Approaches to Teaching the Novels of Toni Morrison*; and *Beloved: A Casebook*. McKay has contributed scholarly essays to literary journals and literary and historical dictionaries.

STEPHEN RAILTON is professor of American literature at the University of Virginia. He is the author of *Mark Twain: A Short Introduction*; *Authorship and Audience: Literary Performance in the American Renaissance*; and *Fenimore Cooper: A Study of His Life and Imagination*.

DAVID N. CASSUTO is a professor at Pace Law School. Before entering law practice, Cassuto was a professor of English specializing in literature and the environment. He has published and lectured widely on legal, literary, and environmental issues. He is the author of the books *Dripping Dry: Literature, Politics and Water in the Desert Southwest* and *Cold Running River: A Ecological Biography of the Pere Marquette River*.

BRIAN E. RAILSBACK teaches creative writing and American literature at Western Carolina University. He has published numerous articles and book chapters on John Steinbeck and published *Parallel Expeditions: Charles Darwin and the Art of John Steinbeck*.

GAVIN COLOGNE-BROOKES is Senior Lecturer in English and Creative Studies at Bath Spa University College, England. He is the author of *The Novels of William Styron: From Harmony to History* and *Dark Eyes On America: The Novels Of Joyce Carol Oates*.

Bibliography

Astro, Richard. *John Steinbeck and Edward F. Ricketts: The Shaping of a Novelist.* Minneapolis: University of Minnesota Press, 1973.

August, Eugene R. "Our Stories/Our Selves: The American Dream Remembered in John Steinbeck's *The Grapes of Wrath.*" *University of Dayton Review* 23, no. 3 (Winter 1995–1996): 5–17.

Bloom, Harold, ed. *Modern Critical Views: John Steinbeck.* New York: Chelsea House, 1987.

Crockett, H. Kelly. "The Bible and *The Grapes of Wrath.*" *College English* 24 (1962): 193–199.

Davis, Robert Con, ed. *Twentieth Century Interpretations of* The Grapes of Wrath: *A Collection of Critical Essays.* Englewood Cliffs, N.J.: Prentice-Hall, 1982.

Davis, Robert Murray, ed. *Steinbeck: A Collection of Critical Essays.* Englewood Cliffs, N.J.: Prentice-Hall, 1972.

DeMott, Robert, ed. *Working Days: The Journals of* The Grapes of Wrath. New York: Viking, 1989.

———. *Steinbeck's Reading: Catalogue of Books Owned and Borrowed.* New York: Garland, 1984.

Ditsky, John, ed. *Critical Essays on Steinbeck's* The Grapes of Wrath. Boston: G.K. Hall & Co., 1989.

———. *John Steinbeck and the Critics.* Rochester, N.Y.: Camden House, 2000.

———. "The Grapes of Wrath: A Reconsideration." *Southern Humanities Review* 13 (1979): 215–220.

French, Warren, ed. *A Companion to* The Grapes of Wrath. New York: Penguin, 1989.

———. *John Steinbeck*. Boston, Twayne: 1975.

———. *John Steinbeck's Fiction Revisited*. New York: Twayne, 1994.

Gere, Anne Ruggles. "Dorothea Lange to 'The Boss': Versions of *The Grapes of Wrath*." In *Making American Literatures in High School and College*, eds. Anne Ruggles Gere, Peter Shaheen, Sara Robbins, and Jeremy Wells. Urbana, Ill.: National Council of Teacher of English, 2001.

Gladstein, Mimi Reisel. "From Heroine to Supporting Player: The Diminution of Ma Joad." In *Critical Essays on Steinbeck's* The Grapes of Wrath, ed., John Ditsky. Boston: Hall, 1989.

Hayashi, Tetsumaro, ed. *John Steinbeck: The Years of Greatness, 1936–1939*. Tuscaloosa: Uninversity of Alabama Press, 1993.

———, ed. *A New Study Guide to Steinbeck's Major Works, With Critical Explications*. Metuchen, N.J.: Scarecrow, 1993.

Heavlin, Barbara. "Judge, Observer, Prophet: The American Cain and Steinbeck's Shifting Perspective." *South Dakota Review* 34, no. 2 (Summer 1996): 92–206

———. "Hospitality, the Joads, and the Stranger Motif: Structural Symmetry in John Steinbeck's *The Grapes of Wrath*." *South Dakota Review* 29, no. 2 (Summer 1991): 142–52.

———, ed. *John Steinbeck's* The Grapes of Wrath: *A Reference Guide*. Westport, Conn.: Greenwood, 2002.

———, ed. *The Critical Response to John Steinbeck's* The Grapes of Wrath. Westport, Conn.: Greenwood, 2000.

Hunter, J. Paul. "Steinbeck's Wine of Affirmation in *The Grapes of Wrath*." In *Essays in Modern American Literature*, ed. Richard E. Langford. Deland, Fla.: Stetson University Press, 1963.

Levant, Howard. *The Novels of John Steinbeck: A Critical Study*. Columbia: University of Missouri Press, 1974.

Lingo, Marci. "Forbidden Fruit: The Banning of *The Grapes of Wrath* in the Kern County Free Library." *Libraries & Culture: A Journal of Library History* 38, no. 4 (Fall 2003): 351–77.

Lisca, Peter. *John Steinbeck, Nature and Myth*. New York: Crowell, 1978.

———. *The Wide World of John Steinbeck*. New Brunswick, N.J.: Rutgers University Press, 1958.

————, ed. The Grapes of Wrath: *Text and Criticism*. New York: Viking, 1972.

L'Heureux, Conrad. "Life's Journey and *The Grapes of Wrath*." *University of Dayton Review* 23, no. 3 (Winter 1995–96): 89–97.

Moon, Michael. "Whose History? The Case of Oklahoma." In *A Queer World: The Center for Lesbian and Gay Studies Reader*, ed. Martin Duberman. New York: New York University Press, 1997.

Motley, Warren. "From Patriarchy to Matriarchy: Ma Joad's Role in *The Grapes of Wrath*." *American Literature* 54, no. 3 (1982): 397–412.

Nakayama, Kiyoshi, Scott Pugh, and Shigeharu Yano, eds. *John Steinbeck: Asian Perspectives*. Osaka, Japan: Osaka Kyoiko Tosho, 1992.

Noble, Donald R., ed. *The Steinbeck Questions: New Essays in Criticism*. Troy, N.Y.: Whitson, 1993.

Owens, Louis. The Grapes of Wrath: *Trouble in the Promised Land*. Boston: Twayne Publishers, 1989.

————. *John Steinbeck's Re-Vision of America*. Athens: University of Georgia Press, 1985.

Parini, Jay. *John Steinbeck: A Biography*. New York: Henry Holt, 1995.

Railsback, Brian E. *Parallel Expeditions: Charles Darwin and the Art of John Steinbeck*. Moscow: University of Idaho Press, 1995.

Rucklin, Christine. "Steinbeck's 'Odyssey': A Reconsideration of Homer's Epic." *Classical and Modern Literature: A Quarterly* 17, no. 2 (Winter 1997): 171–77.

Sanderson, Jim. "American Romanticism in John Ford's *The Grapes of Wrath*: Horizontalness, Darkness, Christ, and F.D.R." *Literature/Film Quarterly*. 17, no. 4 (1989): 231–44.

Sheff, David. "Fifty Years Of *Wrath*." *California* 14, no. 10 (Oct. 1989).

Shillinglaw, Susan, and Kevin Hearle, eds. *Rereading John Steinbeck*. Tuscaloosa: University of Alabama Press, 2002.

Slade, L. A. "The Uses of Biblical Allusions in *The Grapes of Wrath*." *CLAJ* 11 (1968): 241–247.

Sweeney, James W. "The Joads Go Home." *California Journal* 23, no. 3 (March 1992)

Taylor, Walter Fuller. "*The Grapes of Wrath* Reconsidered." *Mississippi Quarterly* 12 (1959): 136–44.

Teisch, Jessica B. "From the Dust Bowl to California: The Beautiful Fraud." *Midwest Quarterly: A Journal of Contemporary Thought* 39, no. 2 (Winter 1998): 153–72.

Timmerman, John. *John Steinbeck's Fiction: The Aesthetics of the Road Taken.* Norman and London: University of Oklahoma Press, 1986.

Wyatt, David, ed. *New Essays on* The Grapes of Wrath. Cambridge, U.K.: Cambridge University Press, 1990.

Acknowledgments

"The Fully Matured Art: *The Grapes of Wrath*" by Howard Levant. *The Novels of John Steinbeck.* © 1974 by The Curators of the University of Missouri. Reprinted by permission.

"*The Grapes of Wrath*: An Achievement of Genius" by Peter Lisca. *John Steinbeck: Nature and Myth.* © 1978 by Peter Lisca. Reprinted by permission.

"From Patriarchy to Matriarchy: Ma Joad's Role in *The Grapes of Wrath*" by Warren Motley. *American Literature* 54, no. 3. © 1982 by Duke University Press. Reprinted by permission.

"The American Joads" by Louis Owens. The Grapes of Wrath: *Trouble in the Promised Land.* © 1989 by G.K. Hall & Co. Reprinted by permission.

"From Heroine to Supporting Player: The Diminution of Ma Joad" by Mimi Reisel Gladstein. *Critical Essays on Steinbeck's* The Grapes of Wrath. © 1989 by John Ditsky. Reprinted by permission.

"'Happy [?]-Wife-and-Motherdom': The Portrayal of Ma Joad in John Steinbeck's *The Grapes of Wrath*" by Nellie McKay. *New Essays on* The Grapes of Wrath. Ed. David Wyatt. © 1990 by Cambridge University Press. Reprinted by permission.

"Pilgrims' Politics: Steinbeck's Art of Conversion" by Stephen Railton. *New Essays on* The Grapes of Wrath. Ed. David Wyatt. © 1990 by Cambridge University Press. Reprinted by permission.

"Turning Wine into Water: Water as Privileged Signifier in *The Grapes of Wrath*" by David N. Cassuto. *Steinbeck and the Environment.* © 1997 by The University of Alabama Press. Originally in *Papers on Language and Literature* 29, no. 1 (Winter) 1993. © 1993 by The Board of Trustees, Southern Illinois University. Reprinted by permission.

"The Darwinian *Grapes of Wrath*" by Brian Railsback. *The Critical Response to John Steinbeck's* The Grapes of Wrath. © 2000 by Barbara Heavilin. Originally in *Parallel Expeditions: Charles Darwin and the Art of John Steinbeck.* © 1995 by The University of Idaho Press. pp. 67–95. Reprinted by permission.

"The Ghost of Tom Joad: Steinbeck's Legacy in the Songs of Bruce Springsteen" by Gavin Cologne-Brookes. *Beyond Boundaries: Rereading John Steinbeck.* © 2002 by The University of Alabama Press. Reprinted by permission.

Every effort has been made to contact the owners of copyrighted material and secure copyright permission. Articles appearing in this volume generally appear much as they did in their original publication with few or no editorial changes. Those interested in locating the original source will find bibliographic information in the bibliography and acknowledgments sections of this volume.

Index